MW00686230

PUBLIC MANAGEMENT
AND THE
RULE OF LAW

PUBLIC MANAGEMENT AND THE RULE OF LAW

JULIA BECKETT

M.E.Sharpe
Armonk, New York
London, England

For my parents

Muriel and Robert Beckett

Copyright © 2010 by M.E. Sharpe, Inc.

All rights reserved. No part of this book may be reproduced in any form
without written permission from the publisher, M.E. Sharpe, Inc.,
80 Business Park Drive, Armonk, New York 10504.

Library of Congress Cataloging-in-Publication Data

Beckett, Julia, 1958–
  Public management and the rule of law / by Julia Beckett.
    p. cm.
  Includes bibliographical references and index.
  ISBN 978-0-7656-2321-8 (hardcover : alk. paper) —ISBN 978-0-7656-2322-5 (pbk. : alk. paper)
  1. Administrative law—United States. 2. Public administration—United States. 3. Rule of
law—United States. I. Title.

  KF5402.B43 2010
  342.73'06—dc22   2009048085

Printed in the United States of America

The paper used in this publication meets the minimum requirements of
American National Standard for Information Sciences
Permanence of Paper for Printed Library Materials,
ANSI Z 39.48-1984.

∞

| EB (c) | 10 | 9 | 8 | 7 | 6 | 5 | 4 | 3 | 2 | 1 |
| EB (p) | 10 | 9 | 8 | 7 | 6 | 5 | 4 | 3 | 2 | 1 |

Contents

Preface

Public management, governance, and law are extremely important. Public servants need to understand how administration, governance, and law are interrelated. Governance includes exercising public authority, representing democratic values, and being aware of serving the public. Law is integral in governing and administration. Law defines, authorizes, and limits public administration through constitutions, statutes, regulations, and court decisions. Laws and legal practices, particularly the judicial reasoning and constitutional due process considerations, are integrated into public administration decision-making. Public servants must recognize that democratic values found in the Constitution and laws are essential for accomplishing policies and providing services to the citizens.

Public managers need knowledge and skills to do their jobs. Part of the training of public managers includes developing competence in public personnel, budgeting, statistics, and other areas. Public administrators also need to have competence in law. This book is a starting point for public administration and public management students to develop the legal competence they need for good governance.

Both the study of public administration and public management emphasize the skills and knowledge public servants need to develop. Public administration is a term used to identify the academic field around the term of the twentieth century, and it is widely used today. Public management also defines the study and practice for public servants, and it often emphasizes the upper level decision-makers. In this book, the terms public administration and public management will be used interchangeably.

There are many excellent textbooks on public administration and public management and there are in-depth books on constitutional law and administrative law, but few books link public law knowledge to public administration practices. This book is written for those students who plan to become public managers, and it provides a general background on areas of law that authorize, delegate, and limit their responsibilities to the public.

This text presents an introduction and overview of how law relates to the values, foundation, institutions, activities, policies, and procedures of public managers. The first chapter discusses the Constitution and the rule of law as foundations for democratic governance. Chapter 2 addresses constitutional authority, structure, individual constitutional rights and how these affect administrative practice. Chapter 3 discusses policy and legislation. Chapter 4 explains the judicial process in trials and appeals, the court doctrines about decision-making, and the process of alternative dispute resolution. Chapter 5 addresses administrative practice and the three main areas of administrative procedure laws: rulemaking, enforcement, and information. Chapter 6 discusses property law. Chapter 7 includes contract law and contracting, and Chapter 8 discusses tort law and sovereign immunity. The final chapter considers how administrators can address legal and governance issues.

Each chapter covers aspects of law, governance, and public administration. The chapters include discussion questions and illustrative court decisions. The cases illustrate legal issues that are related to the materials presented in the chapter. These cases allow readers to understand how courts decide the legal issues, and cases provide readers a chance to evaluate problems with management concerns that may or may not coincide with the legal issues in a case. The cases also illustrate the complex considerations of how an agency may respond when a law, policy, or action is challenged in a lawsuit.

This book is written for master's level classes in public administration, public management, and public policy, and it is also suitable for upper-level undergraduate courses. The book teaches general principles administrators need to understand as they carry out their duties and responsibilities. It provides an important foundation for administrators in gathering information, making decisions, and taking action in a lawful and legitimate manner. Public managers need to learn the law that applies to their job, and maintaining legal competence is an ongoing effort. This book is intended to help students begin building this knowledge.

* * *

I want to convey my appreciation for the many people that helped me write this book. There are a number of people that deserve recognition. First, I want to thank my students. I also want to acknowledge the support I received from my colleagues. In particular, I wish to thank the following for their assistance and encouragement: Heidi Koenig, Nancy Grant, David Rosenbloom, Fred Thompson, Ralph Hummel, Jerry Miller, and Bart Hildreth. Next, thank you to the staff at M.E. Sharpe for your thoughtful suggestions throughout the writing process. In addition, special thanks go to Robert D. Beckett and William J. Miller for reading drafts of the manuscript.

Finally, I want to thank my family. My sons, Jack and Andy Gatti, and my parents provided moral support and good wishes. My husband, Keith Gatti, has been most supportive and encouraging; I appreciate his good humor and patience.

PUBLIC
MANAGEMENT
AND THE
RULE OF LAW

1

Public Management and Understanding Public Law

Law is essential to American government and society, but people often see law as an abstraction or an interference with their activities. Americans both hate and like law and regulations. For instance when a person is driving and sees other cars speeding, tailgating, or trying to beat a yellow light, a common reaction is to ask oneself: Where is a cop when you need one? That is, we want the police to enforce the laws to get the other guy to behave. However, when the recent traffic-enforcement technique of taking photographs of cars speeding or running red lights and then sending the owner a ticket in the mail was introduced, there was public and pundit outcry. The public disliked tickets, and they questioned whether government could legally mail a ticket to the owner rather than citing the driver for traffic infractions. Pundits complained about government interference as they argued there were questions of constitutional and legal authority.

Other recent examples about government administration are the outcries about the lack of regulation, such as the claims that government failed to prevent illnesses related to germs that were introduced in the growing of tomatoes and spinach and the manufacturing of peanut butter. Inadequate regulation or regulatory enforcement are claimed to be a factor in the mortgage crisis. Protesters argue that if government had regulated lenders, then this crisis would not have happened. This blaming-the-government argument conveniently ignores that the dominant political and economic practice in the past decades was based on free markets. Public administrators are often included in these discussions because they are responsible for enforcing the laws and regulations. Often individuals complain about how administrators do their jobs.

Public managers need to understand law in carrying out their governance responsibilities. Public administration, governance, and law are interrelated concepts. They have slightly different meanings, but they share an important core meaning of providing government for the people. Public administration is the general term for the executive agencies and organizations that carry out public activities, services, and duties. Public administration is a field of academic study regarding the practices of government. Public administrators and public servants are the people that work for government in responsible and management positions.

Public administrators are involved in governance, which is more than the exercise of public authority. "Governance includes the traditions, institutions, and processes that determine the exercise of power in society, including how decisions are made on issues of public concern and how citizens are given voice in public decisions."[1] Law is in the foundation, values, institutions, activities, policies, and procedures of public officials and employees. Law is the authoritative and binding requirements, mandates, or orders of society, but law is also a substantive body of knowledge and the area of professional expertise of attorneys and judges. Public law includes the constitution, statutes, rules, regulations, and court decisions that authorize, define, and constrain government. Without law, American government would not exist.

In carrying out their responsibilities public administrators interpret, apply, implement, and evaluate law. Competent public administrators must have the knowledge and skills to accomplish their responsibilities. This book provides a foundation of public law knowledge. This includes: the legal basis of democratic structure and values, constitutional law, legislation and policy, court practices, administrative rulemaking and enforcement, property law, contract law, and tort law. Public administration, governance, and law are integrated in the exercise of administrative skills, especially in decision-making.

A Government Founded in Law

American government is a democratic republic that has its foundation in a written constitution and in laws and regulations enacted consistent with the constitution. Public law in the constitutional, statutory, and regulatory law provides both the structural and philosophical basis of government. Our nation is founded through a constitution, literally and figuratively. Understanding public law is essential to constitutional and democratic governance; understanding public law is an essential competence for public administrators.[2] Public administration law scholars have stressed, first, how law is a philosophical foundation for our society;[3] second, how law pervades and legitimizes administration;[4] and third, how positive aspects of law are useful as guidance, as technique, as perspective, and as process.[5]

The sources of many administrative obligations and imperatives are found in the constitutions, laws, rules, and executive orders—these are called positive law. Court decisions interpret and evaluate administrative actions, and appellate court decisions establish binding precedent—this is called the common law. Both types of law are intimately part of public administration. Public managers and public officials are not expected to be legal experts or lawyers, but they need to have a clear understanding of how public law is integral in governance.

Public managers need to understand the concepts of rule of law that underlie a democratic republic that provides a government under law. Managers need to understand how they must work within and apply the constitutions, legal process, legislation, administrative regulation, and court decisions. They need to understand enough of law to recognize when there may be legal issues and to be able to work with their legal counselors.

The powers, duties, rights, and responsibilities of government and its public managers are contained in the federal and state constitutions. Commonly accepted principles about American constitutional government affect public administration. The Constitution distributes powers to and responsibilities among three branches of government—one writes laws, another administers laws, and the third interprets laws when it resolves disputes. The Federalist Papers, seeking unanimous passage of the Constitution in 1787–88, argued that the three branches—the legislative, the executive, and the judiciary—provided a separation of powers, and this served as checks and balances on government power.[6] This country also has a federal system dividing power between federal and state governments. These structural elements and checks are intended to make government responsive and accountable; the administrative imperative to be efficient must be exercised within this structure.

The Constitution enumerates federal powers, meaning the federal government has limited and specified powers. The Constitution reserves to states all authority except the authority granted to the federal government or specifically prohibited to the states. That means state governments have general powers to protect the health, safety, and welfare of the people. States, in turn, delegate and authorize powers to subordinate governments, such as counties, cities, and school districts. Often the scope of government authority as incorporated into legislation is the subject of public debate or of legal challenges.

Political officials are elected as representatives of the people to make the laws, and this power is sometimes called legislative supremacy. Since the mid-1940s, Congress has passed a number of laws, including the Administrative Procedure Act, to make the executive branch and its bureaucracy accountable to congressional oversight.[7] The traditional public administration approach has emphasized executive power. The broad history of government administration reforms, from the Brownlow Commission in 1937, to the Hoover Commission in 1949, to the new public management of the 1980s–1990s, has emphasized executive authority and administrative expertise and autonomy. Some of these writings, particularly in advancing the new public management, have criticized public law and rules as interfering with effective and innovative managers.[8]

The constitutional duty of the president is to execute the laws, veto or approve legislation, and to serve as commander-in-chief. John Rohr, the eminent scholar of public administration and constitutional duties, has noted these represent dual roles: first as a clerk in executing law and second as a leader.[9] Public administrators are viewed as part of the executive branch, with responsibilities to the executive; administrators have narrow responsibilities in carrying out specialized policies and programs. Public managers are called public servants, public employees, or faceless bureaucrats; often they are simply referred to as the government.

The courts have the role and responsibility to hear cases seeking to enforce or challenge government action. Through litigation and appeals, the courts have the power to review the legality and constitutionality of the actions of the other branches of government and to adjudicate private disputes. All courts have the power to strike down legislative content or administrative practices that violate the Constitution; in addition, they also interpret statutes and rules in ways that conflict with administrative assertions and practices. Courts do not institute these decisions; instead, these decisions are made because advocates challenge government actions through the adversarial process. Often this responsibility is called interference with administration. A more diplomatic viewpoint calls this interaction a type of partnership in achieving democratic values.

Finally, the constitutional and democratic government provides rights to individuals and power to the public. That is, the Bill of Rights and other constitutional amendments provide rights to individuals that can limit government actions. Voters, through electing officials and through initiatives and referenda, can impose responsibilities on government. In executing laws, public administrators should act in the public interest[10] and they should consider equity, fairness, and justice in their day-to-day activites.[11]

Governance and the Rule of Law Philosophy

America has a government of laws, not men, said John Adams.[12] This emphasis on government rule by law and not the will of monarchs nor dictators was unique when the Constitution was ratified in 1788. The founders asserted that the United States was a constitutional republic.[13] The country has endured and, although we now call the nation a democracy which emphasizes a government formed by the people, it just as emphatically is a nation of laws with each of the three branches of government taking roles regarding law: The elected representatives make the laws by writing and passing legislation; the executive branch or bureaucracy enforces and implements the laws; and the judicial branch hears cases that involve challenges to government actions, criminal trials, or suits between individuals based on common law or legislation. The government under law is an enduring and fundamental precept for administrators because the principle of a government under law is part of the democratic values and fabric of government.

Both the press and government officials have emphasized the rule of law in recent years. Here are just three examples of how the phrase is used. The rule of law is essential in a democratic form of government. It implies the need for appropriate legal review of laws and the acts of the government. Even in international relations, the rule of law is essential because it makes global trade predictable and assures nations that contracts and treaties are enforceable.

Principles of the Rule of Law

Although there are a number of definitions of rule of law, the concept can be seen as part of a philosophy of legal and legitimate government. Andrew Altman, an expert in the philosophy of law, presents five basic principles of the rule of law. First, law serves to constrain and regulate the power of government; this means government must have authority to act, and administrators may not operate above the law.

Second, governments operate by laying down and enforcing general rules that apply to the entire population or to particular segments of the population. Government carries out the task of maintaining order and peace for society; it detects and punishes those who endanger society in criminal cases; and it regulates civil matters such as contracts or property rights. Government cannot punish individuals unless it can show that they violated these authoritative rules.

Third, there must be notice and fair warning to the public about the rules. This includes how the rules are made and the form of the rules. The elements of this principle include that the rules must be

1. made public;
2. reasonably clear in meaning;
3. applied prospectively and not retroactively;
4. applied impartially;
5. applied in a manner consistent with their meaning;
6. coherent and possible to comply with; and
7. enacted in a lawful manner.

Fourth, government must give individuals a fair chance to defend themselves from charges and a fair chance to challenge government decisions; this principle requires government to provide individuals due process of law.

Fifth, the political power comes from the people. Neither the people nor government are above the law. Thus, government and its officials must also abide by the laws.[14]

The principles of the rule of law are often incorporated in established administrative practice, but the task of applying these general principles to specific functions or individual situations often involves subtlety and craftsmanship. Although the term "legal-rational approach to public organizations" is often used as a criticism of rigid form, structure, or a bureaucracy, the application of authoritative rules or statutes that enable agencies is rarely automatic or mechanical. The practical tasks for administrators include implementing, interpreting, evaluating, and advocating laws. Here the practical application of rules to individual facts or circumstances also involves discretion, judgment, and compassion. Frequently, court cases that challenge government statutes, rules, decisions, and action involve rule-of-law principles, and courts emphasize the importance of due process of law.

The principles of the rule of law are abstract or generalized criteria that relate to process rather than to the content of the decisions, legislation, or rules. The content of what administrators do is found in enabling legislation and in established standard operating procedures. The Constitution serves as the foundation of the system of institutions and powers and as a source of democratic values.

Administrative and Legal Complexity

American law is complex because there are many types of law, and because when an administrators acts she must act according to what she believes the law requires; that is, administrators interpret the law. There are six types of legal authority in American government; the Constitution is the supreme law of the land and from the constitutional foundations flow the statutes, court opinions, regulations, treaties, and executive orders that form public law. The term public law is used here to denote the laws that public administrators enforce that either mandate or enable administrators to act or constrain the actions of government. Private law regulates the conduct between individuals or businesses. Lawyers often divide the law into a number of substantive or content areas such as criminal law, juvenile law, constitutional law, contracts, torts, property law, and so on. Law also can include agreements and contracts, standard operating practices, as well as community conventions. American law is dynamic in that it allows for changes either in statutes or through court decrees.

Notes on Courts and Public Law

Courts provides for review of government actions for legality, constitutionality, and for developing common law obligations. Although courts are the subject of a later chapter, some preliminary notes are worth presenting here. Courts are the forum for challenging government actions, and they provide one avenue for exercising the right to petition government for redress as guaranteed in the Constitution. Although constitutional and legal challenges affect administrators, these are part of the democratic process. The right of individuals to sue the government to challenge government action is also considered an important element in the rule- of-law philosophy. The ability of individuals to challenge statutes passed by the legislature or actions undertaken by the executive and administrators is part of democratic feedback, and it also is related to the rule-of-law philosophy of no one being above the law.

The court system in the Anglo-American tradition provides for resolving disputes between adversaries before a court. The authority of the trial court is divided between the judge who determines legal questions and manages the case before him and the jury who act as the factfinder to determine the victor or winning party. Individuals can appeal trial decisions based on legal issues, and in a common law tradition these appellate decisions addressing issues of law become precedents and become binding on actions of other individuals and entities.

Administrative Purpose

The purpose of public administration is to carry out public law. "Public organizations exist to administer the law, and every element of their being—their structure, staffing, budgeting, and purpose—is the product of legal authority."[15] This emphasis links administrative duties not to policy or to efficiency but to the statutes and the sources of the delegations of authority. Not only are administrators expected to know the law that applies to them, they are expected to act in conformity with the law. This means administrative actions should be consistent with constitutional and democratic values. As Woodrow Wilson said, the government runs a Constitution.[16] In other words, administrators need to act legally and legitimately. Failure of administrators to act in conformity with the law has legal consequences that can give rise to voiding or overturning government actions, and it can give rise to government or personal liability. Another important consideration is that failure to act in a legal manner can affect the perception of the public about the authority and responsibility of government. When it fails to act within the law, government loses the public's faith in the government's claim to legitimacy.

Often public managers are confronted with situations that affect individuals, the community, and actions of other government agencies. Managers have to consider policy, budget, or public-interest aspects. Public administration commentators use the terms "stakeholders" and "interests" to describe who may be included in agency decisions or how different actors may be affected by a situation. Various techniques for qualitative or quantitative analysis may be used to address a situation. Traditional public administration theory, textbooks, and training emphasize efficient, businesslike management. However, there are often legal considerations that public officials and public managers must include in their decision-making and service-delivery practices.

Government Legitimacy

The legitimacy of government is considered both in the academic sectors and in public opinion. For academics, legitimacy of public administration is discussed in the context of the founding documents of constitutions and charters. There are specific Articles in the U.S. Constitution that define the legislative, executive, and judicial powers. Although the Constitution mentions minor offices and appointments, there is no focused attention given to public administration or public servants in this founding document. After John Rohr drew attention to the lack of explicit constitutional text regarding public administrators,[17] scholars addressed the issue of legitimacy of public administration at the national level. To establish legitimacy, some scholars looked to the "intent of the founders," and often this only includes the Federalist Papers. Some analysts discussed constitutional legitimacy in relation to ethical duties for administrators.[18] Other commentators argued that public administrators were ultimately responsible to the people and must seek the public good that is consistent with constitutional and democratic values.[19]

State constitutions and local charters define their government powers differently than the federal Constitution. State and local founding documents often have specific and detailed references to administrative departments and officers. Yet, many theoretical and conceptual discussions about constitutional legitimacy apply to every level of government. The constitutions and charters define and enumerate the powers of our governments, and without the direct express grant of powers, governments are without authority.

The government legitimacy discussions contain some common themes. These include these concerns: sources of power, clear lines of organizational authority, functional results orientation, public representation, and responsiveness. These formal versus functional debates recur in public administration literature.

The concern of public opinion about the legitimacy of public management action is often linked to skepticism about or hostility toward bureaucracy in general. Challenges about legitimacy relate to lawful, fair process; concerns about legitimacy may be linked to perceptions of unfair or unjust results. Scandal, both at the very top levels of government or from embezzlement allegations about local clerks, can affect views of legitimacy. There may be occasions where administrators have followed the law but public opinion leaders such as politicians, news reporters, or commentators have argued that a particular law is unfair or unjust.

Democratic Values and Administration

Government under the law is another way of expressing the values inherent in a democratic republic founded on a constitution. Democratic values include justice, equity, fairness, and liberty. Philosophers and theorists have enumerated aspects of what the rule of law under a constitution means. They have linked it to democratic values of governance.

Governing under the law requires that a public manager be aware of both managerial concerns and legal context. Government under law means managers need competence in public law. The study of public administration in the early decades of the twentieth century emphasized business management as a foundation and de-emphasized law. One of the first to assert that business, not law, was the proper source of normative values was public administration theorist Leonard White.[20] This "business values" approach to public administration emphasized the idea of neutral and efficient managers; it advocated a separation of politics and administration

More recently, in 1995, Ronald Moe and Robert Gilmour argued public-law principles must be included in the theoretical foundations of public administration.[21] These respected theorists of government developed principles of public administration that incorporated the legal and constitutional framework. Their focus was on the federal government, and they began by stressing the importance of the constitutional structure of congressional supremacy in passing laws and that the executive is responsible for executing the laws. Legislation is essential for proper and effective management of policies and programs. They note how courts hold managers accountable for first maintaining procedural safeguards for citizens and employees, and second for conforming to legislative substantive standards and deadlines. They emphasized how the public administration responsibilities of political and public accountability and achievement of public-policy objectives were related to clear statutory authority and to clear lines of reporting from subordinates to managers.[22]

The public administration principles that Moe and Gilmore discuss reflect rule-of- law principles, constitutional functions, and administrative considerations. They emphasize how law is part of public managers' responsibilities. Many other public administration scholars share this view.

The ability to understand law and judicial reasoning is essential for public administrators. Where ignorance of law may have been acceptable 50 years ago, it no longer is.[23] Just like understanding statistical reasoning or budgetary adoption, understanding law is part of job competence. "A reasonably competent public official should know the law governing his conduct," said the Supreme Court in *Harlow v. Fitzgerald*.[24]

Plan of This Book

Understanding law is an essential competence for public managers because administration, governance, and law are interrelated. There are many types of competence that public administrators need in their jobs. Many books and courses emphasize the general managerial duties and skills that are contained in the acronym PODSCORB (Planning, Organizing, Directing, Staffing, Co-ordinating, Reporting, and Budgeting).[25] As part of the systematic evaluation of the executive branch by the Brownlow Committee in 1937, Luther Gulick contributed PODSCORB which is a foundation of the theory of executive and administrative responsibility. During the 1930s, public administration was deemed to be separate from politics, and this meant laws would be made by politicians and then administrators would efficiently and effectively carry them out.

This book presents an introduction and overview of how law relates to the values, foundation, institutions, activities, policies, and procedures of public managers. This book serves to introduce three general areas where law affects administration. First, this introductory chapter discusses constitutions and rule of law as structural and philosophical foundations for governance. Chapter 2 considers constitutional authority and limits and then how individual rights affect administrative practice.

The next three chapters address public law aspects of the different branches. Chapter 3 discusses policy and legislation. Chapter 4 explains judicial process in trials and appeals and the court doctrines about decision-making; this chapter also considers alternative dispute resolution. Chapter 5 addresses administrative practice and administrative procedure laws.

Then, three chapters include overviews of three substantive areas of common law that often affect government and administrative operations: Chapter 6 addresses property, Chapter 7 includes contract law and contracting, and Chapter 8 includes tort law.

Chapter 9 considers how administrators can address legal and governance issues. This concluding chapter considers administrators and attorney relationships, common criticisms, and democratic responses to legal problems.

Each of these chapters discusses aspects of law and public administration. For chapters 2 through 9, discussion questions and illustrative cases are included at the end of each chapter. These cases were chosen to allow readers to evaluate problems that affect administrators and how courts evaluate the legal issues. In each case, there are management concerns about how to accomplish government goals or how to respond when a government law, policy, or decision is challenged in the legal system. These cases illustrate judicial decision-making that includes a recitation of the legally relevant facts, the court's indication of the legal issue, the legal reasoning—rationale and the holding—or legal result. In the case method used in law schools, students are expected to identify these elements through writing a brief of a case. Although this approach may be used with this book, the intent of these cases is to illustrate how courts evaluate an administrative situation and to provide the reader the opportunity to compare legal and managerial views of the particular situation.

This book intends to teach general principles that related to administrators as they carry out public law. It does not provide authoritative legal advice. Legal advice is provided by attorneys and legal counsel in the form of opinions. Legal advice is often specific to the type of agency, the state or federal legislation and case law, and to the particular facts of a given situation. The intent of this book is not to practice law or give advice but instead to provide a foundation for administrators to work with their council in gathering advice, making decisions, and taking action in a lawful and legitimate manner. This book is a starting place for public managers to act under the rule of law.

Discussion Questions

1. What experiences have you had with law or the legal system? Were these from a course, as part of your job, as a witness, a juror, or a party to a lawsuit? How do these experiences affect your view of law and government?
2. How is the Constitution related to democratic values?
3. What are the six sources of legal authority in public law?
4. How do the rule-of-law principles compare and contrast to public administration principles?
5. How do managers develop and maintain legal competence?

2

Constitutional Concerns

Government Powers and Individual Rights

Although constitutions are very important documents in a democracy, few people read them; constitutions and charters are normally dry reading. They are formative and authorizing documents that express the social contract between the people and their governments, but most people have only a general understanding of constitutions. These documents provide structure, yet it is in the operation of governing that first illustrates what a constitution means. The second approach to illuminating what a constitution means is through court cases, particularly appeals to the highest court. In this setting, what is a constitutional government practice is often based on the facts and circumstances of an individual case that challenges a government statute, rule, or action. Challenges are based not just on the text of the Constitution but on advocacy and reasoning about what the Constitution means. The final determination of what is constitutional rests on the interpretation of narrow questions decided by the highest court of the jurisdiction and for the federal government—this is the U.S. Supreme Court.

Constitutional Law and the Courts

Constitutional law is considered to be the body of Supreme Court decisions on constitutional questions; but states also develop their constitutional law in a similar manner. "Landmark case" is the term for the particularly influential cases that address important questions or change established interpretations. One example of a landmark case is *Brown v. Board of Education,* which found in 1954 that segregated schools were unconstitutional and that this state action denied the equal protection guarantee of the Fourteenth Amendment; this case ruled that the prior judicial test of "separate but equal" was discriminatory.[1] Another landmark case, *Miranda v. Arizona,* provided the statement police must read to criminal suspects to inform them of their Fifth Amendment right to remain silent.[2] The Supreme Court may decide up to 100 cases a year; these include cases that involve federal questions regarding statutes, administrative rules, and constitutional questions. The facts and circumstances, or the subtleties in interpretation, make constitutional law an area for experts. It is not possible for lawyers or public administrators to know all cases. However, there are general aspects of principles of constitutional law that all administrators should be familiar with, and there are other aspects that directly affect the job responsibilities of particular administrators.

There may be cases that raise issues of constitutional law at any level from trial to appellate court, but very few reach the U.S. Supreme Court. This is also true of constitutional cases that reach the highest state court. There are two reasons for this: First, courts avoid making constitutional determinations if a decision can be reached based on statutes or common law. And second, very few cases are appealed all the way to the court of last resort. However, administrators should be familiar with a number of constitutional concepts and provisions.

As part of democratic values, administrators are expected to act in a constitutional manner, but it is not easy to understand opinions that contain many legal issues and where the court's opinion includes lengthy discussion of the legal setting and rationale. At other times, controversial cases may have split decisions between a majority and dissent with multiple concurring opinions; the opinions in some cases approach one-hundred pages. One particular difficulty with understanding Supreme Court decisions is that the courts often use balancing tests to determine whether a particular action is constitutional. Balancing tests are intended to set forth considerations for administrators to weigh and evaluate in similar situations when constitutional rights or authority is in question. For example, when individuals challenge the methods or processes government uses, the Supreme Court in *Matthews v. Eldridge* sets forth this balancing test to determine whether additional procedures are required. There should be a consideration of the cost of the additional procedure sought, the risk of error if it is withheld, and the consequences of error to the person seeking the procedure.[3] It is common when comparing government procedures and individual rights for the Supreme Court to include balancing tests, with some having more than the three steps discussed here. There are difficulties with applying multipart balancing tests in routine administrative decisions and processes.

As the Supreme Court said in *Harlow v. Fitzgerald*, "A reasonably competent public official should know the law governing his conduct."[4] This expresses the responsibility and duty of an administrator. Esteemed scholar of public administration, David Rosenbloom, has repeatedly emphasized the importance of constitutional and legal knowledge for public administrators. Rosenbloom and colleagues call this "constitutional competence," and they have argued that this quote and other constitutional cases require that public administrators have constitutional competence.[5] This chapter provides a starting place for developing this competence. The chapter first discusses constitutional issues involving structure and constraints on authority of federal and state governments. Then, the chapter considers individual constitutional rights that arise under the Bill of Rights and other constitutional amendments.

The study and understanding of constitutional law and authority often includes understanding the general historic setting, the contemporary political environment, as well as the particular factual context of particular cases. A number of textbooks, such as Epstein and Walker's *Constitutional Law for a Changing America*, combine the historic overview and context with cases that illustrate constitutional law.[6] Supreme Court cases are organized and discussed in textbooks by subject matter or themes. In law books, the questions of allocation of power often include judicial review and federal jurisdiction; legislative powers; particular provisions or clauses such as the Commerce Clause and the Taxing and Spending Clause; executive powers and administrative actions; federalism concerns of state power, pre-emption, or concurrent authority. The consideration of constitutional individual rights and liberties includes due process, equal protection, free speech, and search-and-seizure provisions, among others.

Constitutional questions can arise in almost any administrative setting or situation. David Rosenbloom and colleagues organized their text on constitutional aspects of public administration by categories of situations including constitutional structure, liability for violating constitutional rights, privatizing, decision-making, effectiveness, efficiency, economy, and administrative standardization.[7] As this list illustrates, constitutional issues arise in all areas of traditional administrative topics. It is more common to consider issues in relation to legal categories or constitutional clauses.

Governmental Power and Authority

The foundation framework of a constitutional government places inherent and explicit limitations on government action. These limits reflect both the Founders' concerns and current public concerns about democratic governance including: American skepticism about the size, role, and expense of government; the ideal of the need to justify the use of governmental powers; and the appropriate scope of government and society involvement in individual or private activities.

The federal government is defined by the Constitution as a government of enumerated and limited authority. Some of the powers and constitutional provisions were incomplete. For example, the power of the President to appoint officials with the advice and consent of the Senate was included in the Constitution, but an essential aspect of administration—the ability of the President to remove officials he appointed—was not expressed in the Constitution. Thus, a personnel issue of removal of an appointed justice of the peace was the factual situation in the groundbreaking case of *Marbury v. Madison*.[8] This case is better known for the legal holding that the Supreme Court has the final say in determining what is constitutional. The ability of Congress to form agencies and entities was not expressly stated either, and so the formation of a national bank and the ability of states to tax branches of that bank were the questions in *McCullough v. Maryland*.[9] Contemporaneous arguments by Thomas Jefferson and Alexander Hamilton demonstrated that there was no consensus of the constitutional framers about these issues.[10] Questions that were not discussed by the framers and new problems or technology that could not be anticipated by the framers are often brought before the Supreme Court. The manner of resolution of these cases often is built on precedent, advocacy, and pragmatism.

The limited government approach was the dominant view in Supreme Court decisions evaluating federal programs and laws until the late 1930s. The expansion of the administrative state as part of the New Deal introduced numerous laws that broadened federal government agencies to provide methods to regulate commerce, banking, employment, unions, securities, and provide for distribution of social benefits. The New Deal programs first were subject to a number of Supreme Court cases that found that Congress exceeded its authority to regulate under the Commerce Clause and also delegated too much responsibility to agencies to define regulations and enforce the laws. However, in the late 1930s, a shift in the membership in the court facilitated the Court to use the Commerce Clause to be the basis for the administrative state.[11] Now, the scope of very broad federal powers is often based on this clause.

The federal government, by its founding terms, is one of enumerated and limited powers. Constitutional issues and cases often arise in two categories: first the structure, functions, and powers of the government; and second, the constitutional rights of the people and the duties and limits these impose on governments. In contrast, state governments are considered to have broad sovereign powers; they have general governmental powers and the authority to carry them out. State constitutions also address the structure of government and rights, and states are considered to have broad powers. State constitutions are typically longer and more detailed than the federal Constitution.[12]

Although there are federal and state constitutions, most times the discussion of constitutional claims or rights is based on the federal Constitution. This is because, first, as the supreme law of the land, the U.S. Constitution is the foundation and final authority on law. Second, these Supreme Court cases are applicable throughout the nation and state cases interpreting their constitutions apply only to that state. Third, it is traditional in law classes to emphasize the

U.S. Constitution and general legal principles. As a result, public administrators who work for state or local governments develop an understanding of the fundamentals of their state constitution, statutes, and precedent through on-the-job training and especially through updates and advice of their legal counsel on the legal issues and doctrine that affect them.

Local governments have powers that are derived from the state because they are subdivisions of the state; local powers are often granted by state constitutional provisions or legislation. Thus local governments have more limited authority than either state or federal governments. The types of powers and activities a local government may hold depends on the type of government— whether it is a county, city, small town, or special purpose government like a school board; on the size of the government; and on whether the source of powers comes from the constitution or statutes. The broadest type of powers for local government are home rule powers, where the government can establish its power through a charter subject to specific limitations clearly expressed in state statutes.[13]

Constitutional Functions

The Constitution is a foundation. It provides the form and structure of government. It provides for the branches and separation of powers. The text or language of constitutions includes the powers, duties, and limits on government and constitutions provide for individual rights.

State and federal government share the three-branch structure. The important difference in the federal Constitution by its terms is one of enumerated powers. That is, the federal government's authority to act must be linked to specified powers within the Constitution. For example, the federal government's most pervasive power it is to regulate commerce. The Commerce Clause states that Congress has the power "To regulate Commerce with foreign Nations, and among the several States, and with the Indian Tribes."[14] The Commerce Clause is the basis for much of the federal regulatory action since the 1930s. Another important source of federal authority is the Taxing and Spending Clause, which states, "The Congress shall have power to lay and collect taxes, duties, imports and excises, to pay the debts and provide for the common defense and general welfare of the United States."[15] These two separate powers are used to achieve policy purposes; the ability to tax can be exercised to affect people's behaviors. The spending power is also used to achieve policy goals. Congress may impose conditions to federal grants or other spending, and so this power may indirectly regulate activities that federal government could not mandate under other constitutional authority. The courts have upheld these conditions.

The Civil War amendments—the Fourteenth, Fifteenth, and Sixteenth—gave Congress the power to enact legislation to enforce their provisions that included equal protection, citizenship, and voting rights. This is the source of the authority for much of the Civil Rights legislation that prohibited discrimination. Yet, in addition, some Civil Rights legislation is based on the Commerce Clause as well. Thus, the ability to end discrimination in employment is both based on Civil Rights legislation and the ability to regulate commerce among the several states.

There are a number of grants of powers in the Constitution. These include the ability to grant citizenship, to regulate bankruptcy, or to protect intellectual property. The executive's ability to wage war and enter into to treaties are exclusive federal powers.

Although "public administrators" are not mentioned in the Constitution, the ability to appoint minor officers with the approval of the Senate is one of the executive powers. There are other limits on how government and administrators carry out normal activities. For instance, federal taxes and budgets must originate in legislation in the House of Representatives because of the constitutional provision: "All bills for Raising Revenue must originate in the House."[16] It should be noted that in practice, the President develops and proposes the budget, and refers the spending and economic plan to Congress where the House originates the budget bills and then both houses work on the annual budget legislation.

These examples are illustrative and not exhaustive. There are many excellent books on constitutional law and constitution in a democracy. These incorporate historic developments of constitutional powers, the role of Supreme Court, and often consideration of individual rights.

Constitutional Constraints and Public Accountability

Analysts commonly complain that administrators are constrained by law, but limiting the power of government and its public servants is a fundamental aim of constitutions and laws. By their nature and purpose, constitutions form and limit government's powers. These constraints are often included in constitutions and legislation for the purpose of imposing limits and procedures on government as an aspect of public accountability and responsiveness. Often there are legal cases that challenge particular statutes or executive exercises of power. In some situations, constitutional authority and constraints are well-known to administrators because the constitutional limits are interpreted through their incorporation into administrative practice rather than by case law interpretations. This is particularly the situation regarding taxes, and there are different approaches contained in federal and state constitutions. As this section shows, fiscal limits are an important aspect of public accountability and are popular limits on government power that impose procedures and constraints on taxing, spending, and borrowing.

One familiar limitation on state and local governments is the balanced budget requirement. All states but one have constitutional balanced budget requirements that limit the expenditures in a given year to the amount of revenue raised and existing reserves. In other words, state and local governments cannot engage in deficit spending. This constitutional constraint is rarely the subject of court decree or interpretation, but it serves as a limit on executive and legislative action both as a method of public accountability and as a way to limit discretion. Historically, balanced budgets requirements originated from profligate state and local borrowing actions in the 1880s. During that period, many state and local governments issued bonds to invest in economic development. In particular, they borrowed money through bonds to help build railroads. When the economy tanked, that is, when an economic crisis ensued, many governments defaulted on their bonds.

In response to the public outrage, many states adopted three types of constitutional amendments to impose fiscal restraint. States limited the amount of money that governments could borrow, they imposed public referenda before incurring bond debt, and they required governments to operate with a balanced budget. These structural financial control amendments were imposed because of poor decisions that included imprudent exuberance, poor assessment about growth, and a failure to recognize the possibility of economic downturns. These constitutional amendments intended to impose fiscal prudence upon government through providing standards for governments to follow.[17]

The skeptical attitude about government spending and need for control runs deep in American society and history. For a country founded on a tax protest—the Boston Tea Party—the theme of careful government and imposing limits on spending is often reflected in other state constitutional provisions. In 1976, taxpayer revolts began when California voters approved Proposition 13 in a referendum; this complex state constitutional amendment limited the growth of state expenditures in relation to the growth of per capita income, and it also imposed limits on property taxes. Massachusetts soon followed by passing Proposition 2-1/2, which over time reduced property taxes to an amount of two-and-a-half percent of full market value. Other states followed this approach of adopting constitutional amendments to limit taxing and spending. Another dramatic tax limitation was Colorado's 1992 Taxpayer Bill of Rights, or TABOR. Once again, this was a constitutional amendment intended to control government spending. Other states adopted similar measures that include property tax relief through tax ceilings, setting limits on any increase in taxes or fees without voter approval, setting limits on carryover of reserves, and requiring states to issue refunds to taxpayers if revenues exceeded projections or authorized expenditures. These reforms did not reflect a desire for fewer services, instead these constitutional constraints were based on the presumptions that government spending was excessive and inefficient.[18] As part of their design, these taxpayer limits increased the difficulty in planning and accomplishing public goals. Although politicians and commentators have suggested it, the federal government does not have a balanced budget requirement.

State constitutions also have additional provisions that limit public finance. First, government can only issue debt for public purposes, and it is common for suits to challenge whether particular economic development plans serve a public purpose. Second, most states prohibit state or local government from loaning its credit for the aid of any individual, association, or corporation. Since the term "public credit" can be ambiguous and because creative financing plans are often invented to circumvent limits, lawsuits challenging these actions occur.

Not only are there state constitutional requirements for issuing bonds and taxes, there may be legal challenges to taxing and spending decisions alleging unconstitutional purpose; that is, suits that argue that a taxing decision violates a state constitution are brought in a state court. However, the common court practice and common law doctrine presumes that government taxes, borrowing, and statutory actions are constitutional and legal; thus, the individual challenging the action has the burden to demonstrate that it is unconstitutional.[19] When a business received tax relief as an incentive for economic development, a challenge was brought by citizens claiming this affected taxpayer status in federal court, but when the case reached the Supreme Court, the court rejected the suit as lacking federal standing. As Chief Justice Roberts said, "Affording state taxpayers standing to press such challenges simply because their tax burden gives them an interest in the state treasury, would interpose the federal courts as virtually continuing monitors of the wisdom and soundness of state fiscal administration, contrary to the more modest role Article III vision for federal courts."[20] This case is consistent with other federal cases where a challenge to a government decision based on the plaintiff being a taxpayer is seldom considered sufficient for standing to bring a case in federal court.

A final illustration of differences in constitutional budget provisions contrasting the states and the federal government is the line item veto. Many states grant their governors line item veto power and this power has been suggested as a way to reform federal budgets. The line item veto allows the governor to eliminate provisions of the budget, line by line, subject of course to a veto-override by the legislature. Thus line item vetoes are promoted as prudential controls. During President Clinton's administration, Congress passed the Line Item Veto Act in 1996 to permit presidential line item vetoes. This law was first challenged as unconstitutional by Senator Robert Byrd, but his case was dismissed because the senator lacked standing.[21] Then President Clinton exercised the law through vetoing three items, including a Medicaid provision that would benefit New York City. New York sued and the case reached the Supreme Court in 1998.[22] A divided court found that the presidential line item veto interfered with legislative authority to initiate spending. Justice Kennedy began his concurring opinion with "A nation cannot plunder its own treasury without putting its Constitution and its survival in peril."[23] Justice Breyer's dissent viewed the law as novel, but constitutional: "In a sense it skirts a constitutional edge. That edge has to do with means, not ends."[24] But the majority of the justices found the line item veto to be an unconstitutional delegation to the executive, and the opinion expressly stated that for a presidential line item veto power to be valid it would require a constitutional amendment.

Although "states may be the laboratories of democracy," not all governmental approaches can be replicated or applied to other jurisdictions with the same result. It is worth remembering that this famous dictum by Justice Louis Brandeis was argued in a dissent where the Supreme Court overturned a state statute requiring licenses for those in the ice business. The full quote is: "It is one of the happy incidents of the federal system that a single courageous State may, if its citizens choose, serve as a laboratory; and try novel social and economic experiments without risk to the rest of the country."[25] An inventive Congress learned where one constitutional boundary existed when it tried to enact the line item veto.

Individual Constitutional Rights

A number of rights to protect individuals from government action are found in the Constitution, Bill of Rights, and other constitutional amendments. Public administrators, as government actors, can be found liable for violating individuals' rights and so knowledge of the law in this area is important to avoid public harm and personal liability of the manager.

The Bill of Rights of the U.S. Constitution includes a number of provisions that guarantee court review and due process in both criminal and civil actions. The rights to court review and due process are probably the most important for public administrators to know. The Fifth, Sixth, and Seventh Amendments provide for essentials of due process. The Fifth Amendment is broad; it covers indictment for crimes, double jeopardy, and self-incrimination. It also requires due process for government actions and compensation for governmental takings. The Sixth Amendment provides the accused in criminal cases to have the right to a speedy and fair trial, an impartial jury; and right to counsel. The Seventh Amendment guarantees a trial by jury in civil cases. The Fourth Amendment prohibits unreasonable searches and seizures. The Eighth Amendment prohibits excessive bail, fines, and cruel and unusual punishment. State constitutions also provide similar guarantees. In addition, the Fourteenth Amendment requires states to provide equal protection and due process.

Public managers may also be involved in questions of First Amendment separation of church and state or free speech. The separation of church and state arises in situation such as school prayer or in the display of a cross or religious symbols in government buildings, and court decisions prohibit the endorsement of a particular religion. The right to free speech has been interpreted to allow some government regulation and restraints on the time and place on speech. However, courts provide more individual protections for free speech regarding government decisions and public policy, and this is called political free speech. Issues of political free speech may arise in the supervision of public employees: Can a public employee be disciplined for something that they say? Statements to a coworker about the President have been found to be free speech, but public statements about policy decisions about the quality of evidence in a criminal trial are not First Amendment free speech.

The type of constitutional cases involving government actions that frequently are litigated involve individual rights found in the Constitution, particularly in the provisions of the Bill of Rights and other amendments. The purpose of the Bill of Rights was to address important democratic values and aspects of the rule of law that were omitted from the Constitution that was adopted at the Philadelphia Constitutional Convention; and by the time the Constitution was adopted, it was clear that a Bill of Rights was needed and that it would be adopted.[26] Now it seems surprising that these important limits on government power were omitted. Although litigation to enforce the constitutional rights of individuals is often framed as government acting wrongly, the Constitution guarantees individuals the right to bring grievances or to petition their government.

Legislative enactments and administrative practice must not violate individuals' constitutional rights and of all the types of constitutional rights that affect administrators, due process is the most pervasive. The next section will discuss due process that is required under the Fifth and Fourteenth Amendments. In the following sections, these constitutional concerns will be discussed: equal protection under the Fourteenth Amendment, rights of free speech, and assembly under the First Amendment; limits on search and seizure from the Fourth Amendment; and the protection from self-incrimination under the Fifth Amendment. The government eminent domain powers will be discussed in Chapter 6.

Due Process Generally

Of the many constitutional rights, due process of law is the most frequent and pervasive concern affecting administrators. Due process of law is an essential guarantee of individual rights that applies to administrative action. Numerous cases raise the issue of the important judicial and democratic value of due process of law. The first type of due process protects individuals from arbitrary, capricious, or unreasonable government actions—this is substantive due process. The second type of due process involves the methods or means that government needs to follow—this is procedural due process. Although the courts have said that due process does not have a single definition, it has often been considered to mean fundamental fairness. Justice Felix Frankfurter explained due process as "unlike some legal rules, is not a technical conception with a fixed content unrelated to time, place and circumstances. . . . It is not a yardstick. It is a process. It is a delicate process of adjustment inescapably involving the exercise of judgment by those whom the Constitution entrusted with the unfolding process."[27]

In considering due process or other constitutional rights, the first consideration is that these provisions apply to government actions and not to private action. As government delivery of services sometimes involves contractors rather than employees, the distinction between public and private actors may at times be a difficult to determine. The second consideration of due process is that the language in the Fifth and Fourteenth Amendments says that government cannot "deny a person life, liberty or property without due process of law." That means that, if due process is provided, then the deprivation of a protected interest by government action is legal.

The Fifth Amendment was part of the Bill of Rights adopted in 1791, and a number of Supreme Court opinions held that these amendments applied only to the federal government. The Fourteenth Amendment, passed after the Civil War, guaranteed due process protections applied to state and local governments.

Although there is not one set definition of due process, the standards that courts consider are well-established, and often the question of due process of law comes down to a question of fundamental fairness. That is, due process guarantees government fairness and this guarantee is protected by court review of agency actions. Although a fundamental fairness standard provides only limited practical guidance to administrators to determine what procedure is required in particular situations, it does provide a practical starting point. A question to evaluate fairness is: Would a member of the general public, like an elementary school kid, consider the government action to be fair?

Substantive Due Process

The claims that involve substantive due process often assert that the government action is arbitrary or capricious. The courts ask this question: Is the law or government action reasonably related to legitimate government goals? If the answer is no, then it violates substantive due process. If a law is so vague that the official responsible for enforcing it cannot define what constitutes acceptable conduct, then it fails to provide substantive due process. Often state statutes or local ordinances are challenged regarding whether they clearly indicate what is prohibited; other times, the challenge is whether the categories for regulation are fair. When ordinances and statutes are challenged, the courts presume that the law is valid, and the burden is placed on the party challenging it to demonstrate that it is not.

The review standard for "arbitrary or unreasonable actions" is also considered in the context of how a law is applied by administrators. If a statute that may be valid on its face is applied in an unfair way, then courts strike down government enforcement of the legislation. In addition, substantive due process is the category for cases that involve the right of privacy. The Supreme Court began to find an individual had a right to privacy in reproduction and birth-control decisions in 1965, when in *Griswold v. Connecticut* the Court struck down a state law that made it a crime for a doctor to discuss birth control with a patient.[28] Regarding this area of privacy interests, the Supreme Court has imposed limits on what government can regulate. Although the right of individual privacy is not found in any provision of the U.S. Constitution, the case law establishes that there is a right to privacy that emanated from other constitutional provisions.

Procedural Due Process

Legal decision-rationality for government action is based on views of due process and appropriate government action. When considering government action, courts look to the decision processes of managers. Courts consider the following questions to evaluate the informed decisions of public managers. The general legal-rationality criteria found in cases address these questions:

1. Was there a law or rule in existence that the government is enforcing?
2. Was the problem identified and articulated by the agency?
3. Was there disclosure of the problem and facts to those affected?
4. Were facts and information gathered to assist the agency in making the decision?
5. Was the administrator's decision made based on the available facts?
6. Was the basis of the decision explained to those affected?

These criteria are procedural due process requirements that are based on a judicial model of informed and reasoned decision-making. They require managers to act based on research and learning, but they also impose on them the responsibility of explaining and disclosing information to those affected. The foundation for these legal expectations is long established in common law and in constitutional law. Legal decision-rationality has both practical and useable management applications. In general, courts expect and require administrators to use rational and measured processes for making rules and for making decisions. (Due process standards for administrative actions are also discussed in Chapter 5.)

The question of procedural due process often depends on the type of legal situation. Due process in a criminal trial provides the most protection to the individual because the penalty of incarceration or even the death penalty, with the loss of liberty or life, is seen as a severe penalty. Due process in public employment disciplinary actions or termination actions is different from due process for government benefits. For example, due process in public employment allows the opportunity for a hearing, but it does not have to be a formal hearing and the hearing does not have to occur before the discipline is imposed. For termination of government benefits, especially benefits that provide basic necessities for survival, the Court has held that an evidentiary hearing before termination of the benefits is required for due process. Finally, cases involving school or college student disciplinary actions have different and often more lenient due process requirements. For students in elementary and high school, the due process requirements for suspension or expulsion are not as stringent as for cases involving termination of government benefits. The differences in due process standards based on the type of issues involved means that public managers need to work with attorneys to determine what process is due for the particular requirements of the programs that an agency carries out.

Equal Protection and Classifications

Equal protection limits government from making and applying unfair classifications, and this right is found in the Fourteenth Amendment, which limits state and local government action. Equal protection also applies to the federal government under the Fifth Amendment protections. The Fourteenth Amendment says that states "shall not deny to any person within its jurisdiction the equal protection of the laws." This provision was intended to protect the recently emancipated from state-sanctioned discrimination; however, for nearly one-hundred years there were state-sanctioned practices that discriminated against African Americans. Some cases challenged discriminatory practices. For instance in the *Yick Wo v. Hopkins* case in 1886, the Supreme Court held that the city of San Francisco enforcing an ordinance in a discriminatory manner that prohibited only Chinese owners from licensing their businesses was unconstitutional.[29] But in the same era, the court permitted the "separate but equal" argument in *Plessy v. Ferguson* where in 1896 the Court upheld a Louisiana state law mandating separate railway cars based on race.[30] The 1954 landmark decision of *Brown v. Board of Education* found that segregation was not equal and found segregated schools unconstitutional.[31]

After the *Brown* case and with the protests and lobbying from the Civil Rights movement, Congress exercised the authority granted in the Civil Rights amendments to pass laws to enforce those amendments. The Civil Rights laws adopted in the 1960s prohibited discrimination based on race, creed, gender, and national origin. Since then, legislation has extended protected categories to include age and disability. These laws apply to employment, public accommodation, education, and programs that received government funds. Because of the pattern of state-sponsored discrimination and segregation, programs to address past wrongs were adopted; these were called "affirmative action." These remedial programs encouraged government to take steps to desegregate schools and to hire minorities, women, or under-represented groups. But the era of affirmative action to redress past societal wrongs was curtailed when the Supreme Court ruled that affirmative action programs must address past deliberate discrimination by government in the case of *Board of Regents v. Bakke*.[32]

The *Bakke* case, decided in 1972, concerned admissions to a state medical school where the California college officials recognized there were few minority graduates and set aside a number of admission slots for minority applicants. A medical school applicant, Allan Bakke, argued that the admission decision was based not on objective merit criteria but on race and that government decisions based on race were prohibited by the Fourteenth Amendment. The Supreme Court agreed. After *Bakke*, in a number of decisions, the Supreme Court has repeatedly limited the ability of state and local governments, public schools, and universities, to consider race as a factor in the provision of services or benefits. In a recent case involving school districts considering the race of a child when assigning students to attend elementary schools, two cities recognized that the racial composition of their schools was based on where families lived and not on any particular school policies. Although the schools wanted to provide programs to address historic patterns of societal discrimination, the Supreme Court found that these schools could not use programs to assign students to a school if the district considered race as a deciding factor.[33] The important considerations for the court was that there was not clear past discrimination by the government that caused the differences in racial composition of the schools, the remedial plans designed by the schools were not limited in duration, and the dual categories these schools used considering race were not narrowly drawn.

In 2004, the City of New Haven, Connecticut, canceled a promotion list for firefighters because the eligibility for promotion was developed through an exam process that resulted in a low number of minorities passing an exam given in 2003. The city's concern was that the exam results could lead to a lawsuit alleging bias; that is, there was a disparate impact on minorities because of a flawed test. When the exam was voided and the promotion list canceled, individuals who had done well on the exam and who were at the top of the promotion list challenged the city's actions as discriminatory, and this case came before the Supreme Court in 2009. The court found the city's reason for concern about the exam did not have a strong basis in evidence and so it was not a compelling reason to cancel the result of the exam—the promotion lists.[34] As is common Supreme Court practice, when an action raises both a statutory and a constitutional issue, the Court will consider the statutory grounds first. In this case, the Court found that the City's cancellation of the promotion list violated the Civil Rights Act of 1964, and the Court applied Fourteenth Amendment equal protection criteria in reaching its decision.

Many people equate discrimination suits with the constitutional right of equal protection. Equal protection is asserted in more circumstances than racial discrimination. Denial of equal protection of the law has been claimed in cases involving other types of government classifications. For instance, in the landmark case of *Adarand v. Pena,* the question of whether there could be requirements to the contractor to hire minority firms as subcontractors as a condition of awarding a public construction contract; this is called a minority-set aside and it is considered a type of affirmative action. In this case, the court struck down the government's attempts to provide benefits, a set aside, based on race or gender.

The court's discussion in the *Adarand* case serves as the framework for equal protection analysis in government decisions. The types of analysis the court undertakes when a denial of equal protection is asserted falls into three categories. In *Adarand v. Pena*, the Court said that "it follows from that principle that all governmental action based on race—a group classification long recognized as in most circumstances irrelevant and therefore prohibited—should be subjected to detailed judicial inquiry to ensure that the personal right to equal protection of the laws has not been infringed."[35] First, if racial discrimination is alleged then courts treat this as a suspect classification. For a government to prevail, it must show that racial classifications are narrowly tailored to further compelling government interests. Second, in cases that involve questions of gender discrimination, these cases are provided "heightened scrutiny"; this means for the government to prevail, the classifications must serve important government objectives and they must be substantially related to achieving those objectives.

The final category involving government classifications on factors such as age, residency, wealth, distribution of public benefits, or taxation, is considered under an "ordinary scrutiny" standard. Government classifications are generally considered constitutional if they meet the "rational basis test," which requires the government to show that classifications are rationally related to permissible government objectives. Courts presume that government statutes and classifications are valid, and this places the burden of the person challenging them to show unconstitutionality.

It should also be noted that state and local governments must also provide equal protection of the law based on state constitutions and case law. For instance, for tax purposes, statutory classifications need to treat similar property alike. For some types of government actions, the standards that states apply may be different and even more stringent than the rational basis test of the Supreme Court.

Other Fifth Amendment Considerations

The Fifth Amendment also includes a provision that protects individuals from self-incrimination. This right applies to individuals, not entities, but it can be asserted during administrative investigations or by employees during disciplinary actions. The Fifth Amendment limits the government power of eminent domain by protecting individuals from government taking of their property without just compensation. Government using its power of eminent domain will be discussed in Chapter 6.

Protections Against Search and Seizure

The protection in the Fourth Amendment against unreasonable search and seizure applies to both criminal and civil actions. The law in this area is complex. Government officers and their agents can search or inspect public areas where there is no expectation of privacy; they may search some areas of regulated businesses based on statutes, but they may not search or inspect private areas unless they have a warrant. In the criminal setting, before police can execute a search they must have probable cause to obtain a warrant unless there are exigent circumstances that allow an immediate search. The rules for obtaining warrants for searches in administrative investigations and enforcement requires reasonable cause for searches, but there are numerous and detailed exceptions.

The court doctrine regarding search and seizure is complex, but there are some general criteria. First, the fundamental concern is reasonableness. Courts consider expectations of privacy, the intrusiveness of the search, protecting the public from harm, the regulatory scheme, conditions related to licensing or the business, and work rules. Second, individuals can waive the warrant requirement. Routine and unannounced searches or inspections are allowed without a warrant when businesses are pervasively regulated or if the searches are a condition of a license.

When searches are related to employment, the state constitutional protection for employees may be broader than federal rights. The type of job affects the type of protection, beginning first with the expectation of privacy. Workers at airports, schools, or security-conscious environments have lower expectations of privacy. There is no expectation of privacy in public areas or relating to work materials and work areas such as desks and filing cabinets. The concern of efficient and proper operation of the workplace has been considered by the Supreme Court to allow limitations on privacy or to allow searches and inspections. As Justice O'Connor said:

> The legitimate privacy interests of public employees in the private objects they bring to the workplace may be substantial. Against these privacy interests, however, must be balanced the realities of the workplace, which strongly suggests that a warrant requirement would be unworkable. . . .
>
> In our view, requiring an employer to obtain a warrant whenever the employer wishes to enter an employee's office, desk, or file cabinets for work-related purpose would seriously disrupt the routine conduct of business and would be unduly burdensome. Imposing unwieldy warrant procedures in such cases upon supervisors, who would otherwise have no reason to be familiar with such procedures, is simply unreasonable. . . .
>
> Balanced against the substantial government interest in the efficient and proper operation of the workplace are privacy interests of government employees in their place of work which, while not insubstantial, are far less than those found in at home or in some other context. . . .
>
> Government offices are provided to employees for the sole purpose of facilitating the work of an agency. The employee may avoid exposing personal belongings at work by simply leaving them at home.[36]

Searches can be of a location, but the Fourth Amendment also protects government employees from physical searches, such as testing blood for substance abuse. Many public employers subject employees to routine or specific tests for drug or alcohol usage, either periodic or random tests, as a condition of employment. Courts have upheld these requirements when it is related to the job, such as for bus drivers, air traffic controllers, or police officers. In other situations, there must be a reasonable suspicion before requiring testing of employees. The normal and efficient operation of government agencies as compared to rights of employees remains controversial, as does the extent of regulatory inspections.

First Amendment Protections

The First Amendment protects citizens from government abridgement of speech, press, religion, and assembly, but these protections are not absolute. Government may impose place and time constraints on free speech; speech relating to politics or government operations is given broader protection than speech that is profane or incites violence. Regarding religion, cases have raised issues regarding how governments have required the pledge of allegiance or prayer in schools, allowed religious displays at holidays, or permitted inclusion of religious symbols on public monuments.

There are questions of first amendment protections when government regulates commercial speech; advertisements may be regulated to protect the public and ensure that commercial information is not misleading. But there is a view that there is a marketplace of ideas, meaning advertisements, that also inform the public about products. The type of court inquiry regarding regulation of commercial speech involves a two-part test. First, government must show a substantial interest to regulate; and second, government must show that the regulation is not more extensive than is necessary to serve government purposes. Thus, the government regulation of speech must serve to protect the public.

Government employees have First Amendment rights, but these may be narrower than the rights of the general public. Generally, public employees can speak out on issues of public importance, such as letters to the editor or remarks criticizing the President. But rules and practices for effective government operations that may limit freedom of speech have been upheld by the courts. More specifically, government employees do not have a Free Speech right to disclose classified information, and they may not voice their doubts about policies they have been told are not to be challenged publicly. In the *Garcetti v. Ceballos* case, the court upheld the agency disciplining an employee for nonprotected speech.[37] Gil Garcetti was an assistant prosecutor and had reservations about the legality of a search. After a conference with his supervisor, Garcetti was instructed that the search was valid and to proceed with the criminal case. After Garcetti informed the defense and court about his doubts, he was demoted and reassigned by the prosecutor's office. The court found that this was appropriate discipline by the agency managers, and it found that this disclosure was not protected by the First Amendment.

Other areas generally protected by the First Amendment may be the subject of laws that affect public employees. For example, the Hatch Act, which limits volunteer campaign activity that a federal employee can engage in, has been held not to violate the right of political association. Questions of freedom of religion and employment practices are often raised under Civil Rights laws that require reasonable accommodation of religion in job assignments and conditions.

Conclusion

Acting within the Constitution presents a number of difficulties. First, constitutional provisions are often broadly and generally stated, but they have been interpreted to address specific situations. Second, cases that involve constitutional issues often involve not a single constitutional right but a balance of one constitutional right with another, or the cases may raise questions concerning essential democratic or government values. Third, in looking to decisions for guidance, applying the precedent is difficult because courts frequently apply balancing tests or multipart inquiries that are not simple to apply. Fourth, because constitutional right cases involve beliefs and practices that are important to individuals, cases are frequently filed. Finally, the standards courts use often can be framed as: Is the government action reasonable? Was the individual treated unfairly? Was the processes used fair? Standards such as reasonable, unfair, or fair invite courts to consider the facts and circumstances of particular government actions on review.

In addressing constitutional claims and practices, government actors can and should have rational explanations of why they chose a particular action. Constitutional litigation is part of conducting government in a country with democratic values. Public administrators should expect their decisions to be challenged in public discussions and in court; this is part of democratic governance. There will be occasions where government legislation and actions are overturned by the courts. This means public administrators need to keep informed of current court decisions that affect their agency's operations.

Cases

Although the two cases included in this section are old, they deal concisely with important points in cases involving government and individual rights. The first case, *Hesse v. Rath*, raises a question of whether a local government action is consistent with the constitutional grant of powers and authority, and this case was decided by the highest level court in New York, the Court of Appeals. The *Hesse* case raises questions of successful city building, or what we now would call economic development. The two cities Justice Cardozo refers to were across from each other on the Bosporus Strait in the seventh century B.C.E.; Byzantium is the ancient name for present-day Istanbul, Turkey, but Chalcedon was built first in an inferior locale, and this is why it was called the "city of the blind" by the Delphi oracle.[38] The second case, *McMillen v. Anderson,* addresses due process in the context of state tax administration. Here the court found that due process is broader than judicial practice and used common practices rather than citing to legal authority in the rationale. Note the date of 1877 in this case.

Albert O. Hesse v. Fred J. Rath, as Mayor of the City of Utica, et al.,
249 N.Y. 436, Court of Appeals of New York, 1928

Opinion by Cardozo

A statute (L. 1928, ch. 647, amending General Municipal Law, Consol. Laws, ch. 24) authorizes the cities of this State to establish, construct, equip, maintain and operate airports or landing fields for aeroplanes and other aircraft. The local legislative body may regulate the use and establish fees or charges.

The city of Utica, acting under this statute, has contracted to buy 295 acres of land to be used as an airport, and has authorized its officers to issue its corporate bonds in the sum of $120,000 to pay the purchase price.

The Constitution of New York (Article VIII, § 10) provides that no city shall be allowed to incur any indebtedness except for city purposes.

Plaintiff argues that the acquisition of an airport or landing field is not a city purpose, even if a public one, and that the bonds, if issued, will be void.

We think the purpose to be served is both public and municipal.

A city acts for city purposes when it builds a dock or a bridge or a street or a subway (*Sun P. & P. Assn. v. Mayor,* 152 N.Y. 257). Its purpose is not different when it builds an airport (*City of Wichita v. Clapp,* 125 Kans. 100). Aviation is today an established method of transportation. The future, even the near future, will make it still more general. The city that is without the foresight to build the ports for the new traffic may soon be left behind in the race of competition. Chalcedon was called the city of the blind because its founders rejected the nobler site of Byzantium lying at their feet. The need for vision of the future in the governance of cities has not lessened with the years. The dweller within the gates, even more than the stranger from afar, will pay the price of blindness.

The judgment should be affirmed, with costs.

McMillen v. Anderson, 95 U.S. 37, U.S. Supreme Court, 1877

Mr. Justice Miller delivered the opinion of the Court.

The defendant, tax-collector of the State of Louisiana for the parish of

Carroll, seized property of the plaintiff, and was about to sell it for the payment of the license tax of one- hundred dollars, for which the latter, as a person engaged in [the liquor sales] business, was liable. In accordance with the laws of Louisiana, plaintiff brought an action in the proper court of the State for the trespass, and in the same action obtained a temporary injunction against the sale of the property seized. Defendant pleaded that the seizure was for taxes due, and that his duty as collector required him to make it. On a full hearing, the court sustained the defense, and gave a judgment under the statute against plaintiff and his sureties on the bond for double the amount of the tax, and for costs.

Plaintiff thereupon took an appeal to the Supreme Court of Louisiana, and in his petition for appeal alleged that the law under which the proceedings of defendant were had is void, because it is in conflict with the Constitutions of Louisiana and of the United States, and, as he now argues, is specifically opposed to the provision of the Fourteenth Amendment of the latter, which declares that no State shall deprive any person of life, liberty, or property without due process of law.

The judgment of the Supreme Court of Louisiana, to which the present writ of error is directed, affirming that of the inferior court, must be taken as conclusive on all the questions mooted in the record except this one. It must, therefore, be conceded that plaintiff was liable to the tax; that, if the law which authorized the collector to seize the property is valid, his proceedings under it were regular; and that the judgment of the court was sustained by the facts in the case.

Looking at the Louisiana statute here assailed, the act of March 14, 1873, we feel bound to say, that, if it is void on the ground assumed, the revenue laws of nearly all the States will be found void for the same reason. The mode of assessing taxes in the States by the Federal government, and by all governments, is necessarily summary, that it may be speedy and effectual. By summary is not meant arbitrary, or unequal, or illegal. It must, under our Constitution, be lawfully done.

But that does not mean, nor does the phrase "due process of law" mean, by a judicial proceeding. The nation from whom we inherit the phrase "due process of law" has never relied upon the courts of justice for the collection of her taxes, though she passed through a successful revolution in resistance to unlawful taxation. We need not here go into the literature of that constitutional provision, because in any view that can be taken of it the statute under consideration does not violate it. It enacts that, when any person shall fail to refuse or pay his license tax, the collector shall give ten days' written or printed notice to the delinquent requiring its payment; and the manner of giving this notice is fully prescribed. If at the expiration of this time the license "be not fully paid, the tax-collector may, without judicial formality, proceed to seize and sell, after ten days' advertisement, the property" of the delinquent, or so much as may be necessary to pay the tax and costs.

Another statute declares who is liable to this tax, and fixes the amount of it. The statute here complained of relates only to the manner of its collection.

There is a notice that the party is assessed, by the proper officer, for a given sum as a tax of a certain kind, and ten days' time given him to pay it. Is not this a legal mode of proceeding? It seems to be supposed that it is essential to the validity of this tax that the party charged should have been present, or had an opportunity to be present, in some tribunal when he was assessed. But this is not, and never has been, considered necessary to the validity of a tax. And the fact that most of the States now have boards of revisers of tax assessments does not prove that taxes levied without them are void.

Nor is the person charged with such a tax without legal remedy by the laws of Louisiana. It is probable that in that State, as in others, if compelled to pay the tax by a levy upon his property, he can sue the proper party, and recover back the money as paid under duress, if the tax was illegal.

But however that may be, it is quite certain that he can, if he is wrongfully taxed, stay the proceeding for its collection by process of injunction. See *Fouqua's Code of Practice of Louisiana*, arts. 296–309, inclusive. The act of 1874 recognizes this right to an injunction, and regulates the proceedings when issued to stay the collection of taxes. It declares that they shall be treated by the courts as preferred cases, and imposes a double tax upon a dissolution of the injunction.

But it is said that this is not due course of law, because the judge granting the injunction is required to take security of the applicant, and that no remedial process can be within the meaning of the Constitution which requires such a bond as a condition precedent to its issue.

It can hardly be necessary to answer an argument which excludes from the definition of due process of law all that numerous class of remedies in which, by the rules of the court or by legislative provisions, a party invoking the powers of a court of justice is required to give that security which is necessary to prevent its process from being used to work gross injustice to another.

Judgment affirmed.

Discussion Questions

1. Discuss how constitutions and charters both define and limit government authority.
2. The U.S. Constitution is the supreme law of the land. Consider how state constitutions can be different, such as adding tax limit provisions or specifying administrative responsibilities.

3. Discuss how the Constitution provides the philosophical basis for American government as well as imposes requirements on administrators.

4. What are the differences and similarities between procedural due process, substantive due process, and equal protection?

5. Constitutional law is developed through court opinions. What are some recent Supreme Court opinions that have affected administrative practices?

6. There are many constitutional provisions that may not be subject to court decisions, but these affect governance. Review your state constitution and find out if there are public budget or finance requirements.

7. How did the court in the *Hesse* case consider what were constitutional city purposes? Under this definition, what else is a government purpose? Was this decision persuasive?

8. Due process is not just a judicial doctrine according to the *McMillen* case. Consider whether the year of this case, 1877, affects its relevance to current administrative practices. Consider how much $100 would buy in 1877. Would the equivalent amount be considered a fair tax today?

3

Policy, Administration, and Legislation

People's everyday understanding of statutes and ordinances is not the same as how judges and lawyers, or even administrators, evaluate these laws. For example, most people know that there are local ordinances that prohibit people from walking in the middle of the street and prohibit kids from playing ball in the street, but they walk and play in the streets. Sometimes this causes problems and complaints to city hall. One situation occurred when kids were playing ball in the street; when the neighbors complained, the police were sent to respond a number of times. The complaining neighbors wanted the law to be literally and strictly enforced. But the parents argued there were few places for kids to play and since this was a dead-end street, the kids playing there were not a traffic hazard and the parents were able to keep track of where the kids were and what they were doing. The parents argued that the law was not meant to apply to this situation. The police and city hall were stuck in the middle of this ongoing dispute.[1] In this situation, there were two distinct everyday views of the purpose of the laws and how they should be applied.

The question of how to interpret and apply the laws is a frequent concern for public managers. It is connected to how public policy is made and how it is interpreted and challenged. Interpreting policy and law are part of administration and governance. Discussing the importance of legal knowledge for public servants, public administration scholar Rosemary O'Leary said, "If the bureaucrats of tomorrow are to have an understanding of how public policy is made and implemented, knowledge of law is essential."[2] This chapter addresses policy, administration, and legislation.

Policy Focus

Public managers focus on performing tasks and achieving policies as they carry out their public responsibilities. Policy, administration, and legislation are interrelated in governance, although this was not always the framework for discussion. The classical distinction between politics and administration, often presented as a dichotomy, emphasized the accomplishment side of administration and downplayed the policymaking and political aspects. Certainly, no one today would say that public administration has nothing to do with politics or policy. The programs and policies that public administrators are expected to implement come from legislation, but it is far more common that public administration writings discuss policies and programs rather than statutes or laws.

Often discussions of the role of administrators, legislators, and courts reflect the separation of powers and the constitutional structure. Thus the question of roles and duties begins with the idea that the Constitution grants the legislature supremacy in making the laws, the executive carries out the laws, and the courts ultimately determine what the law is when there are legal challenges. Yet the classic discussions of the practice of public administration often begin with the distinction between politics and administration. This distinction is occasionally stated as a dichotomy or a norm to emphasize responsibilities and to emphasize the neutral expertise of the administrator and downplay the policy choices made by the executive branch and bureaucracy. But it has long been recognized that the way public administrators make decisions and perform their duties has acceptable and inevitable political aspects. When agencies select goals, establish priorities, make decisions, and interact with the public, public administrators make policy.

The term "policy" is very broad and extends from passing legislation to administering programs and to court decrees. That is, all branches of the government participate in policy as part of the democratic process. What perceptive individuals will notice is that it is uncommon to discuss statutes as the source of policy or administrative responsibility in most public administration textbooks. Rather than discussing law, statutes, or regulations as the foundation of government actions, the broader and vaguer term "policy" predominates. At other times, the more narrow term "program" is used to discuss a specific approach to achieve policy.

Statutes are relegated to a secondary role to policy for a number of reasons. First, statutes are often one technical part of a policy. Second, a single statute is neither inclusive nor exclusive of all of the policy details because policies develop and evolve over time. Statutes may be one instrument toward a policy and although the statute or legislation is an important and necessary part of policy, it is not complete. Third, statutes are written in technical legal jargon and they may contain a number of parts. Fourth, authority for policy may be located in recent legislative enactments or it may be developed based on new interpretations of established statutory foundations. Finally, academic disciplines that consider legislation and administration adopted the preference of discussing policy rather than statutes or law.

There are some disconnects between the discussions of policy, public administration, and law. Although the general term for academic discussion is policy, practicing administrators are very aware of the types of statutes that affect them. In addition, there are some laws that many individuals are aware of, such as the Civil Rights Act or the No Child Left Behind law. Finally, it is frequently the case that when administrative actions are challenged in trial court or on appeal that it is the specific language of the statutes, as well as the purpose of statutes, that courts evaluate. There are gaps between the common or administrative understanding of policy and judicial interpretation.

Politics and Administration

The connection between legislative policymaking and administrative action is part of the development of public administration studies. During the founding era of public administration studies at the beginning of the twentieth century, a common framework was the politics-administration dichotomy. Public administration doctrine emphasized the neutral expertise for public administrators, but it also served notice to elected politicians that they should make policy and then leave the details of accomplishment to professional administrators. The separation of politics and administration was a normative theory for governance. A second aspect of the early public administration doctrine emphasized administrative efficiency and effectiveness as the metrics for good administration. In the late 1940s, a number of public administration writers argued that a dichotomy was a faulty model. They argued that politics and policy were integral and necessary aspects of the role and responsibilities of public managers. Now the historic aspects of the politics-administration doctrine are recognized, but seen as secondary to administrators acting for the public in ways consistent with democratic and constitutional values.

Policy Process and Studies

A common way to discuss how policy is made and implemented is through the policy process model. Some also consider this model to be a cycle of steps or stages that helps describe policymaking. This model simplifies and describes steps of how a problem moves through the governing process to become a political policy and then an administrative program or action. Although the policy process model may serve better to evaluate how acute problems become programs, it is a common framework that helps describe the interactions between politics and administration.

There are six analytical steps in the policy process, beginning with problem recognition where a situation or problem is seen as worthy of attention from the legislator or executive. This first step is also called "agenda-setting" because it emphasizes that there are many related problems, but they need to be on the agenda or attract the attention of decisionmakers. The second step is to develop alternative policy options; here administrators or analysts may be tasked with investigating and suggesting alternative courses of actions to address the problem.

The third stage is policy adoption where decisionmakers, the legislature, or executive, select an alternative. Sometimes this step is discussed in the context of rational decision-making of selecting the best choice based on evidence and techniques such as cost-benefit or cost-effectiveness analysis. The political tradeoffs for support of legislation or the influence of public-opinion surveys also affect policy adoption. Political or popular aspects often have greater influence on policy choice than the rational, evidence-based policy recommendations.

The next two steps shift from the decision-making to administration. The fourth step is called "implementation," and it focuses on how the policy is put into effect by the bureaucracy. Some of the discussion about implementation highlights the difference between what is intended during adoption and how this may be adjusted, changed, or underperformed by administrators. Other discussions of implementation present the practical procedures or pragmatic steps where administrators take the general policy goals and put them into effect. The fifth step is evaluation where after some period, programs and policies are formally evaluated and reports are submitted to policymakers. The recent attention to government performance can be considered part of this process. To provide more robust evaluation feedback, many analysts suggest that evaluation or performance measures should be included in planning, in policy selection, or in policy implementation.

The final stage is called "policy revision" or "termination." This last step reflects that there often are changes in a policy because of executive attention, budget, or policy evaluation. It is also argued that some policies or programs should be terminated if they have exceeded their usefulness or accomplished their purpose. There may be events that produce major revisions in the policy, or there may be transfer of elements of one program into another policy or program.

In this policy process model, the steps of the policy are described and often policy is studied within one of the steps, but the model is one of a lifecycle or a mechanical process. The first reason for presenting this model is to suggest that it is distinct from how the general public may consider policy. The second is to suggest that this process is distinct from how courts consider policy or make policy.

Enacting Statutes

Not all laws are written in the same way, but there are a few basic patterns that are frequently repeated when statutes are drafted and enacted. First, the bills that propose laws are introduced to one of the two chambers, House or Senate, for the United States and most state governments. (Cities, counties, and special district governments have single-chamber legislatures, as does the state of Nebraska; and in these settings the process is streamlined.) To begin, bills can be drafted or legislative topics can be proposed by individual legislators, the executive, by agencies, by lobbyists, by public-interest groups, or by individuals. Second, bills are typically referred to committees based on the topic of proposed legislation and the committees may collect data and listen to expert testimony before referring it to the full chamber. Third, if a bill passes, it is referred to the other chamber, which again may send the bill to committee. Fourth, if amendments are made in one house, then a confer-ence committee may be formed to work out a compromise bill acceptable to both the House and Senate.

Fifth, once the bill passes both legislative chambers, it is sent to the execu-tive for review. Sixth, the executive can approve the bill and sign it into law; the executive can veto the legislation directly and send a veto message with the bill back to the legislature. If the legislature can muster sufficient votes in both chambers for a veto override, then the bill can become law. If the bill is passed and sent to the President when there are less than ten days in the legislative session, then the executive does not have to send a veto message; the president can sign the bill, but no executive action results in a bill that cannot be overturned by the legislature.

It has become customary for politicians to make speeches and enter state-ments about the bills in the record; these comments, along with changes be-come part of the legislative record. It has also been common for the President to issue signing orders or signing statements that explain how the law is to be interpreted and implemented by the responsible agencies. Signing state-ments became controversial because President George W. Bush included in his signing statements "declarations that he would not enforce parts of the bills he signed." The American Bar Association called this repudiation of parts of legislative enactments "contrary to the rule of law and our constitutional system of separation of powers."[3] As a candidate, President Obama strongly criticized signing statements, but during his first months of office he also used them.[4]

Types of Statutes

There are various types of statutes and various effects. Statutes that establish programs or create new government agencies and describe their powers, responsibilities, and limitations are called either "enabling laws" or "organic laws." Some laws may authorize new duties and responsibilities for agencies or authorize new programs. Annual budget, fiscal authority, and appropriation laws provide for funding and set priorities for agencies. Statutes also may contain amendments, modifications, or recision of existing laws. Many states require statutes to be related to only one subject or substantive area of law.

In the federal government, it has been common to enact omnibus legislation that contains multiple provisions affecting many agencies or functions; when there is pressure to enact budget bills, these often become omnibus laws. It is common to introduce supplemental budget bills to provide for emergencies, such as hurricanes, or to fund activities such as war.

There are some statutes that impose obligations on public officers and administrators throughout government; this is the purpose of overhead laws such as civil service or open meeting laws. These laws are written to apply throughout government agencies unless an agency is specifically excluded; another example of overhead laws is the Administrative Procedure Act. These procedure laws emphasize the ways activities are accomplished, and they address process and method. There are also laws that address substantive areas, and these laws can apply to both government and to society at large. For example, the Civil Rights laws that were passed during the 1960s to prohibit discrimination imposed obligations that apply to governments, businesses, and society in general. There are some statutes that are administered specifically by one federal agency; for example, aviation practices and regulations are administered by the Federal Aviation Administration.

There are some federal acts that are primarily administered by a federal agency but may also have a state agency action as well. For example, the federal Environmental Protection Agency is responsible for enforcing the Clean Air Act and Clean Water Act, but states also regulate these areas. There are some environmental laws and regulations that have mandated responsibilities to all levels of government for clean-ups. These environmental laws affect many local governments in setting standards for trash pick-up, licensing landfills, or providing water services. In addition to administrative practices such as providing grants for clean-ups or imposing penalties for failure to meet regulatory standards, environmental protection is seen as important enough to impose criminal sanctions. Congress included criminal sanctions that can apply to individual administrators if they are convicted of willfully dumping waste. The expansive application of environmental law reflects policy choices about the importance of cleaning up the environment.[5]

Some laws apply to the general public. Legislation is written to apply to defined categories of individuals or apply to specific types of actions. Legislation is to be generally applicable and prospective nature. For example, criminal laws define what is illegal conduct and prescribes penalties that can include fines, imprisonment, or in heinous cases, the death penalty. There are regulatory laws that affect individuals and businesses. There are statutes that establish property rights, contractual relationships, or social obligations.

Once statutes become law, they are often published and bound into books called "Session Laws." Many statutes that are generally applicable and of long duration are also codified or placed in "Code Books." At one point, it was necessary to visit a law library or legislative archives to locate statutes, bills, and related materials, but now much of this information is available online.

Delegation and Discretion

There are ongoing debates about how detailed statutes should be in authorizing and specifying the powers and responsibilities that government agencies and administrators hold. The two terms used in this discussion are delegation and discretion. Delegation commonly means the express authority granted to the agency through legislation. There can be expansive, vague, narrow, or specific delegations of responsibility. Discretion is how administrators use their delegated or implied authority to make decisions, to express policy, or to take action. Sometimes delegation and discretion are presented as problems of governance, supervision, or control. At other times they are presented as tools, techniques, and pragmatic approaches to complex problems.

Courts view vague legislation as unacceptable because it does not provide adequate guidance. Specificity of objectives, methods, and goals in a statute is seen as a way to express democratic and public preferences. The issue of whether delegation is appropriate often revolves around the constitutional and practical question of whether the legislature established clear standards that can be administered. Sometimes this is called "filling in the details for the legislature." Court cases enforce the requirement that statutes have clear, consistent, and articulated standards for the agency to follow or enforce. The consideration from the courts is whether Congress provided an intelligible principle for the agency to apply.

Most analysts agree that delegation of authority should be clear, consistent, and specific, but they differ on whether discretion in executing policies should be strictly defined or expansively authorized. Although delegation may be clear in the goals and objectives, the strong statute approach argues that legislature needs to control the agency's structure and function, and here the allocation of resources, statutory definitions, and detail all serve to minimize the decision points for an agency.[6] Political theorist Theodore Lowi has advocated narrow discretion to prevent the unfettered and undemocratic activity of agencies; in other words, this approach is to control the bureaucracy.[7] Lowi has argued that specific and highly detailed legislation serves democratic accountability purposes by the legislature establishing limited authority and clearly established goals. In response, others argue that this narrow approach limits administrators' ability to adapt to changing circumstances and that it is stultifying and impractical. As legal and policy scholar Jerry Mashaw noted: "Were the Congress to attempt to make statutory meaning uniform over time, it would have to specify the most extraordinarily elaborate criteria for exercising enforcement initiative, for finding facts, for engaging in contextual interpretation, and for determining remedial action."[8]

Some authorities advocate providing broader discretion to administrators to implement policy because such discretion allows processes that include grassroots participation of citizens or street-level bureaucrats in making policy choices. At the center of the broad or narrow discretion debate are questions of control, accountability, competence, and responsiveness. Those who want narrow discretion emphasize control and accountability through established criteria. Those who argue for broad delegations argue administrative competence and public responsiveness.

Techniques to Control Discretion

A number of techniques to control administrative discretion may be applied based on particular types of programs or agencies. Political, managerial, procedural, and court-based techniques are used to control discretion. The political controls can include congressional or executive oversight; these can involve the annual budget process, regular informal exchanges, or program performance reporting. The procedural controls and requirements that are included either in the administrative procedure laws or the specific process requirements are spelled out in the statutory delegation. Managerial controls can include internal agency regulations, executive oversight and guidance, professional norms and standards, or informal organizational culture and practices. In addition, actual or potential legal challenges to government actions also constrain agencies.

Political and procedural aspects of policy may include citizen participation or other grassroots involvement in policy development or implementation. Sometimes critics argue that citizen participation is effective for capacity-building or for providing democratic feedback. In addition, the proponents of participation assert that it allows for better policy design. While a locally customized approach is suggested as being more responsive in policy or services, one shortcoming of local approaches to policymaking is consistency of policy throughout the jurisdiction or nation.[9]

The legal approach to control occurs normally through court cases where litigants may challenge statutes, regulations, or the administrative practices. This role of courts as supervisors of agency action or defenders of legislative

prerogative has been debated. Legal scholar Shep Melnick has argued that
court review makes conflicting demands on administrators because courts do
not understand administration; that court review is decentralized, piecemeal,
and inconsistent from one part of the country to another (in Federal cases);
and finally, that courts need a better understanding of the day-to-day life of
government bureaucrats.[10]

Generalizations about delegation and discretion provide a starting point for
consideration, but the practical application or interpretation of discretion is
often related to a particular agency or program. Many aspects of discretion are
subject to routine supervision and review. More stringent controls on discretion present problems of flexibility, creativity, participation, accountability,
and achievement. Discretion often relates to overall management and policy
implementation by administrators, and in the end, the evaluation of discretion
is considered in the context of the values of democratic governance.

Multiple Sources of Authority

In addition to the complexity of interpreting one statute or policy, public
agencies often have many statutory sources of responsibility and authority.
For example, the police department is formed by the city charter and has its
structure and function set forth in ordinances, but the police enforce state
criminal statutes and traffic codes, they enforce municipal ordinances, and
they must comply with state and federal constitutional mandates.

An agency is formed through the enabling legislation that authorizes and
defines the purpose and scope of the agency. Developing the mission of an
agency is seen as a way to focus its policy and purpose. Agencies develop their
own routines, procedures, and priorities. Then over time programs are added,
responsibilities are amended, and new enforcement duties are delegated. A
practical result of these normal changes is that an agency may have multiple
responsibilities that can conflict. Practical, pragmatic, and political skills are
needed for managers to balance existing duties and new policies.

When asked how an agency will interpret a new law or policy, a midlevel
administrator will often reply, "We pay attention to what the legislative spon-
sor intended, and we will follow that purpose." Agencies pay attention to the
policies and preferences of legislative sponsors and the elected executive. A
public manager must fit new enactments into existing duties within the context
of executive policy preferences and the limits of agency budget and personnel
resources. Agencies also pay attention to the common public understanding
of legislation. Agencies also must develop interpretations and procedures to
implement the new statutes. The agency's interpretation and implementation of
legislation is part of law in action. Yet, when a government action is challenged

in court, it is the language of the statute that the courts find more convincing than the intent of the sponsors and this presents tensions for public administrators.

Agencies and Courts Make Laws

In governing, the political process of making laws becomes the administrative practice of implementation and enforcement. This means that administrators interpret and utilize the statutes that apply to them. However, the method that administrators may use to interpret the law can differ from what a lawyer or judge would use. This section first considers the administrative role and then presents judicial approaches to statutory interpretation.

Agencies Determine What the Law Is

In implementing policy, administrators define and flesh out the legislative intent or they may emphasize certain aspects of a program. This means they interpret law. Paul Appleby argued that public administrators often make policy and determine what law is. Appleby was a highly regarded commentator on government administration with high-level experience in federal administration during the 1930s and 1940s when he served as an administrative assistant to the Secretary of Agriculture and as the Acting Director of the Bureau of Budget. Appleby summarized the interacting roles of legislatures, courts, and administrators as follows:

> Both courts and administrators find in law things Congress or legislatures had never consciously put there. In other cases, both resolve difficulties Congress or the legislature had consciously left for them to resolve.
>
> Congress and legislatures make policy for the future, but have no monopoly on that function, as the courts have no monopoly on the determination of what the law is. *Administrators are continually laying down rules for the future, and administrators are continually determining what the law is, what it means in terms of action, what the rights of parties are with respect both to transactions in process and transaction in prospect. Administrators make thousands of such decisions to one made by the courts.* They act with regard for what the courts have decided and would be likely to decide, of course, but in considerable degree the power of the courts over administration is a reserve power. The power of legislative bodies is in a considerable degree, also, a reserve power over administration.[11] [emphasis added]

Although public agencies may initially determine what the law is, the reserve and supervisory powers of the legislature means elected representatives evaluate agency actions during annual budget review and through informal contacts.

Courts are also called upon during lawsuits to review and evaluate administrative interpretation and implementation of laws. Thus, administrators should understand the approach that courts use to interpret the statutory authority.

Courts Decide What the Law Is

Often the question of how to interpret the statutes is raised in court cases. In many situations the courts will look to the way the agency interprets its statutory powers and if the interpretation is reasonable and within the discretion granted to the agency. As many note, courts have expansive discretion in their interpretation of what law is, but there are some typical steps they take. Courts often follow statutory interpretation doctrines.

Whether someone violated a criminal law or whether a company complied with regulatory criteria may often include a challenge of what did the statute say and mean. In situations where important rights are at stake, such as liberty or imprisonment in a criminal case, courts will take a narrow view in interpreting the statute. The difficulty for administrators and their legal counsel is to determine when the courts will defer to administrative interpretations and when courts will take a stricter approach to statutory interpretation.

Typical Steps in Statutory Interpretation

Most people would assume that if a person takes an airplane without permission and flies it across two states, then the person should be convicted of stealing. However, when the Supreme Court considered this issue in 1931 in the case of *McBoyle v. United States*, the question was whether the federal law made this a crime. Justice Oliver Wendell Holmes, Jr., wrote the decision for the court.[12] The case is included at the end of the chapter, but this section will explain the steps the court used here and in other cases to interpret statutes.

First, look to the plain language of the statute. Holmes quoted the statute and considered the operative term "motor vehicle." Since the definition did not clearly define airplane as "motor vehicle," the Justice considered the next step.

Second, find a common definition or understanding of the term. Holmes concluded that it was common to think of vehicle as something that runs on land but not airplanes or boats.

Third, consider how other statutes have defined the term. Holmes noted that Congress in the Tariff Act specifically excluded airplanes as vehicles.

Fourth, consider what the legislature intended; this may include the legislative history and statements made at enactment. There was no formal history, but Holmes looked at whether Congress considered or could have considered airplanes at the time the law was enacted.

Fifth, look at the statutes or judicial decisions of other jurisdictions as sources or suggestions but not as binding legal interpretations.

Sixth, consider fairness and notice to those whom the statute applies. Part of Holmes' fairness evaluation was whether it would be fair to keep a narrow interpretation or expand the interpretation of the statute. In criminal cases, a narrow interpretation of what is prohibited protects the rights of the accused.

There is an interesting point regarding notice to individuals. Justice Holmes did not require criminals to have actual knowledge of the text of statutes before they acted or in order to charge and convict them. At the beginning of the last paragraph Holmes said: "Although it is not likely that a criminal will carefully consider the text of the law before he murders or steals, it is reasonable that a fair warning should be given to the world in language that the common world will understand, of what the law intends to do if a certain line is passed. To make the warning fair, so far as possible the line should be clear."

This statement seems to present an anomaly. To be fair, the statute should be clear, but it is still fair to convict someone even if they did not know the statute existed? Why then, does the language have to be on the books of what can and cannot be a crime if the alleged crook did not know it at the time of the crime? First, there is an existing legal maxim that ignorance of the law is no excuse, and this means the laws apply if the person could have read the statute or case law. Whether this maxim was considered by Holmes or not, it does not provide a satisfactory explanation about applying law. An alternative analytic approach considers who must know the law to apply it. This makes the crucial consideration government action. The requirements of what is clear in the statute are established for government and administrators to know what they can and cannot do. The statute explains what the government must show or prove. Thus, it is important that the particulars of statutory requirements exist before government can take action and that administrators must understand and work within the statutory language.

The court overturned McBoyle's conviction and some may see this releasing him on a mere technicality, but having clear definitions of crimes on the books before conviction is an essential democratic value. It is also part of the rule-of-law principles. Government, and its agents, cannot act without authority that has been delegated through legislative process.

Other Approaches to Statutory Interpretation

There are many statutes that are left open to agency interpretation. In some situations, the legislature deliberately and clearly expresses agency discretion. In other situations, statutes are left to agency interpretation because they are written broadly. In these situations, the courts will consider the reasonableness of the agency interpretation of the statute. In challenges to statutes regarding delegation of legislative authority or decision-making, courts have considered whether the legislature provided criteria for the agencies to apply. Thus the courts have said that if there is "an intelligible principle" for the agency to apply, then the delegation is acceptable.

The courts then consider whether the agency interpretation and application of the law is reasonable. If agency action is not inconsistent with the legislation, then courts will defer to agency interpretations of these statutes. (Unfortunately, courts often use awkward phrasing like this "not inconsistent" double negative in their standards of review.) Judicial deference serves to allow agencies discretion in policymaking and to leave to executive and legislative consideration whether agency interpretations are consistent with political priorities.

There is one caveat: The type of approach the courts may take in litigation involving statutory interpretation is mutable. Courts may take a narrow interpretation or a more literal view of the statute. Where individuals are subject to fines and imprisonment, the courts' narrow view of statutory interpretation is appropriate to provide fairness. What is a reasonable interpretation of the statute may also depend on the type of governmental activity involved in the situation.

Conclusion

It is common to say that administrators implement policy, and Paul Appleby restated this as: Public administrators make laws. Public agencies and public managers are responsible for the process of taking an enacted law or policy to develop and accomplish actions such as providing services, distributing benefits, collecting taxes, or enforcing laws. This means public administrators are required to read, understand, and interpret legislation.

Cases

Two cases are presented here. The first is the *McBoyle v. U.S.* case. See if you can identify the six steps that Justice Holmes applied within this opinion and expected public officials, law enforcement, and attorneys, to follow in determining if the statute applied to McBoyle. The second case, *Federated Distributors v. Johnson,* is more complex.[13] This case illustrates how statutes change over time and how innovations may not be addressed in an existing law. This case involves a "new product" that does not seem to fit in the statutory definitions which the public administrators had to apply in assessing a tax on the product. This product, a bottled mixed drink of juice and alcohol, had to be evaluated by administrators in reference to the statutory definitions for tax classification. Consider how the agency tried to apply the plain language of the statute regarding the method of manufacture of the alcohol, while the court looked to the legislative purpose of the law. Finally, note that this case involves a question of statutory interpretation under the Illinois Constitution, not the U.S. Constitution. Because the Illinois Constitution uniformity clause requires like products to be taxed alike, the court compared the differences between types of drinks.

McBoyle v. United States, 283 U.S. 25, U.S. Supreme Court, 1931

Mr. Justice Holmes delivered the opinion of the Court.

The petitioner was convicted of transporting from Ottawa, Illinois, to Guymon, Oklahoma, an airplane that he knew to have been stolen, and was sentenced to serve three years' imprisonment and to pay a fine of $2,000. The judgment was affirmed by the Circuit Court of Appeals for the Tenth Circuit. A writ of certiorari was granted by this Court on the question whether the National Motor Vehicle Theft Act applies to aircraft (Act of October 29, 1919, U.S. Code, Title 18, § 408). That Act provides: "Sec. 2. That when used in this Act: (a) The term 'motor vehicle' shall include an automobile, automobile truck, automobile wagon, motor cycle, or any other self-propelled vehicle not designed for running on rails; . . . Sec. 3. That whoever shall transport or cause to be transported in interstate or foreign commerce a motor vehicle, knowing the same to have been stolen, shall be punished by a fine of not more than $5,000, or by imprisonment of not more than five years, or both."

Section 2 defines the motor vehicles of which the transportation in interstate commerce is punished in Section 3. The question is the meaning of the word 'vehicle' in the phrase "any other self-propelled vehicle not designed for running on rails." No doubt etymologically it is possible to use the word to signify a conveyance working on land, water or air, and sometimes legislation extends the use in that direction, *e.g.,* land and air, water being separately provided for, in the Tariff Act, (September 22, 1922, 42 Stat. 858, 948). But in everyday speech 'vehicle' calls up the picture of a thing moving on land. Thus the statute intended, the Government suggests, rather to enlarge than to restrict the definition, vehicle includes every contrivance capable of being used "as a means of transportation on land." And this is repeated, expressly excluding aircraft, in the Tariff Act. So here, the phrase under discussion calls up the popular picture. For after including automobile truck, automobile wagon and motor cycle, the words "any other self-propelled vehicle not designed for running on rails" still indicate that a vehicle in the popular sense, that is a vehicle running on land, is the theme. It is a vehicle that runs, not something, not commonly called a vehicle, that flies. Airplanes were well known in 1919 when this statute was passed; but it is admitted that they were not mentioned in the reports or in the debates in Congress.

It is impossible to read words that so carefully enumerate the different forms of motor vehicles and have no reference of any kind to aircraft, as including airplanes under a term that usage more and more precisely confines to a different class. The counsel for the petitioner have shown that the phraseology of the statute as to motor vehicles follows that of earlier statutes of Connecticut, Delaware, Ohio, Michigan and Missouri, not to mention the late Regulations of Traffic for the District of Columbia, none of which can be supposed to leave the earth.

Although it is not likely that a criminal will carefully consider the text of the law before he murders or steals, it is reasonable that a fair warning should be given to the world in language that the common world will understand, of what the law intends to do if a certain line is passed. To make the warning fair, so far as possible the line should be clear. When a rule of conduct is laid down in words that evoke in the common mind only the picture of vehicles moving on land, the statute should not be extended to aircraft, simply because it may seem to us that a similar policy applies, or upon the speculation that, if the legislature had thought of it, very likely broader words would have been used. *United States v. Thind,* 261 U.S. 204, 209.

Judgment reversed.

Federated Distributors, Inc., et al. v. J. Thomas Johnson (as Director of the Department of Revenue, et al.), 163 Ill.App.3d 27, First District Appellate Court of Illinois, 1987

Justice Linn delivered the opinion of the court.

Plaintiff Federated Distributors, Inc. (Federated), brings this appeal seeking reversal of a trial court order which upheld the constitutionality of an Illinois Department of Revenue (the Department) ruling imposing a $2-per-gallon tax on a product produced by Federated. The tax in question was imposed pursuant to the Liquor Control Act of 1934 (the Act). Under the Act, manufacturers of wine or wine coolers containing less than 14% alcohol must pay a $0.23-per-gallon tax, while manufacturers of "spirits" must pay a $2-per-gallon tax. Federated manufactures "New Products," a spirit-based fruit-flavored drink similar to a "wine cooler." Although New Products contains less than 14% alcohol, the Department determined that because the alcohol in New Products was obtained from distillation rather than fermentation, the Act required Federated to pay the $2-per-gallon tax.

Soon thereafter, Federated requested administrative review of the Department's ruling in the circuit court of Cook County. However, after hearing the parties' respective positions, the trial court affirmed the Department's decision.

Federated now appeals, contending that there exists no real and substantial difference between New Products and wine coolers and that New Products should be taxed at the rate applicable to wine or wine coolers rather than at the rate applicable to hard liquors. Federated asserts that the Act, as applied to New Products pursuant to the Department's ruling, is discriminatory and unconstitutional.

We reverse.

Background

The disagreement between Federated and the Department centers around differing interpretations of the Illinois Liquor Control Act. (Ill. Rev. Stat. 1985, ch. 43, par. 94 et seq.) The following provisions of the Act are relevant to the resolution of this appeal:

> Sec. 1–2. This Act shall be liberally construed, to the end that the health, safety and welfare of the People of the State of Illinois shall be protected and temperance in the consumption of alcoholic liquors shall be fostered and promoted by sound and careful control and regulation of the manufacture, sale and distribution of alcoholic liquors.

> Sec. 1–3.02. 'Spirits' means any beverage which contains alcohol obtained by distillation, mixed with water or other substance in solution, and includes brandy, rum, whiskey, gin, or other spirituous liquors, and such liquors when rectified, blended or otherwise mixed with alcohol or other substances.

> Sec. 1–3.03. 'Wine' means any alcoholic beverage obtained by the fermentation of the natural contents of fruits, or vegetables, containing sugar, including such beverages when fortified by the addition of alcohol or spirits, as above defined.

> Sec. 8–1. A tax is imposed upon the privilege of engaging in business as a manufacturer or as an importing distributor of alcoholic liquor other than beer at the rate of [$0.23] per gallon for wine containing 14% or less of

alcohol by volume, [$0.60] per gallon for wine containing more than 14% of alcohol by volume, and $2.00 per gallon on alcohol and spirits manu- factured and sold or used by such manufacturer, or as agent for any other person, or sold or used by such importing distributor, or as agent for any other person.

Important to the present dispute is the Act's distinction between "wine" and "spirits." Under the Act, wine or wine coolers contain alcohol produced by fermentation, while spirits, or "hard liquors" such as rum and whiskey, contain alcohol derived from distillation.* Wine or wine coolers containing less than 14% alcohol are taxed at $0.23 per gallon, while hard liquor is taxed at $2 per gallon.

In the instant case, New Products is an alcoholic drink which is produced from a combination of water, flavoring, fruit juices, vegetable juices, sugar, corn syrup, artificial carbonation, and fortified by the addition of spirits. The al- cohol in New Products is produced by distillation rather than fermentation.

Prior to introducing New Products to the market, Federated petitioned the Department for an administrative ruling regarding the tax applicable to New Products. It was Federated's position that even though the alcohol in New Products was produced by distillation, nevertheless, the total alcoholic percentage in New Products was less than 14%. Consequently, Federated argued that the $0.23-per-gallon rate should apply to New Products, for New Products was, essentially, a type of wine cooler.

On March 21, 1986, the Department issued a ruling that placed New Products within the same classification as wine and wine coolers. In fact, the Department stated that New Products, "in alcoholic content, are most closely analogous to the category of wine under 14%." That being the case, the De- partment ruled that the $0.23-per-gallon tax rate applied to New Products "regardless of whether the alcohol contained therein is originally produced as a wine or as a neutral grain spirit."

However, on April 24, 1986, the Department reversed its previous rul- ing. The Department stated, "We have re-examined this issue and [have] determined that technically the products that you have described, the [New Products] regardless of the alcoholic content, fall within the present statutory definition of a spirit." The Department then ruled that New Products would be taxed at the rate of $2 per gallon, similar to that placed upon hard liquors.

Federated appealed the Department's ruling to the trial court. In affirming

---

*The Department has previously ruled that wine coolers, which contain alcohol derived from a fermentation process and which contain less than 14% alcohol, should receive the same tax treatment as ordinary wine.

the Department's decision, the trial court found that: (1) New Products contains distilled alcohol and therefore falls within the definitions of "spirits" as set forth by the Act; and (2) the purpose of the Act is to promote temperance in the consumption of alcohol and placing New Products within the higher tax rate helps fulfill that purpose.

Federated now brings this appeal.

Opinion

The parties agree on the case law applicable to the issues raised in this appeal. It is well settled that the legislature has broad powers in the area of establishing classifications to define subjects of taxation, *Klein v. Hulman* (1966), 34 Ill.2d 343, 215 N.E.2d 268. There is a general presumption favoring the validity of classifications created by legislative bodies in taxing matters and the party who attacks the classification has the burden of proving that the classification is unconstitutional *Williams v. City of Chicago* (1977), 66 Ill 2d 423, 362 N.E.2d 1030. The legislature's authority is limited only in that it cannot exercise its taxing power arbitrarily; the legislature must not, under the guise of a "classification," discriminate against one and in favor of another where both are similarly situated. *People v. McCabe* (1971), 49 Ill.2d 338, 275 N.E.2d 407. Classifications created by the legislature must be based upon real and substantial differences of condition or situation between those subject to the tax and those excluded and must bear some reasonable relationship to the purpose of the legislation. *Commercial National Bank v. City of Chicago* (1982), 89 Ill.2d 45, 432 N.E.2d 227. Courts have found classifications unconstitutional where the statute in question included within a class those in fact not within it or have excluded from a class those properly belonging to it. As the Illinois Supreme Court recently summarized:

"[It] must appear that the particular classification is based upon some real and substantial difference in kind, situation or circumstance in the persons or objects on which the classification rests, and which bears a rational relation to the evil to be remedied and the purpose to be attained by the statute. . . ." *Boynton v. Kusper* (1986), 112 Ill. 2d 356, 366–67, 494 N.E.2d 135, 139.

In the case at bar, the parties' respective positions are fairly straightforward. The Department asserts that under the language of the Act, New Products falls within the definition of a spirit as set forth in section 1–3.02. The Department points out, and Federated agrees, that the alcohol in New Products is obtained from a distilling process rather than from fermentation. Therefore, New Products is a "beverage which contains alcohol obtained by distillation, mixed with water or other substance." (Ill. Rev. Stat. 1985, ch. 43, par. 95.02.) That being the case, it is the Department's contention that under section 8–1, New Products is subject to the $2-per-gallon tax, rather than the $0.23-per-gallon tax, for New Products is, under the precise language of the Act, a spirit rather than a wine.

Federated, on the other hand, argues that there is no real and substantial difference between New Products and wine and wine coolers and that to tax New Products as a "spirit" (as defined by section 1–3.02) rather than as a wine-based product is therefore unconstitutional. It is Federated's position that New Products contains the same percentage of alcohol as wine and wine coolers, contains essentially the same ingredients, and is sold to the same consumer base. Federated further contends that the only distinction between New Products and wine and wine coolers is that the alcohol used in New Products is obtained through a different process from that used in wine and wine coolers (i.e., distillation compared with fermentation). Finally, Federated asserts that classifying New Products with other "hard liquors" frustrates the Act's stated purpose; namely, fostering and promoting temperance in the consumption of alcoholic liquors.

Statutory construction demands that a court of law ascertain legislative intent not only from the language employed in a particular statute, but also from the law's purpose as gleaned from the overall spirit of the statute. *Gill v. Miller* (1983), 94 Ill. 2d 52, 445 N.E.2d 330. In so doing, we should be mindful of the subject matter addressed by the statute and the legislature's apparent objective in enacting it. *Chastek v. Anderson* (1981), 83 Ill. 2d 502, 416 N.E.2d 247.

In the present case, we agree with Federated.

To begin, New Products and wine or wine coolers are virtually identical in every aspect except one, the method in which the alcohol in each product is obtained. In wine, the alcohol is obtained through fermentation. In New Products, the alcohol is derived from distillation.

Distillation and fermentation, however, are both simply processes. The purpose of each process, in the world of liquors, is to produce the same object: alcohol. It is the alcohol, not the process from which it is derived, that the Act is meant to regulate. New Products can only be classified differently from wine or wine coolers, therefore, if there exists a real and substantial difference between the ingredients and alcoholic content of New Products and the ingredients and alcoholic content of wine or wine coolers. However, since the ingredients in New Products are nearly identical to that of wine or wine coolers, and since the percentage of alcohol in both New Products and wine or wine coolers is precisely the same, there exists no real or substantial difference between the two types of beverages. To differentiate between two nearly identical alcoholic beverages based only on the process or method used to produce a single ingredient in those beverages constitutes an unreasonable and illogical interpretation of the Act.

Furthermore, it is evident that the Act utilizes the terms "fermentation" and "distillation" merely as a means of clarifying, as opposed to classifying, which beverages fall within the Act's three tax classifications. The presence of alcohol derived from distillation does not automatically result in a beverage's being classified as a "spirit." In this regard, we note that spirits can be combined with wine without causing the wine to lose its favored tax status. (See Ill. Rev. Stat. 1985, ch. 43, par. 95.03.) Thus, the presence of the exact type of alcohol which New Products contains (distilled) can be combined with wine and, assuming the total alcoholic percentage is less than 14%, the beverage can remain classified as a wine. Consequently, if distilled alcohol can be combined with wine and still permit the beverage in question to remain classified as a wine, it is obvious that distilled alcohol can be added to a beverage containing nearly the same ingredients as wine (but having no fermented alcohol) and still permit the beverage to remain classified as a wine; provided, of course, that the total alcoholic content does not exceed 14%. With that in mind, we can discern no real and substantial difference between New Products and wine or wine coolers and we therefore find no merit in the Department's assertion that New Products should be placed in a different tax classification simply because New Products contains distilled rather than fermented alcohol.

The evil sought to be remedied by the Act is also not served by the Department's interpretation. The evil addressed by the Act is the abuse of alcohol. The Act seeks to alleviate that danger by making certain alcoholic beverages more expensive than others. The legislature determined that a greater danger of abuse is posed by these beverages, such as hard liquors which have a higher alcoholic content. As a means of discouraging their consumption, the Act places a higher tax on those beverages. By making hard liquor more costly, the public is discouraged from purchasing it and the evil of alcohol abuse is curtailed. Similarly, a lower tax is placed on beverages with a lower alcoholic content because they pose less danger of abuse when consumed. Wine having less than 14% alcohol is considered to be less dangerous and is, accordingly, taxed at the lowest rate.

Consequently, because New Products is, by its alcoholic content, in the same class as wine and wine coolers, taxing New Products at a higher rate bears no rational relationship to the evil sought to be remedied; a beverage of the least alcoholic content, and thus the least danger of abuse, is being taxed at the same rate as those posing the greatest danger of abuse. To be consistent with the overall theme of the Act, New Products should be taxed at the lowest rate, as it poses the least danger of abuse. By adhering to this taxation structure, the public is encouraged to purchase those beverages containing a lower alcoholic content and the threat posed by alcohol abuse is lessened.

In the same vein, placing a higher tax on New Products runs contrary to the Act's express purpose.

The Act specifically states that "temperance in the consumption of alcoholic liquors shall be fostered and promoted." (Ill. Rev. Stat. 1985, ch. 43, par. 94.) With that goal in mind, the legislature created three different tax rates of $0.23 per gallon, $0.60 per gallon, or $2 per gallon. Which tax rate applies is determined, pursuant to section 8–1, by looking to the percentage of alcohol in the particular beverage. The greater the amount of alcoholic content, the higher the tax charged to the beverage in question.

The Act's elevated taxation scheme reveals the legislature's attempt to promote temperance by making the price of certain beverages more expensive than the price of others. By taxing beverages containing less than 14% alcohol at a lower rate than hard liquors such as rum and whiskey, it is apparent that the Act is intended to encourage (via the differing tax rates) the consumption of some beverages while discouraging the consumption of others. Running throughout the Act, however, is a single consistent theme; the tax charged to a particular beverage is based on the danger of potential abuse which, in turn, is reflected in the percentage of alcohol which that beverage contains. (See Ill. Rev. Stat. 1985, ch. 43, par. 158.)

Based on that legislative purpose, it is apparent that placing New Products in the same classification as hard liquors such as rum and whiskey runs contrary to the legislature's intent. It is uncontroverted that New Products contains less than 14% alcohol. It is equally uncontroverted that the alcoholic content in New Products is nowhere near as great as that present in hard liquors such as rum and whiskey. As a result, under the taxation scheme set forth above, and based on our interpretation of the legislature's intent in establishing that scheme, we are convinced that New Products should be taxed at the same rate as those beverages which it is most similar to, namely, wine or wine coolers. This reading of the statute fulfills the Act's intent of promoting temperance, for a beverage containing the least percentage of alcohol is taxed at the lowest rate, is made less costly, and is therefore more attractive to the consuming public.

In sum, we can find no real and substantial difference between the ingredients and alcoholic content contained in New Products and that contained in wine or wine coolers. Second, placing New Products in the same classification as hard liquors bears no rational relationship to the evil sought to be remedied by the Act. And third, placing New Products in any classification other than that enjoyed by wine or wine coolers is contrary to the legislature's intent of promoting temperance through varying tax rates.

Conclusion

Accordingly, for the reasons set forth above, we reverse the trial court's ruling affirming the Department's decision and order that New Products be taxed at the same rate currently applicable to wine and wine coolers.
   Reversed.

Discussion Questions

1. Public administration emphasizes implementing and evaluating policy. Discuss how implementing policy relates to the law and statutes that the legislators enact.
2. What are the types of enacted legislation and where can they be located?
3. Why are delegation and discretion such important considerations for administrators? How do these actions relate legislation to administration?
4. What is legislative supremacy and how does this affect executive authority?
5. Discuss how legislatures, agencies, and courts all make law.
6. How do the judicial steps of statutory interpretation affect administrative practice?
7. What is your definition of vehicle? Does Justice Holmes's discussion of the ordinary meaning of vehicle in the *McBoyle* case coincide with yours? What steps would you recommend the federal government take after the *McBoyle* decision?
8. Notice the difficulty when an innovation occurs in the *Federated* case in relation to legislative taxing provisions. Is it better for administrators to follow the plain language of the statute or look to the legislative intent? Does the agency have any discretion in developing definitions for taxing products that do not fit the statutory definitions? Would it be better to simply refuse to allow a new product that does not fit within a current tax category?
9. The Department of Revenue appealed the *Federated Distributors v. Johnson* decision to the Illinois State Supreme Court.[14] The last paragraph of the Illinois Supreme Court's opinion is provided below. Consider how this ruling differs from the decision of the Court of Appeals that is printed above.

> In sum, we hold that article VIII of the Liquor Control Act is a revenue measure subject to the uniformity clause of the Illinois Constitution;

that we find no real and substantial difference between New Products and wine coolers; and that, therefore, New Products must be taxed by the Department at the same rate established administratively for wine coolers. Although the Department has administratively ruled that wine coolers be taxed at the same rate as wine, we do not mean by this decision to say that wine coolers and New Products must constitutionally be taxed at the same rate as wine, and to that extent alone we reverse the appellate court. The ultimate determination of taxation levels must be left to the legislature, to be determined within the constitutional limitations and to the end that they promote the purpose of the Act. To the extent that section 8–1 of the Liquor Control Act (Ill. Rev. Stat. 1985, ch. 43, par. 95.03) does not presently establish a basis on which to tax such virtually identical products equally, we declare it unconstitutional.[15]

4

Courts and Dispute Resolution

Most people dislike courts and they want to avoid ever going to court, but conflict and litigation are common parts of public management. Enforcing the laws by implementing policy often involves conflicts.[1] For many public managers, trials are part of their normal duties. For example, dependency and neglect hearings are central to the mission of child welfare departments. Another example is in tax administration where court process is used to collect delinquent taxes. Trials and court processes are tools and techniques of public management.[2] Being a defendant in a legal action also can be part of public administration practice because bringing suits to challenge government actions is part of democratic checks and balances. Therefore, public administrators should understand courts. This chapter addresses trials, appeals, dispute resolution, and judicial norms.

It is common to equate law with judges, attorneys, and the court system. Courts and the judicial system provide an institution for publicly resolving offenses against the community in criminal trials and for resolving public or private civil complaints. Usually, when people talk about a justice system, they mean the criminal justice system that includes prosecutors, probation departments, jails, and prisons. This chapter considers a narrower concept of the judicial system that includes the courts and their administrative staff at the trial and appellate levels.

The public perceptions of law may focus on the stories or factual presentations in a trial, but for judges and attorneys the law developed through appellate cases is distinctive as binding authority. In this judicial view, law is the authoritative statements that are binding on the community. Those trained in law are schooled in the distinctions between factual evidence and the law. Lawyers are trained to locate the legal doctrine found in the common law case decisions, statutes, regulations, and constitutions and argue how this law applies to the particular facts of the case at hand. This advocacy is based on individual circumstances of a situation in the context of binding legal authority.

Role of Courts

There is a strong identification between law and courts, and often individuals use the terms interchangeably. Courts are the constitutional institution for establishing legal relations through litigation, as well as determining what the law is in a particular situation brought before an appellate court. The Supreme Court, since the 1804 case of *Marbury v. Madison*, is recognized as the authority to determine what is or is not constitutional, that is consistent with the law expressed or implied in the U.S. Constitution, when the issue is raised in a case before it.[3] The Constitution is the supreme law of the land, yet there are many legal issues that never come before any court. However, the method of judicial reasoning and the practice of legal analysis and interpretation are expected to be applied to situations involving constitutional rights.

The courts were said to be the weakest branch of government in the Federalist Papers, but the court system is an integral part of American governance. As an institution of government, the functions and logic of the court system differs greatly from the political branches. Courts do not make policy on their own volition; this would violate judicial norms of objectivity and neutrality. It is common to say that courts make policy, but they do not initiate policy decisions and they do not set policy agendas like elected officials in the political branches. Judges and courts make policy when they decide a case, where the issues and facts are framed and argued by advocates. Courts may make policy with an influential case or when they decide a series of cases, but the court system by its role and traditions is not a policy entrepreneur.

Courts are institutions that authoritatively settle disputes between litigating parties, and this practice predates this nation by hundreds of years. Parties must bring cases to the courts and a decision must be made between contending views of a situation. The Anglo-American court system is based on litigants filing cases and suing to enforce law and rights through a highly structured process. Some advocates bring cases to challenge or change policy through a judgment and appellate opinion on what is legal or constitutional.

The logic of an adversarial system is based on the belief that through a process of contested trials and appeals the parties will provide zealous presentation of facts, law, and arguments, and each side will challenge the assumptions and presentation of the opponent. Courts are part of an adversarial system that is based on the belief that civil battle or debate will provide a full and fair airing of relevant information and provide a just result.

Judicial Rational Decision-Making

Judicial rational decision-making includes important conventions and practices. The elements of impartiality, facts, law, reasoning, and disclosure are essential aspects of judicial practice. Judicial practice and legal training emphasize rational, objective, neutral decisionmakers who base their decisions on the advocacy of the parties. The aspects of judicial rational decision-making include presentation of the issues in dispute; clear and detailed evidence; conflict placed in the context of legal authority in statutes, rules, constitutions, and common law; partisan and strong presentation of argument by parties; an impartial, unbiased decisionmaker; and an explanation and record of the decision reached.

The advocates and parties are expected to have a partisan point of view, but the judge and jury need to be unbiased. The impartiality of the judge is an important value and stresses the need to make a decision based on evidence presented and not on external information or personal preferences. The impartial and objective role for the decisionmaker is a due process concern. The explanation of the decision also serves important democratic values of public information and checks and balances. Judicial rational decision-making has a number of purposes. It allows: One, for the parties to understand a decision; two, for objective court review; three, for the legislature to pass statutes in response to decisions; and four, for public understanding or debate. The consideration of an individual case focuses on the individuals before the court. Court proceedings emphasize individual rights and provides for evaluation of equity and fairness considerations in each case. The possibility that courts may limit uses or abuses of power, whether from individuals, business, or government, is another important aspect of court cases. These judicial practices and norms contain essential democratic elements and incorporate constitutional values.

Court Systems

The court system in this country more accurately should be considered a system of courts; there are over fifty-one legal systems in this country. In addition to federal law and federal courts, each state has its own constitution, statutes, and court system. An example of differences between the state and federal systems is judicial selection. Many are familiar with the life tenure of judges in the federal courts, but this is not the situation for states; many states elect their trial judges and appellate justices. There are some generalities, but there are many differences because each jurisdiction has its own laws and processes. In practice, this means that administrators and their legal counsel must be aware of the distinct features of their jurisdiction.

With fifty states having their own legal systems, plus the federal government court system, there is variation in the terminology and in practices. There may be courts of special jurisdiction, such as the federal courts of claims, bankruptcy, or admiralty. Small claims courts are state courts of special jurisdiction to provide for simplified practices when low dollar amounts are at issue. The lowest level of court in a state may be a district court, but there may be municipal or county courts that enforce ordinances from these jurisdictions.

Courts are divided between trial courts and appellate courts. Court administration is also divided by subject matter.[4] Most states divide at the trial level into criminal courts, civil, probate, and juvenile courts. In criminal cases, the state, through the prosecutor, seeks a conviction to punish wrong actions, and the penalty can be fines or imprisonment. The burden of proof in a criminal case is proof beyond a reasonable doubt. This is a heavy burden placed on the state to present evidence and arguments that persuade the jury that it is appropriate to punish someone with imprisonment, fines, and forfeitures.

In civil cases, one party sues another alleging some violation of a law or duty. Individuals can sue individuals, businesses, or the government. Government may use the courts to enforce rules, regulations, and statutes. In civil cases, the burden of proof is the preponderance of evidence, which is sometimes stated that more than half of the evidence must be in favor of the prevailing party. The federal system also includes specialized courts based on the subject matter which include courts of claims, bankruptcy, and admiralty. The structure, jurisdiction, and processes of these court systems have evolved over time and are recorded in statutes and court rules.

The Process of Conflicts, Claims, and Cases

Trials are a visible, and often dramatic, indication of how a government institution affects individuals and society. The courtroom drama is often portrayed in movies and television shows, with the conflicts between individuals, businesses, or government. Often blame, wrongdoing, fault, and responsibility are part of the dramatic arch. The press does not cover all trials; it reports the gossipy or human interest aspects of disputes, and it often reports serious violent criminal cases.

This dramatic and media view of law centers on disputes and litigation, but it is only part of the routine litigation practice. The development of background information, the discovery of facts and evidence, and the legal research that are part of litigation are often glossed over. But it is the underlying factual situation within the context of binding legal authority from statutes and regulations that draw the attention of public managers, and it is the particular actions of individuals that are part of administrative enforcement through administrative and judicial process.

People consider litigation to be the focus of the American legal system. Recently, many commentaries have asserted that there is excessive litigation. Another assertion is that alternative dispute processes are needed to reduce the amount of litigation. However, litigation may be considered as part of a

Exhibit 4.1   **Pyramid of Legal Claims**

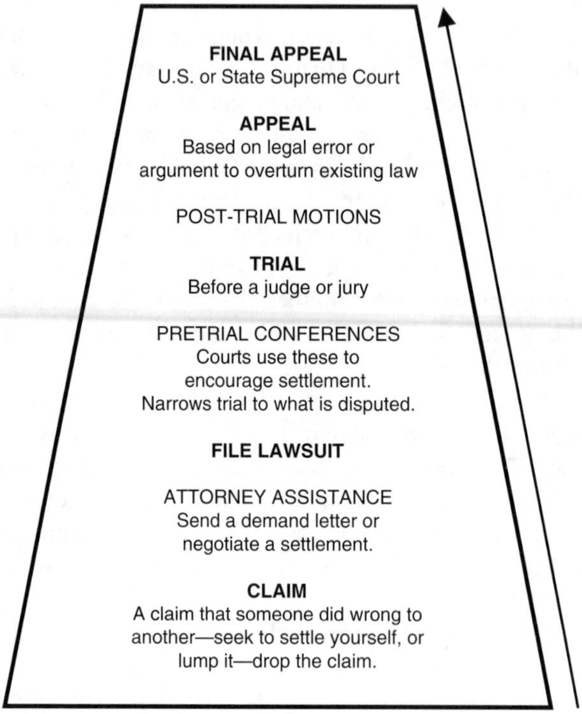

FINAL APPEAL
U.S. or State Supreme Court

APPEAL
Based on legal error or
argument to overturn existing law

POST-TRIAL MOTIONS

TRIAL
Before a judge or jury

PRETRIAL CONFERENCES
Courts use these to
encourage settlement.
Narrows trial to what is disputed.

FILE LAWSUIT

ATTORNEY ASSISTANCE
Send a demand letter or
negotiate a settlement.

CLAIM
A claim that someone did wrong to
another—seek to settle yourself, or
lump it—drop the claim.

pyramid of conflicts where many conflicts are resolved without adversarial process, some are resolved through litigation and others, the very few, may be taken on appeal to the highest court. The way conflicts are addressed can be seen as a series of steps that, like a pyramid, narrows as fewer cases proceed upward. This section discusses this process and Exhibit 4.1 presents a schematic of conflicts, lawsuits, and appeals.

The number of possible claims at the bottom of the pyramid is large. Claims start with an assertion that someone has done wrong—either a criminal or civil wrong. Only the government can bring criminal trials, and the following discussion is built on civil disputes. The beginning of a civil dispute is a claim or request for compensation or resolution of a problem. These claims often begin as informal discussions between individuals, and this discussion may quickly and amicably resolve the claim. The next step for the aggrieved party, if the claim is not settled, is to seek legal advice or to hire an attorney to resolve the dispute. Although individuals can bring suits on their own, they often hire attorneys because of the complexity and specialized aspects of litigation. Public managers at the state and federal level may seek the advice of the agency legal counsel regarding disputes, but often litigation may be handled by a separate office; for example, the Attorney General evaluates and brings all litigation for federal agencies.

Before a suit can be filed, the attorney needs to confirm there is sufficient basis and information to file a case. At this point, the gathering of factual information sufficient to support a court case and a review of the relevant legal authority is done. Informal discussions or negotiations occur between the attorney for the claimant and the respondent—the alleged wrongdoer. Then if negotiations cannot resolve the dispute, it may proceed to an alternative dispute resolution (ADR) or litigation. ADR may be required based on an existing agreement of the parties; ADR may be mandated by law or it is an option the parties can agree upon at this stage. Many claims are resolved at this prefiling step.

The next step is beginning a formal legal claim by filing a lawsuit. The government agency or private party can bring a case as a plaintiff. The plaintiff files a complaint. This filing must allege what occurred, why the filing party believes he is entitled to relief, and to generally state the type of relief sought. The complaint must be served or delivered to the responding party who is called the defendant. The defendant must file a response that addresses the claims by admitting or denying the allegations in the complaint. The response must address each of the claims and present existing defenses. The general term for both plaintiffs and defendants is "parties."

Once a suit is filed, the process of discovery begins. In discovery, the parties seek to gain information that may lead to evidence for use at trial. There are a number of methods of discovery that include requests for documents, interrogatories (which are formal questions), and depositions (which is sworn testimony recorded by a court reporter). Types of information that can be included at trial as evidence will be discussed below. Court rules often require mandatory negotiation and settlement meetings at this pretrial stage. There are also numerous pretrial motions and procedures. Common ones include motions for production of documents and for other discovery. Often, if the facts are not in dispute, there may be a motion for summary judgment or dismissal. The standard for a summary judgment is that there is no issue of any material fact and that the moving party is entitled to a judgment as a matter of law. Many suits are resolved before trial, and some are settled on the courthouse steps just before the trial begins.

The next step is the trial. The trial can have a jury or judge as factfinder. The question of whether the factfinder is the judge or a jury is determined at the time the case is filed; if one party requests a jury, then there will be a jury trial. However, the parties can waive a jury trial and request that the judge decides the case; this is called a "bench trial." Both parties are allowed opening statements to preview what the evidence will show. The plaintiff presents its case with testimony or evidence obtained through questioning witnesses, and the defense may cross-examine each witness. Then, the defendant similarly presents witnesses and exhibits and the plaintiff may cross-examine the defendant's case. During the trial, objections relating to legal and technical points are made to the judge to determine if the objection, or challenge, is proper and if the objection is sustained by the judge, the challenged evidence or question is prohibited; if the judge overrules the objection, this means the challenge fails. At the close of the case the parties may make motions based on law to the judge. At the end of the trial, both parties makes closing arguments to persuade the factfinder to decide in their favor. Jury instructions are developed in which the parties have a chance to suggest to the judge or object to instructions, and then the judge presents the instructions to the jury. The jury deliberates and reaches a verdict; often it is in the form of answering specific points from the instructions.

At the end of a trial, the court must reach a decision. If one party prevails and receives an award of money damages, then the party must seek to collect this amount outside of the courts. That is, courts do not administer the judgments. Once a trial is complete, the parties can accept the judgment and pay damages or comply with the judicial remedy. The alternative in some cases is to bring an appeal.

After a trial verdict, only a small number of cases are appealed. Often the parties accept the verdict. The time and expense of an appeal is also an issue, but a major requirement for an appeal is that there must be an error of law that can be challenged in the appeal and the parties cannot appeal the factual determinations made at trial. This means a small number of parties will file an appeal. There are normally two levels of appeals. The first level is typically called the "court of appeals," and after this court reaches a decision this appellate opinion can be appealed to the highest court of the jurisdiction— most states call their highest court the "supreme court"—which represents the highest level of appeal. For many legal issues arising under state law, it is the state supreme court that makes the final interpretation of the law. Appeals from a state court to the U.S. Supreme Court are not common, and these types of appeals involve a federal or constitutional question. The number of claims that proceed through the legal system gets smaller at each step, and only a very few are resolved at the highest level of appeal.

At every step of the process, fewer claims and cases are considered. Some may drop out and others may settle. There is a presumption that parties reaching an agreement is preferable to a decision imposed by a third party, and so after lawsuits are filed judges encourage the parties to reach an agreement and settle the case between themselves. The expense of litigation compared to returns, a cost-benefit consideration, may result in some foregoing claims, cases, or appeals. For a small number of litigants, pursuing an appeal to win a case or clarify the law is preferred. For instance, when the legal issue involves essential constitutional rights or an uncertain area of law, some litigants will choose to pursue a case to the highest appeal to advocate a change in the law through a precedent that is favorable to their agenda. In many contentious social issues, such as affirmative action or birth control, interest groups fund the litigation to advance their agendas and to seek changes in policy through litigation and appeals; this type of advocacy is called "public-interest litigation."

Trials and Appeals

There are additional aspects of trials and appeals that are worth presenting. Understanding and using the complexities of procedure are part of the technicalities that lawyers use to win cases and appeals and to earn their pay. But there are a number of themes presented here that are relevant to administrative practice: first, the question of jurisdiction or who can address the types of issues; second, the importance of an individual situation and determining what happened, when, and why, or considering the factual setting of an event matters in administration; and third, administrative decisions affecting individual include both the particular factual situations and what they mean within the established laws, regulations, or standard operating procedures.

Procedural Limits on Cases

There are a number of judicial doctrines, as well as statutes, that establish requirements that serve to limit what types of cases trial courts will hear. These requirements serve to ensure that the case is ready to be heard and that important judicial and societal resources are used well. The basic elements that must be present can be discussed as a series of questions: first, who may bring a suit? There are questions of standing or who has the ability to bring a suit, whether there is an injury to that party, and if there is a controversy that arises from a specific factual situation. Second, where to bring suit, or can the court hear the suit? There must be a genuine dispute and this means that the parties stand to gain or lose something from the court's decision. There must be both personal and subject-matter jurisdiction for the court; that means there is authority for that particular case to be tried in a particular venue. Third, when may a suit be litigated? This involves timing questions such as mootness, ripeness, and statutes of limitations (these concepts are defined and discussed below). Fourth, what questions may be litigated? This question goes beyond subject-matter jurisdiction and asks if the type of issue is appropriate for judicial determination.

At the federal level, under the Constitution there must be a case or controversy; this phrase means there must be an active adversarial dispute before the court will hear a case. Some states allow advisory opinions, but issuing advisory opinions can occur only in limited situations to interpret statutes or constitutional provisions. When courts determine if there is a case or controversy, they consider three points: There must be an issue amenable for resolution through court process, there must be a dispute, and there must be a judicial remedy.

These technical and procedural requirements serve to focus and limit the types of cases that appear before the courts, and so the requirements are often raised by the defense as reasons to dismiss the case. The requirement of standing first raises the question of specific harm to the plaintiff. A general allegation of improper policy or harm to the public at large is not sufficient for standing; therefore, suits brought by individuals as taxpayers or citizens challenging federal government spending are often dismissed as lacking particular harm and thus lacking standing.

Courts must have subject-matter jurisdiction or statutory authority to hear the type of case before it. Courts also must have personal jurisdiction over the defendant, which first requires that a defendant must be properly notified of the case by being served with the pleadings. The second consideration of personal jurisdiction is whether it is fair to require an out-of-state defendant to come to court to defend a case; the term for this is long-arm jurisdiction. When individuals travel a great deal in a state or do business in a state, this normally meets the requirement that, to be fair, a defendant must have a sufficient amount of contacts with the state to compel the party to defend the lawsuit in the state.

The question of remedies also serves to focus on what is appropriate or efficient for the courts to address. Damages are the normal type of remedy that plaintiffs seek. Damages is the legal term for monetary compensation for the harm caused. Plaintiffs sometimes seek equitable relief, and they must show that damages are insufficient before courts will use injunctive or declaratory relief. Requests for injunctive relief ask the court to order a party to act in a particular manner; requests for declaratory judgments ask the court to determine rights between two parties. When equitable remedies are being requested, the trial is held before a judge and juries are not allowed.

Timing questions ask if the case was brought too early or too late, which are undesirable because they waste court resources. Moot means that there is no longer a legal issue present that would result in a court decision without an appropriate remedy, and this would mean the judgment would not have any authority. Ripeness is the opposite timing issue from mootness; ripeness means that the legal issue has not reached a point of dispute where it can be resolved by a court. There are statutes of limitation that set a limit of years or months after an event when a case can be filed, and if a case is filed after the statute of limitations has run then it will be dismissed. So if there is a two-year statute of limitations, then a case filed three years after the injury will be dismissed as untimely. Statutes of limitation serve to bring cases when memories are fresher, when it is possible to locate witnesses and collect evidence. Statutes of limitation also serve the purpose of finality and fairness to the parties.

Finally, there are some self-imposed limits on courts. In the case where the government is a party to the suit, the courts may sometimes dismiss the case based on the political questions doctrine. This doctrine serves as part of the checks and balances, and courts use it to recuse themselves from determining cases that are more appropriate for another branch of government to decide. In effect, courts say that some cases are nonjusticiable, meaning the case is not appropriate for judicial consideration. Exactly what is a political question is determined on a case-by-case basis, but examples include legislative reapportionment decisions or disputes between Congress and the President about war powers.

Trials Emphasize Facts

Trials are quite different from appeals. At the trial stage, the parties present evidence to the factfinder, either judge or jury. Trials emphasize what happened, and they apply existing relevant law to determine who is responsible. The system trusts the jury's ability to view witnesses giving testimony and to evaluate the presentation of evidence to reach a just result. The rules of evidence and procedure regulate who testifies, what can be asked, and what exhibits can be entered. It is expected that the attorneys and advocates will zealously represent their clients within the bounds of law. This includes raising issues of whether testimony, exhibits, or legal arguments are consistent with law. Appellate courts provide great discretion to the factfinding and in almost all cases, they defer to the factual determinations made at the trial.

The plaintiff has the burden to present evidence to support the claims made. The defendant presents evidence to dispute and rebuff the claim. The judge rules on various legal motions including objections and on questions of law. Once a judgment is entered, parties can bring post-trial motions. Once the post-trial motions have been ruled on, then either party can bring an appeal.

An additional note about evidence as compared to scientific studies is appropriate here. In social science research and other scientific research, surveys, expert observations, and experiments are considered appropriate or even preferred ways to gather knowledge. The results and generalizations from academic and laboratory research have general respect, but these results are not as important in trials.

In court cases, it is testimony and evidence that is presented to the factfinder. Evidence that differs from social science knowledge includes testimony from witnesses, exhibits such as contracts or photos, and expert witness testimony. The rules of evidence are technical and particular. There is a preference for testimony from a person who observed events that are the facts for the specific case. If documents or exhibits are to be considered as evidence, they must be authenticated by the witness as genuine and accurate. Typical social science research findings may be included in evidence if an expert witness who is properly qualified can testify that both the theory and finding are accepted by experts in the field. This expert witness can be cross-examined on the science and results. The emphasis on eyewitnesses has a long tradition in Anglo-American jurisprudence and is clearly part of the democratic value of confronting ones' accusers. In addition, the ability of the jury and judge to evaluate the witness is seen as a way to seek a fair result. Although memory and observations may be challenged by scientific research as inaccurate, this is not seen as a valid reason to diminish the reliance on witness testimony in courts.

Appeals

The issues presented on appeal must be questions of law that can include interpretations of statutes, constitutions, precedent, or judicial rulings on legal points. What to appeal is decided by the moving parties, but they can only appeal issues that were raised in a timely objection. Objections to evidence or instructions must be raised at the time they occur during trial, or they cannot be raised on appeal. There is a short time period to file an appeal after a verdict or final decision in the case is entered, or it is barred. On rare occasions, some issues may be appealed with permission of the court before a trial begins or verdict is entered; these are called "interlocutory appeals." Either party from the trial can bring an appeal, and the terminology changes to appellant as the party bringing the appeal and appellee as the party responding to the appeal. On appeal, the record of what evidence was presented at trial is considered to be established fact and may not be augmented, except in very unusual circumstances. Although the questions on appeal address legal issues, the decisions of the appellate courts affect which party prevails in a lawsuit.

There are often two levels of appeal with the first being the court of appeals and the final level being the Supreme Court. (In some the states, the names of the intermediate and final courts of appeals are different.) Appellate courts differ from trial courts in that a panel of judges, often three judges, and sometimes the complete court, consider and make the decision. Once an opinion is issued on the initial appeal, either party may appeal the decision to the highest level. If the panel of judges do not all agree on the case then there can be a "majority opinion," which is the authoritative decision, and a "dissenting opinion" which explains why the minority of judges disagree and how these judges interpret the law in this case. Sometimes, judges write concurring opinions—these judges agree with the majority result, but this opinion includes additional discussion of facts or legal points that differ from the majority opinion. Sometimes, the Justices of the Supreme Court do not reach a majority on both the outcome and the legal reasoning; in this case there may be a plurality opinion where a majority of justices agree on the result, but there are concurring opinions that state different rationales (the legal authority or reasoning for the opinion).

There are a number of orders that result from an appeal; the most common are affirm, reverse, remand, and dismiss. The decision to "affirm" means the appellate court approves the lower court ruling. "Reverse" means the prior ruling is overturned. "Remand" means that there are facts or findings that need to be clarified, and so the case is sent back to the trial to decide those issues indicated in the appellate opinion. Sometimes the appeal is "dismissed," meaning a decision was not reached on the merits—meaning the legal issue presented was not determined by the court. When multiple issues are raised on appeal, or if both sides appeal (which is called a "cross appeal"), then the lower court decision can be affirmed in part and reversed in part.

Most jurisdictions have two levels of appeal and a case can be appealed from the intermediate court of appeals to the highest court. For appeals brought to the highest court of the jurisdiction, the court can decide what appeals it must hear and what appeals it will hear. Courts must hear appeals of right—those questions that are required to be heard by statute or court rules. Supreme Courts also hear cases that arise as part of their original jurisdiction. For the U.S. Supreme Court, the process to decide if it will hear cases is called a "Petition for Certiorari"; this is abbreviated as "cert," and it is often stated as cert granted or cert denied. Four Justices must agree to grant a cert petition before it can be placed on the court docket, which is the calendar of cases to be heard. In recent years, the U.S. Supreme Court has heard fewer than 100 cases per year. Thus, the Supreme Court's refusal to hear cases is considered an important way for the court to influence policy. When the Supreme Court refuses to hear a case, the legal result is to leave the appellate court's opinion in effect.

Opinions and Law Making

Common law is developed by a series of court decisions, also called "opinions." It is these published court opinions that decide questions of law by the appellate panel (and sometimes by the trial judge) that are the subject of study for law school. These cases are collected and published in books called Reporters. Reporters are published in series that are organized by type of court, state, or region. The type of cases presented in this book are judicial opinions where the decision affected the rights of the litigants; they are not merely case studies provided as hypotheticals or scenarios for discussion and debate.

There are conventions in writing and interpreting judicial opinions, with typical elements that lawyers and judges look for. First, the names of the parties and the citation are stated at the top. The court then summarizes the facts, any prior decisions, and court process; then it addresses the issues involved. The decision then indicates the area or questions of law to be addressed, which includes the existing statutory, constitutional, and common law authority. As the court discusses the legal authority in relation to the facts and arguments the parties' advocates, it provides the "rationale," which is the primary reasoning for reaching the decision. Often the courts include statements, remarks, or discussion of legal points that are not essential to deciding the case; these nonessential statements are called "dictum." Dictum can be effective in influencing later cases, and the discussions in concurring opinions or dissenting opinions are dictum. The "holding" is the rule for the case, and it is the authoritative statement of the law resulting from the issue in the case. Holdings are binding on subsequent cases; they are precedent.

The effect and importance of court decisions is precedent: Appellate decisions make law. This is part of the longstanding American common law tradition where the legal doctrines that are made through court decisions are called the "common law." There are numerous situations where common law affects governance. Contract law, property law, and tort law are predominantly developed by the common law of a state and this common law precedent applies to government actions. There is no federal common law. The reliance on prior case decisions is an important part of this tradition, and so administrators have to understand and apply the precedent.

Legal Authority and Advocacy

Precedent is an important part of judicial practice because it allows for predictability and reliability in law.[5] The holding of the appellate court, meaning the decision on a legal issue, is precedent. Once a case is determined on appeal, the precedent becomes applicable and binding to everyone in that jurisdiction, unless it is overturned on appeal or replaced by legislation or through a constitutional amendment. Precedent is also called "stare decisis," which means let the decision stand, and this reflects the view that precedent should be respected unless there is a reason to overturn it. Although some suggest that precedent allows for judicial efficiency in having fewer cases brought up on appeal, it also means that cases are appealed because the facts differ slightly and the advocates are seeking new precedent on the more narrowly defined situation. This parsing means that there is growth in the law, and new precedent or changes in the finer points of precedent occur regularly.

Searches for legal authority and precedent are important steps for attorneys. When a dispute arises, attorneys research prior cases to see if the same legal question arose in the same factual situation—this is called "finding cases on point." If there is a case on point then it is binding to those with the same facts and same issues. If asked to give legal advice or an opinion, attorneys also search for statutes or cases that are on point or cases that are closely related.

Attorneys often try to enlist established precedent that is not exactly on point to persuade the court based on assertions that the present case is analogous to a prior precedent that is in their favor, or they attempt to distinguish how their case is different from precedent that does not support their case. Sometimes attorneys argue that the precedent is no longer valid and that it should be overturned. Thus, in motions for summary judgment and briefs for appeals, attorneys argue based on what statutes say, what prior precedent holds, and that this law can determine or support their position.

Precedent is part continuity and part change. If there is a reported case directly on point in that jurisdiction, it is controlling and it can determine a civil case in litigation. It can be controlling and determine a case on appeal. The precedent must be followed until it is superceded by a statute or overturned by another judicial decision. Thus many appeals are brought to change precedent, and a party seeking to overturn precedent must provide persuasive reasons for the court to change its doctrine.

Alternative Dispute Resolution

Litigation has been widely criticized for many reasons. First, the result of a lawsuit is not certain nor predictable; lawsuits are decided by generalist judge or jury rather than someone with expertise and experience. Second, litigation is seen as a battle that will harm relationships. Third, and most common, the time and cost of litigation are criticized. Many of these concerns were used to justify administrative adjudication when the Administrative Procedure Act was passed in 1946, but in the 1980s many innovations in dispute resolution were developed and these encouraged broader use of alternative dispute resolution techniques.[6] ADR are seen as collaborative, consensual, and cooperative approaches to conflict resolution. ADR approaches include arbitration, negotiation, mediation, and minitrials.

There are five reasons suggested for using ADR: It reduces costs; it takes less time; it encourages creative solutions; it improves relationships; and it encourages greater participation by individuals with less control by attorneys. One assumption underlying ADR is that both parties desire and agree to use the ADR process. Another assumption is that ADR can be private and so it is preferable to the delay, expense, and publicness of court hearings.

ADR was adopted as a federal policy for administrative agencies and governments in the 1990s when Congress passed legislation for ADR practices in government. The two congressional purposes for adopting ADR were traditional efficiency rationales: costs less and saves time. Presidents supported ADR practices through executive orders. ADR is used in both internal operations and external relations with the public. There is also a specific process for administrative rulemaking based on negotiated rulemaking.

In addition to ADR, new types of administrative roles were developed to reduce conflicts in the 1990s. Agencies appointed inspectors general or process auditors to investigate internal management processes, procedure, and problems. Ombudsman positions were developed as neutral investigators. Ombudsmen investigate complaints from the public or questions from within an agency, and they produce informal resolution of the complaints. They can also make suggestions on improving government procedures. These process auditor and ombudsman roles provide an organizational structure to develop information-based attempts to resolve misunderstandings before they become full-blown conflicts.

The use of ADR varies by the management and problem context, and managers need to develop the skills to use ADR.[7] Interest-based negotiations, arbitration, and mediation have been used in public-sector personnel management. Often ADR provisions for arbitration are included in public contracting. ADR does not mean avoiding attorneys; many businesses and agencies include their attorneys in ADR situations. The one common prerequisite to ADR is that those involved must agree to participate in ADR. However, in any ADR situation, the complaining party must gather evidence and data to convince both the factfinder and the opponent of the merits of the claim and to persuade them to reach a resolution that the complainant prefers. There are also policy concerns about use of ADR when there are no clear legal precedents surrounding an issue; in these situations, court trials or appeals that result in binding precedent may be preferred to ADR. There are also democratic concerns because ADR, which encourages private resolution, does not promote values of openness and governmental accountability.

Judicial Review of Government Actions

As part of the checks and balances, agencies are sued and courts are called upon to review legislation and administrative practices. Judicial review of government actions depends on the type of issues presented in court cases. What kind of review will be made? This depends on a number of variables including the applicable law in statutes, precedent, or constitution; the type of agency or administrative action (whether the claim is based informal rule-making or adjudication); the facts of a situation; the record made at the time of decision; and the persuasiveness of the advocates presenting the facts.

Judicial review, as public administration scholar Phillip Cooper has explained, usually involves five questions.[8] First, is the administrative action within the agency's authority? The court inquiry considers delegation from the legislation by reviewing the text of the statute itself, or the court may evaluate the administrative interpretation of the agency's authority to act. Courts grant considerable deference to the agencies' interpretations of their enabling or authorizing statutes. If an action is not authorized by statutes, by executive order, or is not inherent in carrying out these duties then it is "ultra vires," which means beyond authority. Ultra vires acts are by definition illegitimate and illegal.

Second, courts ask if appropriate procedures established by the organic statute, by procedure acts, or by agency regulations were followed. Internal agency procedures and rules may be binding on an agency. Judges look to the form and substance of the procedures. Administrators must produce evidence to show what procedures were used. If there is a deviation from normal agency practices, this needs to be explained.

The third question: Was the decision arbitrary, capricious, or an abuse of discretion? Courts do not substitute their judgment for the agency. Courts begin by presuming that administrators act lawfully, and courts consider the record for evidence that the agency considered the laws and facts to reach its decisions.

The "arbitrary and capricious" language is important. The language of judgments may confuse the unwary reader if they encounter phrases like "not arbitrary" or "not confusing." Close reading makes it clear that the court expects the administrators to consider all facts and evidence and demonstrate deliberate and clear reasoning. "Not being arbitrary" emphasizes the need for administrative decisions based on rational consideration of facts and evidence and deliberate and disclosed reasoning. "Not capricious" also considers whether the decision is consistent when compared to similar cases or compared to the standards set in laws. The constitutional guarantee of fair treatment is the foundation of the courts' "arbitrary and capricious" standards.

Courts require systematic and thorough decision-making based on informed decisions, not on emotions. This judicial preference for rational, deliberate, and reasoned decisions does not forestall considerations of compassion, equity, or individual circumstances; instead, it requires disclosure of both the rational and the sympathetic considerations in administrative decisions. Courts look more closely at actions if improper classifications were considered such as race, gender, age, or if the agency failed to consider relevant evidence that was available, or if statutory considerations were omitted. Decisions do not have to be optimal. Agencies do not have to reach the same results as how a reviewing judge would interpret the facts and law if the case originated before the court. Instead, agency decisions have to be supported by evidence on the record and an explanation for the conclusion the agency reached.

The fourth consideration deals with evidence and the record. Was there sufficient evidence in the record to support the results that the agency reached? The agency must examine all relevant data and articulate a satisfactory explanation for its decision, including a rational connection between the facts found and the decision reached. This means agencies need an adequate record; they need to explain what facts were considered and explain the action in writing. In general, the record needs to be contemporaneous with the decision or action of the agency. After-the-fact rationalizations are not acceptable.

The fifth consideration by courts is whether there is a constitutional violation. Administrative hearings must meet the requisites of due process, but the extent of due process may vary based on the type of issue and administrative action. The courts also determine whether constitutional due process was provided in hearings and enforcement; however, the courts have held there is no due process right in the rulemaking process. Constitutional questions of search and seizure and equal protection may also be raised to challenge to administrative actions.

Democratic and Judicial Values

The courts have been called the weakest branch of government, but the court system is an important part of American governance. Courts determine rights between individuals. Courts convict criminals and send them to prison. Courts decide if government officers exceeded their authority. In civil cases courts typically provide damages or a remedy involving compensation for harm, but courts also have the authority for injunctive and declaratory relief. That is, judges may order some action or restraint from action. They may declare a law void. The influence of trial and appellate court decisions can be immense.

The traditional model was one of seeing the judge as a referee and interpreter of law. However, in the last half of the twentieth century, a movement toward more activist or public-interest litigation has argued for judicial intervention because administrators or legislators have failed to address serious social problems. In these situations, some orders for injunctive relief required changing how government provided services in schools, prisons, or mental institutions.[9] In the efforts to remedy discrimination in the public schools, courts supervised school district efforts. Charles Wise and Rosemary O'Leary, two respected public administration scholars, studied one effort by a court to supervise and monitor Kansas City school desegregation, and they detailed how many of the traditional management techniques and problems were present for the court in this type of case.[10]

Elements of constitutionally required protections have been integrated into administrative practices, but they are often used as the reason for challenging government actions. The contestability of government action through court cases is part of the democratic checks and balances. The ability of individuals to sue the government to challenge government action is also considered an important element for democratic government and is included in the rule-of-law philosophy. An indication that no one is above the law is the history of individuals challenging statutes passed by the legislature and actions undertaken by the executive and administrators.

Court review of agency action is both an essential part of democratic governance and a subject of contention. Administrators and theorists alike question when judicial review of agency actions is appropriate. On occasion, statutes may limit judicial review; however, the courts have declared an inherent constitutional power to review petitions that allege unconstitutional bureaucratic actions. It is not surprising that judicial review raises tensions about separation of powers or judicial interference.

Critics offer four kinds of arguments against the court cases and judicial review that they claim interferes with agency actions and prevents an agency from achieving its policy goals. First, court cases divert time, money, and attention away from the agency's tasks; in short, this is an efficiency argument. Second, the types of issues that are litigated and subject to court review interfere with agency discretion or impose burdens on agencies, or this is an effectiveness argument. Third, these cases make administrators cautious in making decisions so they take a narrowly defined view of problems and actions to avoid possible litigation or conflict; this is the excessively bureaucratic or legalistic argument. Fourth, court review and a rules-based approach interfere with achieving innovation or accomplishing goals. This is a liberation management position which is a utilitarian argument, where the officials should be judged by results and achieving goals rather than considering the methods and processes along the way.

Of course, supporters of judicial review offer five kinds of arguments defending judicial review as essential and vital. First, judicial review is part of an individual's right to petition and seek court review to defend rights found in the constitutional limits on government; this is a constitutional values argument. Second, judicial review is a policy choice made through legislative enactments. It is included as part of many administrative procedure statutes, tort liability waivers, and other enactments. This is a legislative policy argument. Third, court cases and judicial review are part of the transparent and open evaluation of official government action that allows for disclosure of activities to public scrutiny and publicity; this is the public information argument. Fourth, since administrators are not elected, neither executive nor legislative supervision may be able to evaluate and review administrative action in the same way as an individual bringing a lawsuit. Thus, this type of advocacy serves as an additional check on government action, or this is a bureaucratic constraint argument. Finally, legal challenges and court review are part of the constitutional structure that provides litigation as an avenue to influence government policies expressed in legislative acts or bureaucratic practices; this is a policy advocacy argument. The five arguments all build on the belief that judicial review and supervision are essential values for democratic and constitutional governance.

Conclusion

The court system is an important constitutional institution. This chapter presented the process of trials and appeals, but it is the facts and merits of what happened in a lawsuit that is determined at trial. In considering disputes, courts evaluate three kinds of matters in detail—matters of fact, persuasive arguments presented by the attorneys for each side, and the legal authorities—statutes, rules, precedent, and constitution—relevant to the points at issues. Even when public administrators carry out their responsibilities, conflict is inevitable and normal. The court system and the legal process provide a location and method for administrators to enforce the law, and the courts serve important democratic and constitutional values.

Cases

The two cases presented in this section address interesting, as well as recurring problems that arise in public administration. Equally important, they illustrate how courts consider cases. The first case, *Buckley v. New York,*[11] illustrates how a precedent is first adopted based on social norms and how a series of case and legislative actions are considered in the decision to change the precedent. The second case, *Ethredge v. Hail,*[12] illustrates a management situation involving individual political speech in contrast to unit morale. However, the legal issue discussed is mootness, which considers whether after a change in circumstances if there still is legal issue that the court can resolve.

Terence Buckley v. City of New York; Anthony Lawrence v. City of New York, 56 N.Y.2d 300; Court of Appeals of New York, 1982

Opinion by Gabrielli.

Each of the cases involved in these appeals presents the question of whether the fellow-servant rule continues to apply in New York. In each case an employee of the City of New York, who was injured through the negligence of a coemployee, brought an action against the municipality. In *Buckley v. City of New York*, a police officer was accidentally shot in the leg when a gun being loaded by a fellow officer discharged in the station house locker room; and in *Lawrence v. City of New York*, a fire fighter was seriously injured when a fellow fire fighter threw a smouldering couch from the second story window of a fire-damaged building and struck the plaintiff while he was standing in the yard. In each case the plaintiff secured a jury verdict of liability against the city on a theory of vicarious liability and the city's motion to dismiss the complaint on the basis of the fellow-servant rule was denied. The Appellate Division has affirmed the judgments in both instances and leave has been granted to appeal to this court. We now affirm the orders below.

Under the rule of respondeat superior, an employer will be liable to third parties for torts of an employee committed within the scope of his employment (*Sims v. Bergamo*, 3 N.Y.2d 531). By virtue of the fellow-servant rule, however, if an employee is injured by a fellow employee in the workplace he will have no recourse against the employer in respondeat superior. Succinctly stated, the rule provides that "where a servant is injured through the negligence or fault of a fellow servant, engaged in a common business and employment, . . . and the master is himself free from fault, the master is not responsible for the injury" (36 *NY Jur*, Master and Servant, § 130).

The fellow-servant rule had its origin in England in 1837 (*Priestly v. Fowler*, 3 M & W [Meeson & Welsby's Exch. Rep.] 1, 150 Eng. Rep. 1030) and was adopted in the United States shortly afterward (*Murray v. South Carolina R.R. Co.*, 1 McMul. [L. Rep.] 385; Prosser, *Torts* [4th ed.], § 80, p. 528). The rationales attributed to the rule are varied; the most convincing is that the rule promotes the safety of the public and of the workers by encouraging each employee to be watchful of the conduct of others for his own protection. It has also been suggested that the rule was based upon the notion that an employee assumes the risk of negligence on the part of his fellow servants or, more fundamentally, that the rule simply reflected a 19th century bias by the courts in favor of business (see Prosser, *Torts*, 4th ed., § 80, pp. 528–529). The theoretical underpinnings of this rule have, to a large extent, been discredited in recent years (see *Poniatowski v. City of New York*, 14 N.Y.2d 76, 81; *Crenshaw Bros. Produce Co. v. Harper*, 142 Fla. 27, 47). Logically, there appears to be little reason for denying an employee the right which a third party possesses to recover from the employer in *respondeat superior*, since for one thing, in both instances the employer might have avoided the injury by selection of more careful employees. Moreover, the class of persons most frequently endangered by the negligence of an employee—his fellow workers—should not, without compelling reason, be denied a remedy accorded to the general public.

The over-all effect of the fellow-servant rule was drastically curtailed by the advent of workers' compensation legislation, for the rule, involving injuries sustained in the course of one's employment, provides no defense to a demand for this remedy (Prosser, *Torts*, 4th ed, § 80, p. 531; see *Workers' Compensation Law*, § 11). Nevertheless, the rule has not yet been completely obliterated since there are some areas of employment, such as those involved in the present appeal (see *Matter of Ryan v. City of New York,* 228 N.Y. 16; *Matter of Krug v. City of New York,* 196 App. Div. 226), where the Workers' Compensation Law does not apply.

In *Poniatowski v. City of New York* (supra), our court signaled the beginning of the end of the fellow-servant rule in New York. There, a police officer was injured in a motor vehicle accident through the negligence of a fellow officer. Although the plaintiff's cause was sustained in our court on the basis of a statute which obviated the necessity of directly confronting the fellow-servant rule, we referred to this rule in passing by stating that "[the] inherent injustice of a rule which denies a person, free of fault, the right to recover for injuries sustained through the negligence of another over whose conduct he has no control merely because of the fortuitous circumstance that the other is a fellow officer is manifest. . . . This may well suggest the desirability of abolishing the rule but we leave decision of that question to the future. It is sufficient at this time to decide only that we should not extend it into an area in which it has not previously been applied" (*Poniatowski v. City of New York,* supra, at p. 81, note omitted). Today we are squarely presented with the question left open in *Poniatowski*—whether the fellow-servant rule is to survive in New York. The rule had its birth in the 19th century, was severely crippled with the advent of workers' compensation, and was dealt an almost fatal blow in this State in *Poniatowski*. Today, in rejecting this rule entirely, we inter its remains.

In constructing its argument for retention of the fellow-servant rule, the defendant city has largely abandoned the rationales originally underpinning the rule and, instead, the city asserts that the rule should be retained primarily because it has enjoyed a lengthy tenure in our jurisprudence. While the longevity of a rule of law requires that its re-examination be given careful scrutiny, it does not demand that its effect be given permanence. The continued vitality of a rule of law should depend heavily upon its continuing practicality and the demands of justice, rather than upon its mere tradition. Although the policy of stare decisis is not to be lightly cast aside, this court has previously noted that "[it] was intended, not to effect a 'petrifying rigidity,' but to assure the justice that flows from certainty and stability. If, instead, adherence to precedent offers not justice but unfairness, not certainty but doubt and confusion, it loses its right to survive, and no principle constrains us to follow it"(*Bing v. Thunig,* 2 N.Y.2d 656, 667).

Furthermore, we make it abundantly clear that we do not subscribe to the view that the abolition of the fellow-servant rule is strictly a matter for legislative attention. The fellow-servant rule originated as a matter of decisional law, and it remains subject to judicial re-examination. As this court observed in *Woods v. Lancet* (303 N.Y. 349, 355), "[we] act in the finest common-law tradition when we adapt and alter decisional law to produce common-sense justice."

The fellow-servant rule serves no continuing valid purpose in New York, but instead merely works an unjustifiable hardship upon individuals injured in the workplace, and we must thus conclude that the fellow-servant rule is no longer to be followed in New York.

Accordingly, the orders of the Appellate Division should be affirmed, with costs.

Jesse Ethredge v. Robert Hail, Deputy Base Commander, 996 F.2d 1173, U.S. Court of Appeals, 11th Circuit, 1993

Opinion by Kravitch

Appellant Jesse Ethredge seeks review of a district court order denying his request for a preliminary injunction prohibiting enforcement of an Air Force administrative order. That administrative order forbids Ethredge to display on his truck certain remarks about the President of the United States while on Robins Air Force Base in Georgia. Because we conclude that the issues raised on appeal are moot, we dismiss the appeal, vacate the district court order, and remand the case to the district court for further proceedings.

I.

Ethredge is a civilian aircraft mechanic who has worked at Robins for more than twenty-five years. He drives onto the base for work approximately four to six times per week.

From 1984 through 1988, Ethredge displayed on the back window of the truck he drove to work a sticker reading "HELL WITH REAGAN." Ethredge designed the sticker as a protest to President Reagan's policies regarding unions and the civil service retirement system, especially those involving air traffic controllers. In 1989 Ethredge changed the message on his truck to reflect the new administration of President Bush. Ethredge's anti-Bush messages read "READ MY LIPS HELL WITH GEO BUSH" and "FORGIVE BUSH NOT EGYPT HE LIED." These statements were intended to focus criticism on President Bush's agreement to raise taxes notwithstanding contrary campaign promises and his decision to forgive certain debt owed by Egypt.

In 1991 Major General Richard F. Gillis, the Robins base commander, directed appellee Hail, the deputy base commander, to order Ethredge to remove the anti-Bush stickers while on base. Hail issued the order as directed. The order provides, in relevant part:

1. As Robins Air Force Base (AFB) is a military installation, bumper stickers or other similar paraphernalia which embarrass or disparage the Commander in Chief are inappropriate as they have a negative impact on the good order and discipline of the service members stationed at Robins AFB.
2. You are hereby ordered, while at Robins AFB, to remove all bumper stickers that contain disparaging or embarrassing comments about the Commander in Chief of the United States of America.

Rather than remove the stickers, Ethredge began to drive a different vehicle to work at the base. He then filed the instant lawsuit. Ethredge alleges that the order is an unjustified, viewpoint-discriminatory restriction on his speech which violates his rights under the First Amendment. He seeks both preliminary and permanent injunctions against enforcement of the order, as well as a declaratory judgment that the order is unconstitutional.

Following a hearing, the district court denied Ethredge's request for a temporary restraining order and a preliminary injunction. The court held that Ethredge failed to show a substantial likelihood of success on the merits of his claims. Id. Specifically, the court concluded that the administrative order is viewpoint-neutral and that Ethredge's stickers present a "clear danger to the discipline, loyalty and morale of Air Force personnel" at Robins.

Ethredge took an interlocutory appeal to this court; see 28 U.S.C. § 1292(a) (1) (1988). On January 20, 1993, after the parties' briefs were filed but before oral argument, President Bush left office.

II.

A.

When a case becomes moot after the district court enters its judgment but before this court has issued a decision, we are divested of jurisdiction and must dismiss the appeal and vacate the underlying judgment. U.S. Const. Art. III; *Lewis v. Continental Bank Corp.,* 494 U.S. 472, 477, (1990); *Wahl v. McIver,* 773 F.2d 1169, 1174 (11th Cir.1985). A case is moot when it no longer presents a live controversy with respect to which the court can give meaningful relief. E.g., *United States v. Certain Real & Personal Property,* 943 F.2d 1292, 1296 (11th Cir.1991).

In his motion for a preliminary injunction, Ethredge requests only that the district court "[enjoin] defendant from enforcing a Robins Air Force Base administrative order requiring Plaintiff to remove a bumper sticker from his truck *simply because it is critical of President Bush.*" The crux of Ethredge's argument in support of preliminary injunctive relief is that the base commander imposed a viewpoint-discriminatory restriction on his political speech by forbidding his anti-Bush messages while allowing "pro-Bush, pro-Republican and conservative bumper stickers." In short, by its terms the motion for preliminary injunction seeks relief solely as to Ethredge's anti-Bush stickers. But former-President Bush is no longer in office. Consequently, the administrative order no longer forbids Ethredge's anti-Bush stickers. It does not appear that Ethredge is being precluded from displaying his anti-Bush stickers notwithstanding the order's inapplicability to them. Thus, no live controversy remains with respect to Ethredge's request for preliminary injunctive relief.

We hasten to add that our dismissal of the appeal as moot is necessarily limited to the specific order before us in this proceeding: the district court's denial of Ethredge's request for a preliminary injunction. As we recently wrote, "[this] case reaches us . . . as an *interlocutory* appeal from an order denying a preliminary injunction. 'Consequently, only the action on the preliminary injunction is presently reviewable.'" *Cafe 207, Inc. v. St. Johns County,* 989 F.2d 1136, 1136–37 (11th Cir.1993) (quoting *Scott Paper Co. v. Gulf Coast Pulpwood Ass'n,* 491 F.2d 119, 119 (5th Cir.1974)) (other citation omitted) (emphasis in original). Still pending before the district court are Ethredge's seemingly broader requests for a permanent injunction and a declaration that the administrative order is unconstitutional. The issues raised by those prayers for relief may remain live notwithstanding President Bush's departure from the White House.

B.

Ethredge proffers several arguments why this appeal is not moot, or, if it is, why an exception to the mootness doctrine should apply. First, he argues that he retains a stake in the litigation because the administrative order remains in effect and he "has a proven propensity to criticize Presidential policies." This argument is unavailing for the very reason we hold above that the appeal is moot. The motion for preliminary injunction is specific to Ethredge's anti-Bush stickers. The likelihood that Ethredge will criticize President Clinton or some future president may be relevant to the larger question whether Ethredge's remaining requests for permanent injunctive and declaratory relief present a live controversy. Such future criticism likewise might justify Ethredge seeking leave of the district court to amend or supplement his pleadings in this case. In view of Ethredge's specific contentions in his motion for preliminary injunction, however, that the Robins order was issued and enforced against him solely because his messages were anti-Republican and anti-conservative, we decline to recast the motion as a more general allegation that the order was issued and enforced against him because his stickers were "anti-Commander in Chief." Cf. *Wakefield v. Church of Scientology of California*, 938 F.2d 1226, 1229 n. 1 (11th Cir.1991) ("This court reviews the case tried in the district court; it does not try ever-changing theories parties fashion during the appellate process.").

Ethredge also argues that the issues raised in the motion for preliminary injunction are "capable of repetition, yet evading review." See, e.g., *Naturist Society, Inc. v. Fillyaw*, 958 F.2d 1515, 1520 (11th Cir.1992). Although we agree that the issues are capable of repetition, we do not think they are so transitory in nature as to likely evade review. Critical remarks abound for the full duration of every president's administration. Such commentary is not confined to the relatively short timeframe of the political campaign. Ethredge himself is proof of this obvious truth; his anti-Reagan and anti-Bush stickers were displayed on the back of his truck for more than eight years. Hence, a First Amendment challenge to a military restriction on speech that is critical of the president is not likely to stay ripe only for so short a period of time as to elude full judicial review. It is mere happenstance that in this case Ethredge sought his preliminary injunction less than nine months before the change in administrations and thus was not able to obtain review in this court before his motion became moot.

Ethredge next argues that he has satisfied the exception to mootness for "an appellant [who] has taken all necessary steps to perfect the appeal and to preserve the status quo before the dispute becomes moot." *B & B Chemical Co. v. EPA*, 806 F.2d 987, 990 (11th Cir.1986). This exception, however, is an extremely narrow one that has been limited primarily to criminal defendants who seek to challenge their convictions notwithstanding that they have been released from custody. "The fundamental argument for review [in such cases] is that the stigma of conviction of itself justifies review." 13A Wright, Miller & Cooper, *Federal Practice & Procedure* § 3533.4, at 302 (2d ed. 1984). In *B & B Chemical* we cited with approval the opinion of the Third Circuit in *In re Kulp Foundry, Inc.*, 691 F.2d 1125 (3d Cir.1982). *B & B Chemical*, 806 F.2d at 990. *Kulp Foundry* described the "all necessary steps"exception as an extension of the traditional mootness exceptions to cases in which the appellant has been released from custody or has served his sentence and has taken all possible steps to have his order of confinement promptly reviewed prior to his release. 691 F.2d at 1129. The court explained that the exception is "grounded on the important personal liberty interest at stake" in such cases. Id. The court did not understand the exception to extend to cases in which no personal liberty interest is at stake. Id.

This limitation on the "all necessary steps" exception is only logical. To review every otherwise-moot case simply because the appellant took all necessary steps to prevent the case from becoming moot would be to graft a fault requirement onto the doctrine of mootness. This would water down the doctrine almost to the point of impotence. Dilution of the mootness doctrine, in turn, would be inconsistent with the constitutional mandate that federal courts hear live cases and controversies. Thus, the "all necessary steps" exception does not save the appeal in this case from dismissal for mootness.

Finally, Ethredge argues that the district court's order will have dangerous collateral consequences if not reversed. See, e.g., *B & B Chemical,* 806 F.2d at 990. In particular, he fears that if the order remains as published precedent it will affect the decisions and actions of the military and of individuals wanting to exercise their First Amendment rights in future cases. In view of our decision to dismiss the appeal as moot, however, we vacate the district court's opinion. See, e.g., *In re Federal Grand Jury Proceedings 89–10,* 938 F.2d 1578, 1580–81 (11th Cir.1991); *Wahl,* 773 F.2d at 1174. This action will prevent the district court's opinion from spawning precedential consequences. E.g., *County of Los Angeles v. Davis,* 440 U.S. 625, 634 n. 6, (1979); *Curtis v. Taylor,* 648 F.2d 946, 947 n. 1 (5th Cir.1980). Any consequences that might derive from the district court opinion's lingering persuasive value are neither personal to Ethredge nor sufficiently certain to warrant an exception to the mootness doctrine in this case. See *B & B Chemical,* 806 F.2d at 991 (holding asserted possible collateral consequence "too speculative").

III.

For the foregoing reasons, Ethredge's appeal is Dismissed, the judgment of the district court is Vacated, and the case is Remanded to the district court for further proceedings consistent with this opinion.

Discussion Questions

1. Discuss how there are differences in how courts influence public policy compared to politicians or administrators.

2. What are the steps of judicial rational decision-making?
3. How are trials different from appeals?
4. What is precedent and why is important to judicial practice?
5. Discuss how ADR techniques are used by administrators instead of litigation.
6. What are the five questions judges use to review agency action?
7. How are litigation and advocacy part of democratic constitutional values?
8. In the *Buckley* case, consider how history and different views in society influence precedent and provide the rationale for a change in precedent. Consider how the fellow-servant rule indicates management responsibilities and compare this with current public personnel management practices. Consider why workers compensation does not apply to the *Buckley* case and following this case, are there any changes New York local governments might desire in legislation or management practices?
9. The *Ethredge* case was dismissed because of mootness. How does this affect the order issued by the base commander? How do you compare Ethredge's rights to free speech and the government's concern for morale and employee behavior? Are there any changes you would suggest to the base commander to balance the individual and organizational concerns?
10. Note that in the two cases the courts cite to cases, the Constitution, statutes, a legal encyclopedia (*NY Jurisprudence*) and a treatise (Prosser, *Torts*). Some are cited as authoritative and others are cited as guidance.

5

Administrative Practice and Administrative Law

Not so long ago friends could walk their traveling pal down the concourse to the airport gate and watch the plane take off, but that all changed after September 11, 2001. Security became more stringent as it became the responsibility of the Transportation Security Administration (TSA), a branch of the new federal Homeland Security Agency.[1] Only ticketed passengers are admitted to a concourse after screening. Each passenger goes through metal detectors; their baggage, coats, and shoes are all X-rayed. Signs are posted that list the items that cannot be carried onto planes, and the signs explain that only those containers of medicine or grooming supplies that hold three ounces of liquid or less and that fit into a one-quart-sized bag could be carried onto planes. Many airports supply these clear quart bags for travelers.

This airport-screening example illustrates major aspects of the administrative process. The authority to require passengers to take off shoes and jackets and to limit liquids was developed through regulations.[2] The signs posted to inform travelers are part of the public-notice provisions that inform individuals of acceptable and impermissible conduct. The way screening is conducted is a type of administrative enforcement that is now part of routine travel. But when a grandma is frisked or asked to disrobe or another person is detained, the manner in which these safety provisions are carried out is subject to criticism, complaints, or even litigation. This feedback also is part of normal administrative practices.

This chapter considers the types of administrative activities and the three major categories of administrative law: rulemaking, adjudication (enforcement), and public information. The federal administrative process has been the subject of greater study, so this chapter will follow convention and discuss federal administrative law. Federal rulemaking, adjudication, and information processes differ from the states but the many state administrative procedure acts incorporate many steps and requirements for public notice, executive supervision, and legislative oversight.[3]

Administrative Activities and Regulation

One way to understand governance and administrative practice is to describe the types of activities that are assigned to agencies. Some activities are internal to the continued operation of government. There are many other activities that are external, including regulating actions of industries or providing information and assistance to individuals. Carrying out these activities and policies from statutes is the responsibility of public administrators.

The range and scope of government activities is enormous. Some activities are specific to a single agency, but many are common agency practices and will be performed by many agencies. The details of the common operating practices for an agency may be determined by the types of activities and the traditions of each agency. The following description includes categories of administrative actions.[4]

Licensing: Perhaps the most common license granted by the state is the driver license. Governments license activities and often require tests or training for the applicant to show a minimum competence before a license is granted. Professions that are licensed include engineers, nurses, teachers, barbers, hairstylists, lawyers, and accountants. Some professions must pass tests given by the state, and others pass tests given by a national association. Business may be required to get a license to operate that may include registering information about the owners.

Provide services: Local governments provide many services that are consumed by individuals including water, sewer, and schools. The federal government provides services to individuals such as business advice, student loan guarantees, flood insurance, and disaster relief. The federal government provides general public services such as national security and military, Internet development, and census and economic data. Cities and states provide general services, such as public health, police, and fire protection. Some government services such as parks and recreation can be considered either individual or general services.

Distribute benefits: Governments provide and distribute benefits to individuals. These include workers compensation, unemployment, food stamps, housing vouchers, Medicare, Medicaid, and Social Security Death and Disability benefits. Individuals must apply for the benefits and demonstrate that they qualify for the programs. Many benefits are administered through combined state and federal authority.

Taxes: Tax administration and collection provides for democratic support of government activities, and taxes are used to affect the behavior of individuals and businesses. The methods of tax calculation, notice, collection, and resolution of improper filing are all well-developed administrative routines at the local, state, and federal levels, even though the types of taxes differ. Some tax problems that agencies have to address may result from the improper completion of a form, and usually these can be resolved through an exchange of letters. Other tax problems may be more complex and involve whether the proper amount of taxes were paid; these are often are settled through a notice and compromise. Tax disputes may proceed to a formal hearing, and very few may be referred for administrative or criminal sanctions.

Internal operations: Many government activities are internal operations and may not directly affect or involve the general public. Once these were referred to as housekeeping, but many of the internal functions are essential for government operations. The internal roles for administrators include budgeting, planning, personnel, supervision, performance monitoring, and recordkeeping.

The word "regulation" has two major meanings when discussing administrative practices. The word regulation stands for the governmental activities that affect and control the behavior of individuals and businesses. The federal government regulates clean air, clean water, standards for food, childcare, nursing homes, drugs, securities, radio broadcasting, and employment practices. State and local governments regulate weeds, vermin, home construction, and insurance sales. Regulation may include providing standards to protect public safety, such as food processing; regulation may provide economic regulation of markets or industries, such as the securities regulations. In addition, some analysts call benefits a type of "social regulation." There are numerous types of administrative activities that are called "regulation." In other words, bureaucrats regulate, and unfortunately both terms, "bureaucrat" and "regulation," have negative connotations. Usually the term bureaucrat is used to criticize public administrators, and regulations are often viewed by critics as government intrusions into private behavior of individuals and businesses. As a broad activity, regulation may include enforcement through informal means, through administrative hearings, or even through criminal prosecution.

The second major meaning of regulations is found in administrative procedure laws, and in this definition, regulations are a type of rules or are seen as a systems of rules that affect an industry or activity. Under the federal Administrative Procedure Act (APA), "regulation" is the formal term for what most people would call a rule; regulations that are promulgated under the APA that have the force of law are called "substantive regulations." Unfortunately, there is no way to avoid the confusion between the two kinds of regulating, but in this chapter the broad administrative activity will be called "enforcement" or regulating and the rule-type regulation will be noted.

The many different administrative practices are affected by informal and formal rules, enforcement activities, administrative adjudication, and information disclosure. These administrative practices have distinct policy origins and established procedures that affect governance.

Historic Transition from Administrative Law to Administrative Procedure

Historically, what was called "administrative law" applied to almost all aspects of government, but the term administrative law now means something much narrower following the passage of the Administrative Procedure Act. What once was administrative law, meaning the constitutions, statutes, and common law that affected governments, is now referred to as public law. Administrative law now means the APA, or state administrative procedure laws, and the cases interpreting these statutes. As this section details, the shift is part of the development of the field of public administration.

The development of the modern complex administrative state has its beginnings in the late 1880s, but the federal administrative state had its expansive growth during the New Deal, from 1932–1942. Early major involvement of the federal government into regulating began when railroads became essential to the national economy and when state regulations were inconsistent across the country. The federal government intervened and established the Interstate Commerce Commission (ICC) in 1887 as a major national program affecting commerce. The Commission established uniform rates, schedules, and shipping procedures for railroads. To establish uniform train schedules, the ICC mandated standard time zones. (The ICC was terminated in 1995 following the deregulation movement of the 1980s). Another milestone event was the establishment of the U.S. Food and Drug Administration in 1906 after a long struggle to have uniform standards to provide for pure food; the act prevented adulterated and misbranded food and drugs. Many attribute the establishment of the FDA as a policy response to concerns about the meatpacking industry made notorious in the 1906 novel, *The Jungle;* however, concerns about pure food and drugs had been a national issue for decades.[5]

At the end of the nineteenth century, administrative law meant the study of government management. In this view, the entire structure, functions, statutes, and procedures for administration were integrated, and the emphasis was on accomplishing public objectives. This expansive administrative law was based on a public administration point of view, as evidenced in 1893 when esteemed scholar Frank Goodnow wrote *Administrative Law*, a groundbreaking treatise comparing the governments of America, England, France, and Germany.[6] Goodnow's book reflected the view that law and public management were intimately related. As the administrative state grew with increased regulation by city, state, and national governments, there was ongoing debate about how regulation and enforcement were conducted by government actors.

The move from Goodnow's unified view of administration and law began as part of the development of the specialization of the field of public administration in the early twentieth century. The separation of administrative law from administrative practices took two distinct paths. Some legal scholars took a view that promoted training for law students that emphasized the lawyer's role in accomplishing public objectives.[7] The more common view, based on professionalization, separated law from administration. Early public administration texts emphasized that public administration and law were separate spheres and that administration should have its basis in management, not law.[8]

As the activities of federal and state regulation expanded during the first three decades of the twentieth century, businessmen and attorneys complained that administrative processes were not consistent and there was no readily available public access to agency rules. However, it was events during the New Deal that made administrative procedure an issue that concerned constitutional administrative practices and democratic governance. There was a large public debate about what should be done with the rapid and unruly expansion of federal agencies, and therefore federal influence, during the 1930s. The expansion of federal activities under President Franklin Roosevelt's New Deal was not only criticized politically, but the activities were also challenged in court. In the 1935 and 1936 court terms, the Supreme Court found administrative practices under the New Deal were unconstitutional in eight cases. For the Supreme Court, this is an overwhelming number of related cases in a short period of time, and this series of cases lead to a political crisis.[9]

The first part of the crisis was that major elements of Roosevelt's economic recovery were struck down by the court. The President's response of proposing to increase the size of the court where he would appoint justices favorable to his policies became a second part of the governmental crisis. Here are two examples of the type of administrative practices found unconstitutional. In the "Hot Oil Case," *Panama Refining Company v. Ryan,* the use of administrative orders to impose quotas on sale of oil was struck down as an improper legislative delegation;[10] and in the "Sick Chicken Case," *Schechter Poultry Corp. v. U.S.,* both the government regulations for sales of chicken and the mode of enforcement were found unconstitutional.[11] The administrative procedures of promulgating regulations, enforcing, and issuing orders were found to be unconstitutional delegations of legislative authority. Both cases, decided in 1935, involved the National Industrial Recovery Act, and the Supreme Court found major portions of the act unconstitutional in *Schechter Poultry.* Not only did these cases strike down important provisions of the New Deal, the issues in these cases were central in a debate about the administrative role and power of the executive branch consistent with the Constitution.

In December 1938, the Attorney General sent a letter to President Roosevelt recommending forming a committee to investigate ways to reform administrative procedure. When the President authorized the committee in February 1939, he emphasized two themes: protecting rights and effective administration. In this systematic study of all federal agencies, the committee focused on administrative practices of regulation and enforcement. Robert Jackson, as Attorney General, submitted the report to the Senate in 1941. "The Attorney General's Report on Administrative Procedure" proposed a statute to reform agency practices. The proposed law contained the three major categories of the administrative law framework: developing regulations, administrative adjudication, and public information.[12] This report became part of the heated debates about presidential power and the administrative state.[13] Although a law was not passed in 1941, the categories of proposed reforms from this report were useful in crafting the Administrative Procedure Act (APA) that was enacted during the legislative reforms of 1946.

A brief review of the debate over administrative procedure is appropriate because many of the issues and positions remain as concerns for constitutional and democratic governance. The proponents justified the APA based on four points: administrative expertise, legislative limits, judicial practice, and public access.[14] The first rationale was that public administrators were experts in the subject matter that was the subject of both rulemaking and enforcement and this expertise could be more efficient, effective, and flexible in administrative processes than through legislation or court review. The second rationale was that there were limits in the legislative capabilities and processes; legislators passed general laws because legislators lacked the time and expertise, and the legislative process presented difficulties in enacting laws with specific applicable provisions. The judicial practice concerns reflect that administrative enforcement was an alternative to the slow courts and adversarial practices; in addition, it was argued that judges as generalists needed more time for understanding some complex, but routine, administrative topics. Finally, the public-context argument emphasized the need for practices that were consistent and understandable to the public. Routine practices of centralized notice and publication would provide transparency. Administrative process could simplify processes as well as provide flexibility in responding to changing public concerns and needs.

The critics argued against the APA because it encouraged large government, it expanded executive powers, and administrators were not elected and thus not responsive to general public concerns. However, the most severe criticism was that the APA was unconstitutional because it was an improper consolidation of all three types of constitutional powers. Combining legislative, judicial, and executive powers in unelected and unsupervised administrators was considered dangerous and undemocratic, and the statutory process and oversight would not be sufficient to overcome the flaws of improper centralization of authority.

Rules and Regulations

The development of rules and regulations is often considered an essential bureaucratic function to provide for the uniform and systematic operation of an organization. The word "rule" often connotes a mandate or required practice. Regulations have long been the subject of debate regarding the need, substance, and effect. A fundamental dispute about the role of government and its public administrators is in the context of appropriate use of rules and regulations. But the underlying critique of whether rules and regulations reflected public interest and public policy, and are transparent and fairly applied, are issues of which administrators need to be aware. Public managers also need to be familiar with the classification of regulations and the way regulations are developed.

Three Types of Rules

Within the context of administrative law, the term "administrative rule" has three general meanings: substantive regulations, interpretive rules, and procedural rules. Substantive regulations, also called "substantive rules" or "legislative rules," have the force and effect of law. The APA defines rules as "the whole or part of an agency statement of general or particular applicability and future effect designed to implement, interpret, prescribe law or policy or describing the organization, procedure, or practice requirements of an agency."[15] Substantive rules are binding on private parties and the government. Substantive rules must be based on a legislative delegation, and they must be promulgated, meaning developed and approved, through the rulemaking process set forth in the APA. Substantive rules are normally prospective; that is, they go into place after the rule has been promulgated. These rules must be generally applicable to the circumstances or group. Substantive rules may be based on specific technical findings, such as defining the percentages of ingredients in products that are called "peanut butter," setting standards for drug dosages, or determining how much of a pollutant may be permitted in filtered water. There must be sufficient technical findings and scientific data evaluated by the agency to justify adopting a substantive regulation. These regulations must be promulgated according to APA procedures that include public notice and comments.

Interpretive rules and regulations may be general statements from the agency that set forth how the agency interprets its authority or how it will apply laws and regulations. Interpretive rules are not intended to establish or alter legal rights and obligations. Agency guidance and general statements of policy may be considered interpretive rules. At one point, these interpretive rules were seen as a way to clarify and inform the public about an agency's general positions in a simple and quick manner. Interpretive rules are published, but there is no APA requirement for public participation or public comments in making interpretive rules. There are numerous types of agency releases that are intended for the general public that do not fit the definition of a substantive regulation; one common type is called "guidance."

Guidance can be quite pervasive and influential in affecting businesses, individuals, or state and local governments. For instance, the Federal Emergency Management Agency (FEMA) has issued a National Response Framework for state and local governments to prepare for all hazard emergencies; although it is not a binding substantive regulation and falls under the category of guidance, if state and local governments do not develop their own plans, they may be ineligible for federal grant funding to recover from disasters.[16] Another type of pervasive guidance that is followed would be guidance issued by the Center for Disease Controls. In providing information on hygiene and public health practices in response to the 2009 Novel Flu emergency,[17] many local schools relied on the guidance issued by the federal government in their decisions to close schools.[18] This short discussion about guidance illustrates that interpretations and government advice can be extremely influential, even if they do not have the same enforcement provisions as substantive regulations.

Finally, procedural rules are internal rules that affect the management of the agency. Standard operating procedures are one type of internal rule. Internal procedural rules may serve as institutional memory; they may be developed to govern the operations and organization of the agency in a consistent, routine, and efficient manner. The scope of internal rules can range from establishing priorities in enforcement to developing agency employment practices. Under the APA, agencies can issue procedural rules without public notice. There are other types of managerial decisions that are exempt from the APA; these include contracts, loans, and property management.

The Rulemaking Process

The development of rules and regulations should be seen as an important policy and management function of an agency and the executive; rules are not just made by a single administrator. This is one aspect of administrative law that has highly developed policy and political controls; rulemaking is an agency activity. Federal agencies make substantive regulations with additional requirements and review established and implemented through overhead management practices from the Executive Office of the President. Developing rules requires not only comment from the public but numerous comments, edits, and evaluations by other federal agencies.[19] Lawyers are involved throughout the rulemaking process to evaluate the technical language and to anticipate legal challenges; thus, the administrators involved in the rulemaking process need not be legal experts but they do need to understand the substance of the proposed regulation thoroughly. Administrators need to understand the ways the proposed regulation can be implemented, and they need to evaluate whether the draft regulation will achieve the policy and technical goals. Wide participation of interest groups and affected individuals is possible but not common. However, one concern in rulemaking is that the interest groups, the agency experts, and legislators may work as an iron triangle or a network and unduly influence the rulemaking process.[20]

There are two types of substantive rulemaking included in the APA: formal and informal. Formal rulemaking involves a trial-type procedure to present facts and collect evidence before a rule is issued. For example, this type of rulemaking occurs in setting rates for public utilities.

The most common type of rulemaking at the federal level is informal rulemaking, or, as it is commonly known, notice and comment rulemaking. As this section illustrates, in practice the way regulations are developed has a number of deliberate steps that require evidence, evaluation, public participation, and factfinding. Although the process may be labeled informal, it is certainly not casual or relaxed. The requirements for administrators under the APA include publishing a notice of the intended rulemaking in the *Federal Register*, providing opportunity for public comment, and considering those comments before the final rule is issued. In practice, the process can be even more complicated.

The federal process and politics of rulemaking is highly elaborate, interactive, and complex. The public administration scholar and expert on administrative process Cornelius Kerwin has analyzed and described eleven stages of rulemaking summarized below:

1. Rulemaking authority exists in the statutes.
2. There is an origin of or need for individual rulemaking.
3. Agency mechanisms exist for approval to start work on a new rule.
4. Planning the rulemaking includes investigation, gathering evidence, and evaluating legal requirements.
5. Develop the draft rule.

6. Internal review of the draft rule, both horizontal and vertical.
7. External review of the draft rule includes OMB, Congress, interest groups, and other agencies.
8. Revising the draft rule and then publishing it in the *Federal Register*.
9. Public participation through written comments, public meetings, and then agency review and analysis of the public input.
10. Actions on the draft rule. Agency options include: prepare final rule, another round of public participation, start over, or abandon rulemaking.
11. Agency post-rulemaking activities include staff interpretations, technical corrections, responses to petitions for reconsideration, and preparation for litigation.[21]

These stages of rulemaking involve far more emphasis on the development of the rule and clearance within the agency and the administration than what is typically described as notice and comment process.

The complexity of federal rulemaking evolved because of the numerous political and executive steps that have been added to APA requirements. There is a high degree of lawyer involvement in drafting, promulgating, and defending substantive rules, and there is a high degree of interaction within the executive branch before rules are finally adopted. The political and policy aspects of rulemaking are now intertwined with the traditional, rational, "fact-based," management decision-making.

Since the establishment of the Executive Office of the President in 1939, the federal rulemaking process is centrally supervised by the Office of Management and Budget (OMB). In addition, a number of presidents have issued Executive Orders that have imposed criteria on development of regulations. For example, Ronald Reagan established OMB regulatory review through Executive Order 12291 in 1981, which included a rational and information-based evaluation of the need for regulations and mandated agencies to consider alternatives to rulemaking.

One of the most extensive groups of requirements was added in 1993 by President Bill Clinton when he issued Executive Order 12886 imposing regulatory planning and review that reflected principles of new public management theory. Agencies were required to consider twelve steps:

1. Identify the problem the agency intends to address.
2. Assess existing regulations in relation to the problem.
3. Identify alternatives to direct regulation such as economic incentives, user fees, marketable permits, or making information available to the public.

4. In setting regulatory priorities, also consider risks.
5. Determine what regulation is the best available method of achieving its goals.
6. Weigh costs and benefits of the intended regulation, and make a reasoned determination that the benefits justify the costs.
7. Base decisions on best obtainable technical scientific, economic, and other information.
8. Assess alternative forms of regulation and identify performance objectives rather than specifying the behavior the regulated entities must adopt.
9. Seek the views of state, local, and tribal governments if regulations will substantially affect them.
10. Avoid inconsistent or duplicative regulations.
11. Impose the least burden on society.
12. Write the regulations simply, in easy to understand language to avoid both uncertainty and litigation.

In 2007, the George W. Bush administration, through Executive Order 13422 "Agency Good Guidance Practices," required that guidance that has a substantial effect on the economy, an industry, or state and local government must be cleared by OMB; and, in effect, agencies need to follow procedures similar to substantive rules. One of the first actions that President Obama took regarding administration was to issue a Memorandum to all department heads on January 30, 2009, to make recommendations to OMB for developing a new executive order to "improve the process of regulatory review."[22]

In addition to executive oversight, rulemaking is often challenged in court cases. As the prior discussion indicates, it is assumed that there will be legal challenges by parties affected by the rule. Although there is no one approach to judicial review, courts often review these substantive rules in the context of whether the rules are consistent with legislative mandates or authority and whether administrators followed appropriate notice and rulemaking procedures.

There is also legislative oversight of rulemaking that requires agencies to notify Congress of completion of rulemaking activity. As an attempt to supervise agency actions, Congress developed the technique of including legislative veto provisions that authorized Congress to nullify administrative actions. Although this was a creative attempt to exert congressional control that was first used in 1932, legislative vetoes raise constitutional questions about legislative process and separation of powers. In 1983, when a one-house congressional veto of administrative hearings was considered in *INS v. Chada*, the Supreme Court struck the statute down as unconstitutional because it violated the separation of powers.[23] Now legislative vetoes are considered invalid, but Congress oversees agency actions through other means such as constituent services, committee hearings, annual budget reviews, and through investigations by the Government Accountability Office.[24]

Contrasting Promulgating Regulations to Enacting Legislation

Many analysts compare the development of substantive regulations to enacting legislation. This general comparison is somewhat useful, but this is often an inaccurate description in the specifics. Legislatures are constitutionally authorized to determine policy and pass laws. Legislative purposes, if they are related to promoting public health, safety, and welfare, are not subject to the same evidence-based deliberations and disclosure that courts require for rulemaking. Administrative development of regulations is a derivative power that is subject to appropriate delegations of power from the legislature and to executive oversight. Although rules often address policy concerns and administrative viewpoints, administrative rules are subject to oversight in the federal government by the required OMB clearance and through submitting rules to congressional committees.

   The process of developing regulations is highly centralized and politicized at the federal level. It involves legislative delegation, sometimes very broad and sometimes very specific, to develop the regulations relating to a substantive area of agency expertise. Developing regulations often involves technical studies and evaluations. Developing regulations includes public involvement, normally in the form of comments from interest groups, but it often includes political and legal challenges.

   An underlying issue in administrative law practice is whether there are more objective ways to discuss rules and regulations. How do administrators use rules and regulations? How do rules and regulations affect administrators and the public? The use of rules as policy instruments has focused on inducements, information, rights, powers, tools, guidelines, and rationales.[25] Administrators and the public use rules to understand what is acceptable and what is not; they provide reliable and predictable guidelines; they provide an institutional memory and public notice. Rules are pervasive in modern society and, although they are frequently criticized, they are also useful.

Administrative Enforcement and Adjudication

Administrators often enforce standards on a case-by-case basis. That is, the normal situation has one person or business involved and there are distinct facts and circumstances to the event. Some examples: granting or suspending one person's drivers license; rejecting applications for disability benefits; inspecting a swimming pool; grading food at a factory; recalling dangerous toys made by a company; and so forth. Such types of administrative actions are commonly called "administrative enforcement." Although there are generally applicable regulations and statutes to provide for the public health and welfare, how they apply is based on individual circumstances. Therefore in administrative enforcement and adjudications, many of the judicial practices are adopted and due process and other constitutional protections apply. The steps of investigations, settlements, and hearings are called "administrative adjudication," which are part of administrative practices.

As the earlier discussion shows, there are many differing roles and methods that agencies use to accomplish their responsibilities. Although voluntary compliance is expected from the public, there are occasions where the statutes or regulations are clearly violated by individuals or businesses. Administrators are expected to enforce regulations and laws in the public interest, and so when there is an outbreak of food-borne disease from farming spinach or from the manufacture of peanut butter, there are common questions. First, why did the government not prevent this? Second, will the government punish the wrongdoers? Third, how do we develop better ways to provide for the public health and safety? Agency enforcement is one answer in situations where the conduct of a business or regulated party needs to meet legal standards to protect the public. Two types of agency actions that lead to administrative adjudication will be discussed below: inspections and benefits application cases.

Enforcement and Inspections

A common agency enforcement technique relating to public safety is inspections. Business activities subject to inspections range from food processing, restaurants, daycare, or nursing homes to nuclear power plants. First, the public servant goes to the factory or business to conduct a walkthrough, a review of process and evaluation of documents, or even testing of materials or food. For some industries and activities, inspections may be a regularly scheduled event, and in other cases, inspections are conducted based on complaints. In some instances, a warrant is required under the Fourth Amendment search-and-seizure provisions before an administrative inspection. Typically, there is a report made from the inspection indicating whether standards and requirements were or were not met.

Second, if the manufacturer or inspected party is not complying with the laws and regulations, then the report may also become a complaint or a request for compliance. The content of the complaint must inform the party of what the standards are and what conduct did or did not meet the standard; these are aspects of notice required by due process. Often the agency practices allow the inspected party to be given a short period of time to come into compliance and then be subject to a reinspection. This approach is used because the emphasis is on having businesses comply with health and safety rules rather than punishing them, and so working to achieve a settlement that gets a business up to standard is seen as a reasonable method to achieve public objectives.

Third, if there is serious noncompliance or if compliance is not achieved, then the agency may proceed to an agency hearing and administrative adjudication. At this point, it is fair to call these activities "cases." The agency preference is toward a voluntary settlement of cases. If a case is not settled, then it proceeds to a hearing—either an administrative hearing or it could lead to criminal prosecution.

Benefit or License Actions

A second category of agency actions, application cases, often involves individuals applying for some type of government benefit, license, or decision. For instance, the decision to award or deny veteran's benefits or determining full disability and qualification for Social Security Disability benefits fall within this category. Decisions to terminate benefits also are considered under this category. When a person applies for a benefit or license, the agencies are expected to make a decision within a reasonable time period and inform the applicant of their decision. This written information should include the statute or rule they are acting under and the evidentiary facts they rely upon to reach their decisions. An agency decision can either be the award or denial of the benefits or license. If the applicants object to the agency's decision, they may request reconsideration and then they may proceed to administrative adjudication by requesting a hearing.

Administrative Adjudication

Different types of administrative actions have different legal requirements for administrative hearings. The term "administrative adjudication" is used in the APA. The procedures an agency must follow in administrative adjudication are based both on statutory requirements and on constitutional due process. As a general rule, agency adjudications are not as rigorous or as formal as trials before a judge, because they were intended to be an alternative to litigation. Administrative adjudication was intended to allow for agency expertise and specialization to be considered. They were intended to serve as policy instruments. The result of an enforcement action is an order or a decision.

There are a number of different types of procedures used in administrative hearings; some are less formal and in some situations the hearing resembles a formal court trial. The requirements of the organic statutes, agency rules, provisions of the administrate procedure laws, and precedent can be distinct for an agency or differ between programs in a particular agency. The most elaborate requirements are for a trial-like full hearing, and these will be detailed below. There are also many situations where less-formal hearings are the norm. For instance, in some states the procedure to suspend a driver's license can proceed in a hearing using documentary evidence presented through a complaint with official records of accumulation of points against a license, or the documentary evidence can be an affidavit from a police officer stating that the person refused to take a breath test. The decision can be made based on these documents. That is, no one has to testify; the hearing is based on documentary records. Often the procedures for employee termination or student discipline are less-formal types of hearings.

Formal Adjudication or on the Record Adjudication

This section considers the steps for formal adjudication that are set forth in the APA. This formal adjudication is also called "on-the-record adjudication." Again, there can be variation on the details of administrative adjudication based on an agency's programs, practices, and traditions. Section 554 of the APA requires a hearing on the record, and it has an extensive number of detailed requirements. These include:

1. Persons who are entitled to notice of hearing shall be timely informed of (a) the time, place, and nature of the hearing; (b) the legal authority and jurisdiction under which the hearing is to be held; and (c) the matters of fact and law asserted.
2. The agency must provide parties with an opportunity for submission and consideration of the facts, arguments, offers of settlement, or proposals of adjustment when the time, the nature of the proceedings, and the public interest permit.
3. The party has the right to be represented by an attorney, but the government does not need to provide an attorney to any party.
4. Government discloses to the party the facts and evidence it has relating to the hearing.
5. The party has an opportunity to present his or her case, including defense by oral or documentary evidence, submitting rebuttal evidence, and conducting cross-examinations.
6. The hearing is conducted before an impartial hearing officer, who is called an "Administrative Law Judge" or ALJ.

7. A decision is made based on substantial evidence in the record.
8. The agency must maintain a complete record of the hearing, with a recording or transcript of testimony.
9. The ALJ must promptly notify the parties of the outcome of the hearing.
10. The outcome must be a written a statement of the findings and conclusions and the reasons for the findings that are based on all material issues of fact, law, or discretion presented on the record.
11. Finally, the party can have judicial review of the final agency action.

The formal adjudication described here looks very much like trials in court, and a frequent comment is that this has "judicialized" agency enforcement. The steps for an APA formal hearing are similar to the types of due process procedures discussed in the Supreme Court case, *Goldberg v. Kelly*.[26] During the long discussion of different administrative settings, the Court said that due process requirements varied in different administrative settings. However, the court found that a full trial-type hearing was required before welfare payments could be terminated by a state because the payments were essential to the basic survival of the individual.

Follow-up to Administrative Hearings

Administrative hearings are not self-implementing. There are a number of steps that can occur after the final resolution of a formal or informal hearing. Often, the result of an administrative hearing is not a final decision like a trial court would enter. Instead, the administrative result is either a provisional or recommended order issued by ALJ that does not become final until it is reviewed by the agency. The purpose for the ALJ issuing a provisional order is to allow for political review of decisions, and it also allows for consistency across a number of different hearing officers. This review step demonstrates a large difference between administrative hearings and trials in the justice system: The product of an administrative hearing is an institutional decision. It is not the opinion of one judge or the verdict of a jury. This process provides a means for oversight and accountability.

In addition, the requirement of having a final agency order before seeking judicial review also provides another opportunity for an agency to review and make a decision on a particular administrative case. In the courts, this step is called "exhausting one's administrative remedies," and courts refuse jurisdiction if a party has not exhausted his or her administrative remedies. Once a party exhausts all of its administrative remedies, then the party can challenge the agency's findings in court. Sometimes the district court is acting as an appellate body and evaluating the findings of the agency; at other times the review is "de novo," meaning the court can reconsider the evidence and make findings of fact based on the evidence.

The APA requires "substantial evidence" for formal rulemaking and formal adjudication, and this term is not clearly defined but courts may take a more rigorous review in determining if the evidence meets this standard. "The court wants to know whether there was enough evidence of the kind that reasonable people are accustomed to relying upon in serious matters that the administrator reasonably could have reached the conclusion reached by the agency. . . ."[27] In informal actions the substantial evidence standard may not apply, but there needs to be evidence on the record as a whole to support the decision. The record on the whole needs to support the administrative action.

The oversight mechanisms for the executive and legislature are not as routinized for agency enforcement and adjudication as they are for substantive rulemaking. The movement toward government performance and outcome measures may indicate how many inspections were conducted or how quickly or efficiently benefits applications were processed. However, these indicators may not measure how well, fairly, or effectively an agency carried out enforcement actions or adjudications. However, when individuals challenge these administrative adjudications in court, the courts are diligent and thorough in their reviews.

Comparing Rulemaking and Enforcement

It is common to discuss government administrative practices and process based on: the focus of the action, the types of facts and rules followed, type of rationality, when it applies, who it affects, due process requirements, the participants, and oversight measures. The following table, Exhibit 5.1, summarizes the major differences between rulemaking and administrative enforcement using these factors.[28] Sometimes distinguishing between rulemaking and enforcement is not easy or obvious. In situations where it is not clear if an action is rulemaking or adjudication, it is better for the agency to treat the action as adjudication and provide due process protections to the affected party.

Information Aspects of Administrative Law

Public access to information is now seen as an essential part of democracy. In this view, information has many beneficial attributes. It provides for an informed public that can contribute its opinions in the policy process. It provides access for the press to publicize government policies and programs.

Exhibit 5.1   **Comparing Rulemaking and Enforcement**

	Rulemaking	Administrative enforcement
Focus	Policy concerns, resembles legislation, rule applies to group	Individual; resembles court trials
Type of facts	Legislative facts; facts gathered from scientific study	Adjudicatory facts of individual conduct, situation, or motive
Type of rationality	Comprehensive rationality	Incremental
When it applies	Prospective or future; effective after the rule is made	Retrospective or evaluation of existing behavior
Who it affects	Applies to general class; binding like legislation	Applies specifically to parties in dispute, then generally applied like precedent
Procedure and due process	No due process rights in rulemaking process; follow requirements in APA	Due process applies
Participants	Wide public participation is possible, but normally interest groups and affected individuals are involved—iron triangle	Often involves only the agency and defendant; the moving party bears burden of proof
Oversight	Detailed requirements, OMB review before rule is made and legislative review before rule goes into effect	Flexible, few systematic political review mechanisms, but reviewed by courts if decision is appealed

It provides factual foundations to question and debate government actions, statutes, policies, and programs. Public information serves as a control when self-interest or privilege are made public. Finally, it may help contain fraud, waste, abuse, and bad judgment.

There are a number of statutory provisions in state and federal laws that require administrators and legislators to provide information and access to the public. These include publication, information-access requirements, and open meetings. First, requirements for publishing public information about government activities, decisions, and policies are included in both the rulemaking and adjudication provisions in administrative procedure laws. The codified statutes in the *U.S. Code* and codified substantive regulations in the *Code of Federal Regulations* provide public access. The publication of notices in the *Federal Register* provides for public access to proposed rulemaking and to guidance and informal rules. Now many of these official records are available online.[29]

The second approach to information allows the public access to government records. There is general access to many documents in libraries, and some materials are included in government archives. There are also provisions to request specific materials. The procedures for the public to gain access to government records are found in the Freedom of Information Act (FOIA).[30] Individuals can request copies of existing public documents and information. Although there is freedom of access for scholars and the media, often individuals seeking information pay large sums. In recent years, many governments have taken to publishing information on Web pages to allow readily searchable public access. To balance concerns of government security, individual privacy, and trade secrets, government agencies may be exempted from disclosing certain types of information.

Public administrators express frustration with public records requests. The efforts to provide public records involve administrative expenses that are not considered part of the core mission or values of an agency. The record requests may be seen as an additional task or irritation because they are not seen as accomplishing the routine job duties or within the agency's primary responsibilities. They often involve large expenses that are not reimbursed because most public information laws limit charges for the cost of photocopies and do not allow charging for staff time. In addition, the large expenses of developing public-information systems, such as computerized mapping or databases, are frequently not allowable costs in charging for copies of public information. In court cases regarding access and fees for information, courts see the development of this information as part of normal government operations; and without express statutory authority, these costs cannot be factored into developing user fees.

There are a number of complaints by the public about FOIA administration. First, the "normal" delays in getting a response can involve years. There are huge backlogs in federal, state, or local responses to requests. Some backlogs are based on a lack of employees assigned to this task. However, some government delays in FOIA responses can be tactical and politically oriented. For example, agencies determine who is exempt from charges and they limit the number of fee exemptions thus increasing the costs to requesters; this tactic may be used to discourage reporters or researchers from requesting information. Despite the laws and general policy that encourage release, disclosing information can embarrass agencies, and agencies have an unwritten rule that says: Do not embarrass the agency. Finally, the enforcement provisions under FOIA are weak. Federal FOIA laws allow for suits for injunctive and declaratory relief, but the law does not allow for fines or damages for delay, even if there is administrative bad faith or misconduct.

The third method to providing public access to government is through open-meeting laws. These are also called "Government in the Sunshine laws," and they typically require that legislative meetings and hearings be open to the general public. These laws have raised practical questions for public officials; for example, if all the city council members are invited to a Fourth of July party, do the press and public have a right to attend under public meeting laws.

Although there are open-government laws, the application and use of these laws varies. Many times, it is the media that seeks this information to provide news reports or in-depth stories. Other times, government watchdog groups follow certain activities. When the media or watchdogs cannot get information, they sue. In short, there is ongoing friction involving information, openness, and public participation.

Conclusion

Often legislative policy and statutory requirements establish what the agency must do and what it can do. Sometimes the issue is how laws that seem neutral on their face are applied by administrators in particular situations. Sometimes the statutes specifically delegate powers to the executive branch agencies, and at others times statutes provide grants of broad discretion. There may be many laws that affect an agency; one may be the organic law that established the agency, and another may be a statute that defines the requirements of a program.

The pragmatic decision to allow administrators to make rules and enforce laws became subject to administrative procedure laws in the 1940s as a way to impose controls on administrative actions. The concerns of whether agencies have too much concentrated power as they carry out their responsibilities are ongoing. That is why there are oversight provisions exercised by the executive, the legislature, the courts, and the public in reviewing administrative practices.

Cases

The following two cases illustrate a number of the aspects of general APA procedure and specific statutory interpretation. Note also how the cases raise aspects of the interactions among the three branches in the federal government in relation to administration of federal benefits in the Social Security system. The first case, *Ezell v. Bowen*[31] allows a non-attorney to represent claimants for disability benefits, and this case considers grounds for and the administrative process for removal. Notice the steps in the administrative hearing in the first case and the relationship between legislation and court review. The second case, *Lauger v. Shalala*, illustrates interaction between administrators and claimants for benefits. Pay attention to when events occur in the Lauger case because timing is important.

Before considering the cases, a brief overview of Social Security programs may be useful. Most Americans pay into the Social Security system as part of payroll deductions. There are differing benefits under the programs. These include disability benefits, Old Age and Survivor Benefits, and burial benefits, and these are explained on the Social Security Web site. In 2005, a total of 835,000 people received disability benefits and of these 727,000 were children. The amount paid out was 10.155 million dollars ($10,155,000,000).[32]

To be eligible for disability benefits, an individual must apply and provide information that demonstrates that the person has earned enough credits to be insured and that the person meets the definition of being disabled. There are also forms and requirements for other benefits, and they must be filed in a correct and timely manner. The Social Security Administration is responsible for determining benefits, and claimants may request a hearing if they are either denied benefits or if they wish to challenge the amount awarded.

The local Social Security Office makes a determination of eligibility for benefits and if benefits are denied, the applicant has a right to appeal. The applicant can have a representative on appeal; this representative can be a lawyer or a person approved by the Social Security Administration. The representative advocates for the applicant. The representative can be paid up to 25 percent of past due benefits or $5,300, whichever is less. Thus, the credentials of representatives matter.

Sheryl Ezell v. Otis R. Bowen, in his capacity as Secretary of Health and Human Services, 849 F.2d 844, U.S. Court of Appeals, 4th Circuit, 1988

Per Curiam.

Sheryl Ezell appeals the district court dismissal of her complaint challenging the decision of the Secretary of Health and Human Services prohibiting her from representing claimants seeking benefits pursuant to the Social Security Act and the Federal Coal Mine Health and Safety Act. We affirm.

Section 206(a) of the Social Security Act provides that non-attorneys may represent claimants if "they are of good charater [sic] and in good repute." 42 U.S.C.A. § 406(a) (West 1983). Ezell, a non-attorney representative of claimants, was notified in August 1984 that the Secretary was initiating proceedings to suspend or disqualify her from further representation of claimants. The Secretary's actions were based upon Ezell's September 1983 felony conviction of two counts of filing false claims for job-related expenses. *United States v. Ezell*, No. 83–107-A (E.D. Va. September 8, 1983).

Following a hearing an administrative law judge suspended Ezell from representing claimants for a period of five years. The Social Security Administration's Appeals Council affirmed that decision, but found disqualification rather than suspension to be warranted. Ezell then filed suit in district court challenging the constitutionality of section 206(a) and the statutory authority for her disqualification. She contended that in addition to the lack of authority for the disqualification, the standard of good character and reputation required of non-attorney representatives denied her equal protection and due process. She based her equal protection argument on the claim that the good character requirement unconstitutionally distinguishes between attorneys and non-attorneys. Due process was allegedly denied because the requirement was ambiguous and vague. Ezell also alleged that the Secretary's actions were arbitrary and exceeded statutory authority because the actions for which she was disqualified did not involve representation of a claimant.

The district court dismissed Ezell's complaint pursuant to Federal Rule of Civil Procedure 12(b) (1), finding that the court lacked subject matter jurisdiction. 669 F. Supp. 141. The court held that judicial review of the Secretary's decision was precluded by section 205(h) of the Social Security Act, which provides:

> The findings and decision of the Secretary after a hearing shall be binding upon all individuals who were parties to such hearing. No findings of fact or decision of the Secretary shall be reviewed by any person, tribunal, or governmental agency except as herein provided. No action against the United States, the Secretary, or any officer or employee thereof shall be brought under Section 1331 or 1346 of Title 28 to recover on any claim arising under this subchapter.

42 U.S.C.A. § 405(h) (West 1983). The district court rejected Ezell's argument that section 205(h) does not foreclose judicial review of the action due to the presence of her constitutional questions, stating that Ezell's "constitutional claims [were] 'inextricably intertwined' with her challenge to the Secretary's decision to suspend her."

Ezell contends that section 205(h) does not apply because it only pertains to claimants seeking recovery of benefits under the Social Security Act and not to disqualifications of representatives. We need not address this argument because we find subject matter jurisdiction lacking due to Ezell's failure to raise a colorable statutory or constitutional claim.

As the district court noted, the regulations implementing section 206(a) do not provide for judicial review of the disqualification decision. 20 C.F.R. §§ 404.1745–404.1799 (1987). And, judicial review of a decision of the Secretary is foreclosed unless it is an "initial determination." 20 C.F.R. § 404.902 (1987). One administrative action which is not an "initial determination" subject to judicial review is "disqualifying or suspending a person from acting as [a] representative in a proceeding before [the Social Security Administration]." 20 C.F.R. § 404.903(g) (1987).

These regulations do not absolutely foreclose judicial review because federal courts are always free to examine whether the Secretary has acted arbitrarily or exceeded his authority. *Garcia v. Neagle,* 660 F.2d 983, 988 (4th Cir. 1981), cert. denied, 454 U.S. 1153 (1982). However, before subject matter jurisdiction arises for review of the propriety of the Secretary's actions, there must be more than a bare allegation of unconstitutional action. *Thomason v. Schweiker,* 692 F.2d 333, 336 (4th Cir. 1982). The court in *Thomason* determined that the district court had properly dismissed an action for lack of subject matter jurisdiction where there was no "colorable" claim on constitutional, statutory or regulatory grounds. Id. This result is consistent with the Supreme Court's declaration that a "substantial" constitutional claim is required for invocation of federal subject matter jurisdiction. *Hagans v. Lavine,* 415 U.S. 528, 537 (1974).

Ezell's contentions fail to meet these requirements. She entered a guilty plea for two counts of filing false claims for expenses following her dismissal from employment with the federal government. The action of the Secretary disqualifying Ezell for lack of good character was clearly warranted in light of this felony conviction and Ezell failed to assert a colorable statutory challenge to this decision. Further, her claims of violations of constitutional protections are clearly unsubstantiated.

Affirmed.

Muriel Lauger on behalf of John Lauger v. Donna E. Shalala,
820 F. Supp. 1239, U.S. District Court, Southern Dist. of California, 1993

Opinion by Huff.

The plaintiff appeals the [Secretary of Health and Human Services'] denial of the application for disability benefits. Both the plaintiff and the defendant move for summary judgment. Because the court finds the denial of benefits did not violate substantive or procedural due process, the court grants the defendant's cross-motion for summary judgment.

The plaintiff's husband died on August 8, 1990. At the time of his death, the plaintiff was suffering from neck pain and was recovering from a hysterectomy performed in April 1990. In December 1990, she learned of Social Security burial benefits and contacted the social security office. An interview was arranged with the Social Security office in Oceanside for February 20, 1991. Prior to that time, a Social Security employee contacted the plaintiff and informed her that, in addition to burial benefits, she may be entitled to Title II Social Security disability benefits. On February 15, 1991, she submitted an application for the disability benefits, but her application was denied on February 20, 1991, due to untimeliness.

The plaintiff seeks reconsideration of the denial of disability benefits. After a hearing, an Administrative Law Judge (ALJ) reaffirmed the denial of benefits, and the Appeals Council affirmed the decision. The plaintiff now seeks judicial review from this court.

42 U.S.C. § 423(a)(1) provides for the payment of disability benefits if an application is filed within three months from the date of death. The section makes no exceptions for late filings. The plaintiff argues this time limitation is arbitrary and, thus, unconstitutional. Specifically, the plaintiff argues there is no rational basis for refusing to excuse late filings based on good cause.

The court must uphold economic regulations against constitutional challenge if the statute "has a rational relationship to a legitimate goal of government." *Price v. Heckler,* 733 F.2d 699, 701 (9th Cir. 1984). Courts generally must be deferential to the government's determination of preferable means of regulation and will overturn such a determination only if it is "wholly arbitrary." *City of New Orleans v. Dukes,* 427 U.S. 29 (1976). The Supreme Court has granted a strong presumption of constitutionality to legislation conferring monetary benefits because the Court believes that Congress should have discretion in deciding how to expend necessarily limited resources. *Mathews v. DeCastro,* 429 U.S. 181(1976).

The court cannot hold that Congress's imposition of a time limit upon the receipt of benefits is arbitrary. The imposition of a time limitation ensures that the Social Security Administration will know with certainty the demands made upon a particular fund. The amount necessary to pay disability benefits would become substantially less certain if a good cause exception was allowed. Section 423(a)(1) does not become arbitrary merely because Congress has allowed longer time limitations in other sections governing the receipt of Social Security benefits. 42 U.S.C. § 402 provides for a "lump-sum death payment" if an application is filed within two years after the date of death. This longer time limitation does not necessarily render more restrictive time limitations irrational. For example, the payment under section 402 is limited to $255 per person. Disability benefits, however, are determined according to a complex formula set forth in 42 U.S.C. § 415. These payments could substantially exceed $255 per person. Thus, Congress may have determined a more restrictive time limitation is necessary in order to budget for larger expenditures. The court, therefore, finds the three-month time limitation is not arbitrary.

The court also finds the statutory section comports with procedural due process. To determine the procedures needed to comply with due process, the court must consider (1) the private interest affected by the governmental action, (2) the risk of an erroneous deprivation of such interest through the procedures used, and (3) the government's interest, including the fiscal and administrative burdens, that the additional procedure would entail. *Mathews v. Eldridge*, 424 U.S. 319, 335 (1975).

The plaintiff has received full hearings on whether she is entitled to disability benefits and, specifically, the constitutionality of section 423 before an ALJ and this court. Contrary to the plaintiff's allegation, due process does not require the Social Security Administration to provide notice to all individuals who may be entitled to some payment of Social Security benefits. First, it is the plaintiff's burden to demonstrate eligibility for benefits. *Mathews*, 424 U.S. at 336. Further, the cost in terms of resources and money to the Administration would be astronomical. This cost would substantially reduce the amount of benefits available for disabled individuals. Although the court is sensitive to the plaintiff's situation, the court finds procedural due process has been satisfied in this case.

Accordingly, the court grants the defendant's cross-motion for summary judgment and denies the plaintiff's motion for summary judgment.

Discussion Questions

1. What types of government activities and regulations affected you today?
2. Discuss the political and pragmatic reasons for the approval of administrative procedure laws following the political crises in the New Deal.
3. Consider the distinctions between substantive regulations, interpretive rules, and guidance.
4. Consider the steps for promulgating regulations under the APA, the additional routine steps described by Kerwin, and those included in President Clinton's Executive Order. How do they compare and differ? What are the purposes for the additional guidance and requirements?
5. Consider how many activities of administrative enforcement are informal and never reach the step of adjudication.
6. Compare the oversight mechanisms for rulemaking and adjudication. Should there be additional procedures for either administrative function?
7. Discuss how the rules for public information and open meetings address the concerns of efficient government compared to transparent government.

8. In both the *Ezell* and *Lauger* cases, consider: How do the laws or procedures protect the public? How are the laws applied?

9. In the *Ezell* case, consider if Congress should limit courts from reviewing certain agency actions. Consider if there are ways to improve the process for licensing or certifying non-attorney individuals as representatives for claimants.

10. In the *Lauger* case, consider the role of the administrators and the differing categories of benefits. Consider the administrative processes and hearings. How did the court balance individual circumstances and governmental considerations? Finally, consider if a benefits clerk should be allowed to make exceptions to statutory deadlines.

6

Property Law

Public and Regulatory Aspects

Owning property and amassing wealth are important to Americans, but the ownership and use of property often involves and affects others. A fundamental purpose of state and local governments is to protect the health, safety, and welfare of the public and often this affects private property interests. Governments determine acceptable uses, require permits, inspect property, and prohibit activities. Governments also tax property. All of these governmental actions involve balancing the individual uses of property with concerns about the community and the general public welfare in developing policies and in enforcing them. Governments also are involved when there are disputes between individuals about how property may be used. The government's ability to define property, to determine property ownership responsibilities between private parties, to determine how government could tax or regulate private property, and the uses of public property are the four aspects of property law considered in this chapter. These first two topics relate to private property rights; the second two consider governmental or public aspects of property law.

As a substantive area of common law, property law has a long history. Today many aspects of private property law still are found in common law doctrine and precedent, but there are also many aspects of property law that are found in statutes. In the American system, property ownership and property rights are almost exclusively determined by state laws, but property rights are an important part of the democratic constitutional system. The preamble of the Constitution states a purpose of government is to "promote the general welfare," but the idea that government should protect property is often linked to the text "the pursuit of life, liberty, and happiness" that is in the second paragraph of the Declaration of Independence. In the Constitution, ownership of property was a prerequisite to vote. One type of property exclusively granted by the Constitution is intellectual property: the constitutional power of Congress to protect and promote science, inventions, and the useful arts.[1] The Fifth and Fourteenth Amendments protect individual private property from government actions without due process of law; the Fourth Amendment protects property from search and seizure, and the Third Amendment prohibited government from housing troops in people's homes. The founding principle of no taxation without representation also relates to government's ability to affect property and mandate tax contributions by individuals and businesses to support government.

Property Law Generally

There are many things that are included as property; the two main categories are real and personal property. Real property has to do with land, as well as the permanent attachments made to the land; real property is often called real estate. Governments require the recording of real property ownership interests. The owner files a deed when property is transferred, and claims against the property—such as mortgages, tax liens, or workman's liens—must be filed to be enforced. Any lease or ownership interest that extends over a year needs to be filed with the recorder's office. The purpose of this filing is to secure ownership and provide notice about obligations that attach to the property. Most people associate owning real property with owning a house or land, but in law the ownership interest in real property can be divided among individuals. A real property interest can be as the full owner and also as partial owner, such as renter or as mortgage holder. Divided or shared ownership is common under property law, and the person in possession of the property may not have the largest ownership interest. Thus, requirements about recording help protect those with various interests and protect potential buyers by informing them of claims against the property.

The second category is personal property, which includes everything that is not real property. Your shirt, your car, and your dog are personal property. These examples are all tangible personal property, meaning corporeal; that is, the property can be touched or seen. Many types of personal property are categorized as intangible property. Intellectual property is one sort of intangible property. Ownership of bank accounts, corporate stock, and contracts are types of intangible personal property. Some types of government benefits are considered property, and the civil service provisions that provide tenure or job security are also intangible property.

Ownership or interest in personal property can be divided as well. The old childhood taunt of "ownership is nine-tenths of the law" is simply wrong. You may own the shirt on your back, but with books that you purchase you only have partial ownership. You own the physical book, but the writer or publisher owns the copyright—a type of intellectual property—that is a form of ownership in the book; this copyright limits the commercial uses of the content. Much of the law of property involves how someone obtains and protects property. The law of property is extensive, and the following summary provides a brief overview of the elements of ownership.

Elements of Ownership

The law involving real property and tangible property developed over a long time. The development of property rights predates the American colonies and traces back to medieval England. The questions of who owned the livestock that grazed on the commons and who owned the lamb or calf borne of livestock on the commons were practical and important problems in the preindustrial era. One of the earliest sets of codified laws, Hammurabi's Laws, which date between 1728–1686 B.C.E., considered and regulated owning property and obligations if property was damaged.[2] The questions of who owned land or property and how it could be transferred to another were other practical problem that often involved documentation. As the commercial markets developed, the question of providing security for loans or mortgages added to the complexity of transactions. The connection of owning property and wealth were important aspects of capitalist societies and global trade.

To deal with the complexity of the law of property, legal doctrine discusses elements of ownership, and often the language about property rights sounds decidedly old-fashioned. These elements are also referred to as incidents of ownership or property rights. The common metaphor used to discuss and categorize these elements of ownership is a bundle of sticks, or it is sometimes referred to as a bundle of rights.[3] The seven elements of property ownership include the right to

1. use,
2. enjoy,
3. dispose,
4. possess,
5. control,
6. exclude others, and
7. receive benefits of the property.[4]

Not all of these elements of property need to be present at one time to determine if someone owns property or an interest in the property. However, discussions of property rights often relate to one or more of these elements.

The rights to use, possess, and enjoy property are descriptive terms that are amenable to common sense and common understanding. The rights to control property and exclude others from using the property also fits commonsense understandings. The right to dispose of property includes the right to destroy or give away property. The right to benefit from the property means that the products from that property, be it the apples from the tree or the royalties from the sale of a song, belong to the owner of the property.[5]

Conditions and Limits on Ownership

The way law considers property rights is often a question of ownership, use, or value. In law, someone's pet cat or dog is property and is treated accordingly. So if a dog is hit by a car or poisoned and there is a civil suit based on property, the court looks at the sale value of the dog and not the sentimental attachments of the owner. The linking of property to its capacity for producing wealth also relates to how property is expected to be used, and it relates to consideration of differing property ownership interests.

Preferences and Ownership Attributes

Property law evaluates rights between partial owners in a piece of property in interesting ways. A longstanding tenet is that property should be used currently to produce wealth. Historically, when coal and oil were found beneath the surface of land and they were determined to be valuable, then the use or exploitation of these resources was considered good public policy. The law developed that mineral rights could be severed from the other ownership of the surface, and the preference developed that encouraged mining and extraction. Since the mineral rights were deemed to be the dominant property rights, then it was acceptable both to remove the surface to extract the minerals and to give preference to those who owned the minerals which could mean forcing the surface owners to move. This historical approach to encourage producing wealth was categorized as a type of highest and best use. The idea of resource extraction now often conflicts with social preferences for environmental and ecological protection, and the sustainability and green movements would change preferences or priorities about acceptable or preferable property uses.[6] The debates about environmental protection versus extracting and developing wealth are issues about this fundamental assumption about incidents of property. There are also other legal doctrines that one cannot use one's property in a way that harms others. There are common law doctrines, agreements, and government regulations that affect the use of one's property and how it affects others.

Private Nuisance

Although the cliché is "a man's house is his castle," this is not always the case in law. An individual cannot always use her property as she sees fit. Quite simply, an individual cannot use property in a manner that bothers and harms others; this area of law is called "private nuisance," and it falls within the substantive area of tort law. If an owner leaves dangerous conditions on his property, he can be liable for damages if someone is harmed when on the property. This helps explain why stores may put up signs near the entrance that say "Danger, Slippery When Wet" on a rainy day.

Some courts have found that the property owner may have to pay damages if a trespasser is injured by a dangerous condition. For instance, even if a swimming pool or trampoline are behind a fence, some courts have found the owner liable if someone comes on the property to play because these amenities may be called "attractive nuisances." The enforcement of private nuisances can take place in situations when one person may sue his neighbor asserting that the way the neighbor is using property is causing harm. Harm here might be physical, such as hearing loss, or it might be economic harm or loss of property value. Sometimes, private nuisance suits are brought by individuals alleging that a state or local law is being violated, and the plaintiff may be seeking injunctive relief of removing the nuisance.

In the alternative, some individuals will complain and demand that the government enforce laws, ordinances, or regulations. This may be a way for citizens to avoid talking to their neighbors about problems such as loud noises or leaning fences; that is, rather than neighbors seeking informal ways to address concerns, they call governments and file complaints. In other situations, there can be longstanding difficult relationships between neighbors. Sometimes, citizens may pursue both private nuisance and public enforcement.

Deed Restrictions and Ownership Associations

Private individuals can place conditions and limits on property when they transfer it; transfers include gifts or sales. Currently, in real property law, an owner can place restrictions on the deeds that can control or limit how the current and future owners use her property. There is the ugly history of some developers imposing covenants that prohibited sale of property to individuals who were not white, and these deed restrictions that discriminated on race were found to be unconstitutional and unenforceable.[7]

Yet many other types of allowable deed restrictions limit the appearance or uses of real property. Deed restrictions that limit the type of roof materials, the color of paint, and parking on the street have been included for homes in subdivisions. These deed restrictions are attached to the property and can remain indefinitely. Another approach is to have a set of rules or conditions that are included with development of subdivisions; these are called "common-interest developments."[8] The difference is that they allow a process to consider, add, or change the conditions; the provisions may also include election of a homeowners' association to amend the conditions. It is also common to include the right of the developer to vote or have weighted voting that allows the developer to maintain a type of appearance or use until the subdivision is built out. A condominium where someone may own a home or apartment, but share ownership of common areas and there are mandatory maintenance fees typically has binding rules that limit one's use of property or even require permission for leasing or sale of the property. In addition to use restrictions, the condominium associations may establish rules and regulations regarding appearance and upkeep of individual units.

Although the actions of the common interest developments or the conditions of subdivision associations and condominium association may look like governmental actions, the method of voting and enforcing the rules is considered by many courts to be private actions of associations or the enforcement of contractual and voluntary agreements. These restrictions raise questions about whether it is democratic for a corporate owner-developer to impose these conditions on the buyer of a new home, but they are even more troublesome when one owner can impose restrictions on future owners in perpetuity.

Government Regulating Property—Generally

There are numerous aspects of private property that are subject to government actions and regulations. The question of how to prove and track ownership of real estate led to states requiring recording of deeds, leases, mortgages, and other interests. The license plates on cars and mobile homes serve both to identify ownership, to regulate transfer, to regulate pollution, and as a way to raise revenue. Governments may require licenses for the practice of certain businesses. Some licenses are considered property and some are not.

Taxes, or the ability of government to raise revenues to support government policies and programs, often affect property. Sales tax is imposed on the value of goods sold. Property taxes are used to provide general revenue for a local government, or they may be imposed for a special purpose such as road repairs. In addition, governments regulate property to protect public health and safety, such as prohibiting fireworks, but these constraints must generally apply and they cannot single out one person or business.

Numerous laws and ordinances affect how individuals use their property. For example, states require automobile safety evaluations and auto air-emissions standards for private cars. Enforcement provisions of these regulations limit the use of the car such as to prohibit driving it on roads, unless it meets certain safety and health standards.

The Constitution gives Congress the right to protect and promote useful inventions,[9] and this authority to regulate intangible property has been implemented through copyright, trademark, and patent laws. These regulations or laws define and protect ownership of intellectual property and provide individuals rights against public encroachment on their property without payment. Thus, laws regulating property may be to protect the general public or to protect individual's property rights.

Government regulations often are written in response to community preferences or social problems. It is fairly common for local governments to regulate real property through land use restrictions. Other types of local regulations have to do with uses of types of personal property. A common restriction is on the types of animals that can be housed in residential areas; farm animals are often prohibited and when pot-bellied pigs became fashionable as pets, owners argued that they should get to keep their pet pig. Many cities require pets to be licensed and kept under the control of the owner. These leash laws may require a dog to be in a fenced yard or on a leash. To protect the public and keep the peace, many cities limit the use of guns. Although the Supreme Court ruled in 2008 that a city could not prohibit carrying a gun,[10] many cities have ordinances that make firing weapons in their communities a misdemeanor offense. These regulations can be justified as reasonable regulations that serve valuable or desirable public purposes, but they all limit the individual's use or enjoyment of his property.

Local Government Land Use Regulations

Most local governments have land use regulations.[11] These include requirements such as defining lot size for buildings, specifying location or size of structures, and requiring building permits and inspections prior to construction or remodeling. Real property is often subject to zoning and land use restrictions. For over a hundred years, cities have regulated certain types of land uses based on geographic zones. This Euclidean zoning, named for the city of Euclid, Ohio, aims to plan for and control certain types of land use based on categories of uses. For example, it is common to zone land for use as residential, commercial, industrial, agricultural, or mixed uses. Typically the land cannot be used for a use that it is not zoned for, and this means that factories are prohibited in residential areas and commercial uses are separate from agricultural uses. There may be subcategories of uses as well; residential purposes can include categories such as multifamily or single-family structures. It is also common for a city to limit the number of unrelated individuals that may live in one apartment or house as part of zoning controls. Another approach is to limit the number of residents based on square footage or bedrooms.

Often the unrelated individual clauses in residential zoning have become controversial for the way they have been enforced against certain ethnic groups, or because these have been used to limit the number of college students living in a dwelling. Zoning techniques, especially limits on houses per acre, lot footage, or number of residents, are criticized for being designed to provide elite enclaves that exclude the poor, immigrants, or students. This critique argues that zoning is not egalitarian. The influential urban commentator Jane Jacobs criticized zoning because it reduces the vibrancy or dynamics of city life.[12] There are alternative approaches developers use called "planned-unit developments" that are designed to mix zoning uses, but the designs and zoning uses must be approved before a construction permit is issued.

The way zoning and building codes are enforced also raises concerns. For example, if an individual or a business constructs a fence without a permit or if the fence is too tall, too close to a street, or in some other manner does not comply with building codes, then the city can enforce these ordinances through citations and fines or through orders to remove the nonconforming structure. The extent of zoning enforcement often raises challenges. For instance, builders or individuals cannot construct a house unless they are in compliance with building and zoning codes. Delays in issuing permits or completing inspections are often the subject of friction or citizen complaints.

One type of zoning or land use restriction prohibits home-based businesses. For example, individuals who teach piano lessons out of their homes have been cited for violating the residential use zone. Although it may seem fairly common and innocuous for an individual to give music lessons out of his home, it often technically violates the residential-use only definitions in a zoning code. But in practice, cities often only respond when someone complains about using a residence as a business. A home business can increase the amount of car traffic on the street, and this may bother the neighbors. Whether the home business such as music lessons is a commercial use that damages the property value of the neighborhood involves questions of fair use of someone's property and interference with someone else's use of their property. Thus, the enforcement problem for a city is the dispute can involve individual beliefs, values, preferences, and even someone's livelihood. These land use disputes between neighbors can be emotionally charged.

Another common concern for enforcement includes the appearance of property. Some communities want restrictions on the use or display of signs in yards in residential zones. This restriction is applied during election time where some communities may limit the size of political notices or limit the dates when campaign signs may be displayed (such as signs may only be displayed within two weeks prior to the election and must be removed within two days after the election). The objection to campaign signs is often that they make the neighborhood look cluttered, but the countervailing concern is whether the First Amendment right to political free speech allows limiting or even prohibiting campaign signs.

When an appellate court evaluates whether restrictions on the use of land should be upheld or rejected, it begins by determining whether the restrictions are related to a public purpose. If they are, the regulations will normally be upheld. When issues affecting constitutional free speech arise, then total prohibition of signs or speech is problematic, but reasonable time and place limitations have been upheld by courts.

There are some provisions for exceptions and although individuals may petition for nonconforming use, the movement toward land use planning for an entire community during the 1980s and 1990s has encouraged communities to develop long-range land use plans that relate to capital development and economic growth. This policy of long-range planning of the urban environment often discourages permitting nonconforming uses.

Another consideration about planning and zoning is whether an entity is required to comply with these regulations. For example, land uses that pre-existed the current zoning are often allowed to continue, which is known as grandfathering a use. Most state laws and local government ordinances also allow exemptions of certain uses from zoning. If a property is owned by a government and is used for governmental purpose, such as an elementary school, then it is exempt from zoning. Public purposes often include schools, churches, government buildings, and public parks. Because buildings with public purposes often attract high volumes of visitors during certain days, residents may not like them in their neighborhood. This phenomenon is called either LULU or NIMBY. LULU means locally unwanted land use, and NIMBY means not in my backyard. Thus, attitudes and emotions about a community or how the neighborhood looks can add to challenges in governance.

Property Issues and Constitutional Rights—Generally

The problem of community standards that are required on behalf of public health and welfare may also raise concerns. For example, most people would agree that weeds are unattractive. Governments regulate weeds or the height of grass based on arguments such as that high grass attracts or serves as cover for vermin, and thus can cause disease or other public health problems. Another regulation established in the nineteenth century had to do with fire risks and building materials; protecting public health and welfare was accomplished by licensing or prohibiting locating laundries in wooden buildings. Although courts might uphold this type of regulation as it was written, the Supreme Court in the 1886 case of *Yick Wo v. Hopkins* found that laws that appeared valid on their face could be an unconstitutional denial of equal protection because of the manner of enforcement. In this case, out of 320 laundries in San Francisco, 310 laundries were in wooden structures. The city denied 200 applications for licenses, and all but one of those people denied a license was Chinese. The court struck down this law.[13]

Many types of property are subject to due process protection. There may be differing standards of review. Again, it is worth emphasizing that courts often review due process in terms of process, and consider whether adequate procedures were used to provide individuals with notice, an opportunity to be heard, and a fair decisionmaker. That is, courts in some due process review situations try to balance the tasks of government management and operations with individual rights. Thus, in employee disciplinary situations, in which the expectation of continued employment is either a property right defined by agreement or the right to a hearing, is guaranteed by civil service laws. The due process right requires a hearing before the discipline or termination is final.[14] However, not all employment—even government employment—is property that is protected by due process.

Constitutional Rights and Eminent Domain

Governments have the inherent right and power to take private property for public uses; this is called "eminent domain." However, under the Fifth and Fourteenth Amendments, governments are constitutionally required to pay just compensation for taking property for public use, whether it is real or personal property. This constitutional provision of the right to compensation is called the Takings Clause.[15] Governments prefer to negotiate a purchase of property they want to take, but if the government cannot reach an agreement with the property owner then the government can pursue an eminent domain action in court. These actions are also called "condemnation hearings," and normally the question at the hearing is the value of the property; although it is possible to challenge the taking as not being a public purpose, the courts have interpreted public purposes broadly. The government's power of eminent domain is justified as allowing governments to act in the public interest in constructing schools, roads, or government offices, and in providing for water, sewer, or power lines. Government can take, with compensation, important scarce resources such as drugs, vaccines, or protective equipment. "Without the power of eminent domain, individuals could block government programs, such as the interstate highway system, by refusing to sell property to the government or demanding unreasonable compensation, holding the government project for ransom."[16] However, some people are skeptical about how government uses its eminent domain powers. As one analyst stated, "Condemnation poses a threat of majoritarian ganging-up because the interests of so many can outweigh the interests of the few. In condemnations involving the taking of private property, this possibility is mitigated by the requirement that just compensation be paid."[17]

Governments with eminent domain powers include the federal government, states, cities, and counties. Most states allow entities with public purposes to use the power of eminent domain; these entities include government corporations, state colleges, and public utility companies. In addition, eminent domain situations occur where one government seeks to take property of another government, and in this situation there may be conflicts of priority between two public uses.

Eminent domain occurs when government takes the complete piece of property, and this typically is done through the condemnation hearing. Governments must also compensate owners when there is a partial but permanent occupation of private property by the government. The individual right to just compensation for government takings applies in situations where government laws or actions diminish the value of property, and these cases are called "inverse condemnation cases." Two situations where inverse condemnation is found include, first, when government regulation of property removes all economic value and the regulation is not closely connected to protecting public health, safety, and welfare. The second inverse condemnation situation applies when the regulation or other government activities severely reduces the economic value of property, and then the owner is entitled to compensation. However, the courts reviewing takings cases often do not provide compensation when the laws and regulations are enacted to protect the health, safety, and welfare of the public. Thus, the question of the purpose and effect of regulation often is a complex issue in these cases. The law and practice of eminent domain, government takings, and inverse condemnation is very complicated.

Often there is a fine line between state regulation of land uses and a government taking of property. In a case involving the installation of cable TV lines and a junction box on apartment houses in New York City, the Supreme Court explained:

> [The Supreme] Court has often upheld substantial regulation of an owner's use of his own property where deemed necessary to promote the public interest. At the same time, we have long considered a physical intrusion by government to be a property restriction of an unusually serious character

for purposes of the Takings Clause. Our cases further establish that when the physical intrusion reaches the extreme form of a permanent physical occupation, a taking has occurred. In such a case, "the character of the government action" not only is an important factor in resolving whether the action works a taking but also is determinative.[18]

The court found in this case that the city required landlord property owners to allow cable TV installation on the building for the benefit of the tenants, and this resulted in a permanent taking of a portion of the building and so the owner was entitled to compensation.[19]

Certain types of regulations that permanently take or deprive an owner of the use of property are found to be government takings and that reasonable payment is required for public taking of private property. One situation where regulations were found to be a taking of private property occurred when, as a condition of a building permit application, the property owners were required to provide public access across their property to get to the ocean.[20] Another example, when a business wanted to expand, the city required the business owner to dedicate part of her property for flood control and build a greenway for recreation.[21] Again, the Supreme Court found that the conditions on the permit violated the business owner's right to compensation. All three of the situations just described included an acceptable public purpose, but the extent of the regulations permanently deprived the property owners of some access, use, or enjoyment of their property, and thus the Supreme Court found that reasonable compensation for these takings must be provided to the private property owner.

The 2005 case of *Kelo v. New London* raised contentious policy considerations of individual property uses versus local economic-development improvement plans. The Supreme Court found that a redevelopment project that included a shopping-hotel complex that was intended to help the town's economy and increase the tax base was a public purpose. Thus, the Court allowed taking of an individual's house by the city to allow a builder to construct the commercial development. Because the Court found that the type of economic uses or public purposes were a matter of state laws, many state legislatures responded by enacting more stringent criteria to limit taking of property from one owner to promote a more lucrative taxable use.[22]

Often the question in eminent domain is not whether the government can take private property, but instead the question revolves around what is just compensation. At other times there are questions whether types of government regulations result in a taking because the regulation may limit the way private property is used. Issues about taking property also have included situations involving licenses or location of a public right of way. In these situations, whether this is regulation of the use or a taking of ownership rights often become a constitutional question.

Government as Property Owner

Governments are the owners of property—real property and personal property, tangible and intangible property. However, the role of government as property owner may be different from the role of an individual or corporation owning property. The historic view of property was that it was wealth that should be used to produce more wealth. This meant that using the standard of highest or best use, rather than leaving a beautiful meadow, courts preferred to encourage building a coal-pit mine to hasten the extraction of the ore. However, government is not the single owner of property. Instead, government owns or holds property as the steward or trustee for the public. This stewardship interest obligates the government not just to manage the property for the current public but also to preserve it for future generations. Thus, when government owns property, it cannot just think of the current use but also has to think about future uses. There are a number of contentious administrative and political issues that this raises.

Some states distinguish whether government properties are held for a public purpose or for private purpose, and some states only allow property to be tax-exempt if the property is held for inherent governmental purposes. Some governments hold properties for investments or as part of a city capital-improvement plan that has not yet been implemented. Some state courts have held that if a government owns property that is outside its boundaries, then the property is subject to taxes of the jurisdiction where the property is located. There are a number of times where governments may lease real property, such as office buildings for governmental purposes, and here the landlord property owner may still be subject to paying property taxes. Some state constitutions establish tax exemptions for governments or nonprofits and others allow taxation. Although governments may be tax-exempt under Federal income tax laws, this type of exemption is not binding on states determining tax status, except of course, the federal government is exempt from state and local tax since the 1819 case of *McCulloch v. Maryland*. That case found under the Supremacy Clause, in Article IV of the Constitution, that the federal government was not subject to state or local taxes.[23]

The question of whether a government nonprofit is exempt from taxes presents problems in equitable provision of public services. The issue is whether a nonprofit entity, such as schools or churches that do not pay taxes, should pay for the government services that they use. It would be difficult to change the tax laws, but local governments have considered alternate funding arrangements. Some local governments have entered into agreements with other governments or nonprofits for payments in lieu of taxes, sometimes abbreviated as PILOTS. For instance, a state college may be exempt from taxes but it desires to maintain roads nearby so that students can get to classes and it still needs timely fire and ambulance services for emergencies. Recognizing the need for these public services and applying the benefits-received financing principle, the two governmental bodies—the municipality and the college—may enter into an agreement for payments in lieu of taxes to make sure there are adequate levels of services.

Government acting as the steward of public resources raises many practical challenges. For instance, government owns many types of property, such as art works or parkland. These properties are often held for the enjoyment of the current citizens, but the properties are also seen as part of an important national or community heritage that should be maintained and available for future generations. Not only do public administrators owe a duty to manage the property for current use, but they also have the responsibility that they do not damage or harm the property in a way that prevents future use or enjoyment. This question of current and future uses has been the subject of many political and legal challenges. For instance, during the construction of the interstate system the federal government often tried to build highways through city parks—often the road would bifurcate the park. Building a road, of course, is a public use but here the dispute was between alternative views of public uses. Many groups and communities objected and some sued. One group, the Citizens of Overton Park, prevailed in their challenge of the government's interstate construction taking much of a prominent city park in Memphis, Tennessee, for the roadway. The group prevailed, at least in the short term, because the federal administrator failed to explain the reasons for the administrative order approving construction.[24]

The disposition of government property through sales can raise policy and legal concerns. The area of concern for government as property owner becomes more apparent in tough economic times where cultural institutions such as museums, heritage centers, libraries, and parks are often seen as both expensive to maintain and as a repository of assets that can be liquidated. The temptation to sell or lease government assets to balance a budget may raise issues of whether the property is held in trust for current and future generations' enjoyment. Another situation arises when a government or public organization receives a gift or bequest, such as land or a piece of art, with conditions included with the gift. Often the donors impose conditions on the gift such as providing public access, requiring certain upkeep, or prohibiting the sale of the property. Although sometimes the conditions are negotiated before a gift is accepted, these conditions may present challenges for management at a later time. Heirs of the donor often challenge a government's proposal to sell a bequest, or they may seek to require the government to follow the terms of the bequest.

Although government holds property for public benefit, it certainly can manage and restrict property uses by implementing time or place limits, imposing reasonable fees for the use, and prohibiting public access to offices or other secure sites. Governments can protect property or enforce conditions by a number of means; for instance, they may prosecute individuals for trespass or misuse of public property. Another consideration for a state or local government's property management might be federal mandates such as the Americans with Disabilities Act (ADA)[25] and environmental protection laws.[26] For example, under the ADA local governments are required to install elevators in public buildings like courthouses, and cities must construct ramps in sidewalks so individuals can get across the street without obstacles. Transportation districts and schools need to provide buses with handicapped accessible lifts or provide assistance for those who have physical disabilities. Meeting some of these ADA accommodations does require remodeling or rebuilding, and the expenses are considered necessary to promote a type of civil right—public access. Many environmental laws have imposed great expenses on local governments; for instance, developing new water treatment plants so that the water meets state and federal clean water standards. The necessity of building or maintaining landfills so that they do not pollute is another major concern for local governments. The lack of budget capacity or the fact that the federal government did not fund these mandates has not been considered by courts to be an adequate defense for governments who delay implementing these laws.

Community Preference and Individual Rights

The balancing of community preferences for property use restrictions may be based on health concerns such as weeds, safety concerns such as height and location of fences, or to aesthetics such as appearance or smell. Communities regulate because of safety concerns. They demand property not create a hazard and require owners to lower, move, or remove fences. They reflect local concerns about aesthetics, such as appearance or smell. These preferences and restrictions are policy considerations that involve politicians and public administrators. However, the situations where these can occur often are not simple; frequently there are a cluster of individual interests, rights, and preferences that must be evaluated. The following scenario illustrates the challenges relating to government property regulation, policy, and private rights.

This was the problem. In 1995, people bought 52 new homes in a subdivision in the town of Black Jack, Missouri. One of the attractions of this area was that it was on the rural edges of St. Louis County. With beautiful countryside, it was away from the busy city and crowded suburbs. But when spring came, these newest residents were surprised to discover that their new homes were right next to a pig farm. The new suburban residents were greatly upset that they could not sit on their decks or be outside without smelling the farm or being bothered by flies. As is common in pig-farming operations, there was a barn that housed the pigs and an open lagoon that contained the pig sewage. Although most could not see the lagoon, some neighbors were concerned there could be runoff from the open pig-sewage lagoon that could cause environmental damage to a small creek that ran next to the farm and through the town. The neighbors made numerous complaints to town hall.[27]

Then the dispute made it into the newspapers. A newspaper editorial made three points. First, that the farmer was the victim of poor planning by city officials who never should have let the developer build homes within a few yards of the hog-feeding operation. Second, if the city had properly zoned and managed their undeveloped land, the situation would have been avoided. Third, that cities, in general, give preference to houses and commercial development because these uses bring in more tax revenue than agricultural land.[28]

The farm had been in existence for 146 years, but it was now within the town limits. The subdivision neighbors demanded action, and so in June, the City Council considered enacting an ordinance to make it illegal to have a pig farm within the city. The farmer wanted to keep his pigs until October when he said that the hogs would be ready for market. There were discussions of the city compensating the farmer to end his pig farming and end the stink from the farm.

Here is how this situation can be analyzed or evaluated. This situation presents a familiar collision between development and tradition. It illustrates what in the abstract is called suburban sprawl. But this was a situation with a real conflict that public managers had to address; it is a conflict between subdivision residents and a rural business. This situation also includes a number of concerns about the intersection between public management and public law that must be included in the analysis and decision-making. These concerns are: What authority does the city have to act? How does city hall handle the phone calls in situations like this? Does the city proceed with city inspections for zoning or environmental violations with enforcement practices of citations, hearings, and fines? Doesn't an individual have a right to conduct farming? Can the neighbors force the farmer to lose his livelihood? Is this a governmental problem for managers, for the elected officials, or for the city attorney? The city residents involved directly in this case include the subdivision residents and the farmer, but what about the other residents and taxpayers? Whose interests are most important now? What are some of the legal and constitutional concerns here? How do you reach a fair result? How do you provide justice? Does a manager look at this situation differently than a lawyer or a judge?

This pig-farm situation involves a number of themes and issues that demonstrate the practical and political situations that managers face. It involves relations between members of the community and how they expect government to act to address their concerns. It also involves a number of issues that affect how government is perceived. Practical concerns may relate to the town's budget and policy practices. There are a number of legal issues presented here. Some of the legal issues are about the relationship between the citizens. Some of these can be expressed as common sense and common practice. But in law, it is the individual rights of the farmer to have due process or fair compensation for his pigs that can be enforced through litigation with the city.

There is not one simple answer to problems like the pig-farm situation; there are no easy answers either. There is not a single answer based on review of constitutions, statutes, or court decisions. The resolution of the pig farm situation like many issues of public management and law depends on the situation, and this includes understanding the law, the community, and the factual circumstances of the problem. Although the public managers in this situation are not legal experts, they need to have a good understanding of the public law aspects. Resolving a civic problem like this involves careful consideration of the facts, individual interests, and the practical and governance issues. However, resolving civic problems must be done within the rule of law and this requires understanding the legal authority, legal processes, and constitutional constraints.

Conclusion

Property and public safety are important to Americans, and often public law issues involve balancing property rights in relation to public purposes. Understanding the types of property is important because property is a right protected by the Constitution, and how government regulates or takes property is often litigated. In addition, public administrators should be mindful that they are stewards of public property for the benefit of current and future citizens. Finally, governments are often asked to enforce laws that regulate one person's property interest at the request of a neighbor.

Cases

The following two cases involve two different aspects of property law that could affect public administrators. In the *Lawrence School v. Lewis* case, the school is seeking a building permit and a zoning ruling. In this court case, note the number of government actions that begin with zoning, exemptions, and land use regulations and how they affect a school. This case also illustrates political pressure from neighbors and the difficult question of whether public officials acted in an appropriate manner. *Campbell v. Champaign*, the second case, considers a different type of property and an internal management concern. The legal question of whether a type of public employment is property that entitles a public employee to a hearing before termination has interesting management implications.

In the Matter of Lawrence School Corporation v. Harold Lewis et al., 578 N.Y.S.2d 627, Supreme Court of New York, Appellate Division, 1992

Opinion by Harwood.

This appeal provides the opportunity to remind municipalities that because educational institutions presumptively serve a beneficial public purpose, local governments may not unreasonably prohibit accessory uses of school premises. Since the appellants failed to recognize the petitioner's special status when determining its application for a variance to enable it to install swimming facilities, we agree with the Supreme Court that their determination absolutely denying the application must be annulled.

The appellants are members of the Zoning Board of Appeals for the Village of Hewlett Bay Park. The Village's zoning ordinance authorizes only residential uses of property (see, Hewlett Bay Park Code § 146–6), although property owners are permitted to construct swimming pools as long as the Village Board of Trustees issues a permit after determining that "the public health, safety, comfort and welfare will be secure and that such swimming pool will not be detrimental to the general character of the district or to the orderly development of the village" (Hewlett Bay Park Code § 146–9 [C] [2)]). The petitioner is a day school located on almost 10 acres within the Village. Its existence predates enactment of the zoning ordinance and its use is thus a nonconforming one.

In 1988 the petitioner applied for and, following hearing and imposition of various conditions, the Village Board of Trustees granted a permit authorizing it to build two swimming pools on its nearly 10-acre plot. Community opposition erupted, however, and the permit was revoked on the stated ground that the petitioner intended to operate a summer camp rather than an educational program. The petitioner commenced litigation challenging the revocation as arbitrary and capricious and was initially successful. However, the Village amended the zoning ordinance concerning continuation of nonconforming uses to provide that "no such use, building or structure shall be altered, enlarged or otherwise expanded" (Hewlett Bay Park Code § 146–3). The Supreme Court subsequently ruled that, in light of the amendment, reargument should be granted and the proceeding by which the petitioner challenged the revocation of the permit was dismissed. That determination was affirmed by this court on the limited grounds that the petitioner had acquired no vested rights in the permit and that it had shown no basis for an estoppel (see, *Matter of Lawrence School Corp. v. Morris,* 167 A.D.2d 467).

The petitioner applied for a variance of the prohibition against altering, enlarging and expanding its use of the school. At the outset of the hearing on this application, the Village Attorney acknowledged that environmental review and a referral to the Nassau County Planning Commission were required (see, ECL art 8; see also, General Municipal Law § 239-m), although it appears that no referral and no review of the petitioner's environmental statements has been made. The petitioner presented evidence of its financial need to increase its summer enrollment, that it expected that the addition of the swimming pools would enable it to do so, that it had present capacity for 800 students, that current enrollment for its already-existing summer program was 157, that it hoped to expand its summer program to a maximum of 450 students, that its summer program would be academic in nature and would include courses in reading, music, home economics, art, astronomy, geology, and computer programming and usage, and that there would be athletic instruction and recreational activities, including soccer, softball, field hockey, lacrosse, and swimming. The petitioner also presented expert evidence as to the negligible impact the addition of the pools would have on traffic patterns and on the value of neighboring properties. Some residents spoke in favor of the application. Although the school itself is apparently in keeping with the character of, and is generally acceptable to, residents of the Village, and although the appellants concede that the petitioner may lawfully expand its summer educational program by increasing its enrollment to full capacity, most residents who spoke opposed construction of the swimming pools. One such resident stated that she sold real estate in the area and that property values would fall if the pools were built.

The Zoning Board of Appeals denied the application on the ground that the petitioner's financial hardship, if any, was self-created and that the adverse effects of the pools on the community in any event mandated denial of the application. The Board also found that the proposed "activity" was a "commercial camp in disguise," declined to determine whether the environmental assessment forms that the petitioner had submitted were sufficient and complete, and declined to make a referral to the Nassau County Planning Commission, ruling that the environmental review procedures were not necessary because the application was being denied.

Upon the petitioner's judicial challenge to this determination pursuant to CPLR article 78, the Supreme Court ruled that the denial of the variance was arbitrary and capricious and, in effect, directed the appellants to issue a special permit for construction of the pools after further hearings as to the conditions to be imposed. It also directed the appellants to conduct an environmental review and to refer the matter to the Nassau County Planning Commission, although it made no provision for the possibility that either process could culminate in recommendations or findings that the pools should not be allowed. It further directed that the appellants complete these processes and render a decision within a specified period of time. This appeal ensued.

Although the function of the courts in reviewing determinations granting or denying variances is somewhat limited (*Matter of Fuhst v. Foley,* 45 N.Y.2d 441; *Matter of Perlman v. Board of Appeals,* 173 A.D.2d 832), a determination which is arbitrary and capricious or unsupported by substantial evidence will not be upheld (cf., *Matter of Perlman v. Board of Appeals,* supra). But while we agree with the Supreme Court that the determination at issue here cannot stand, we also conclude that a directive that the appellants presently authorize the construction of the swimming pools is premature.

It is established law that educational institutions, like religious institutions, enjoy special treatment with respect to residential zoning ordinances because these institutions presumptively serve the public's welfare and morals (see, *Cornell Univ. v. Bagnardi,* 68 N.Y.2d 583; see also, *Matter of Diocese of Rochester v. Planning Bd.,* 1 N.Y.2d 508). It is also established law that a school offering a summer program need not exactly duplicate the September-to-June curriculum in order to retain its "educational" character (see, *Rorie v. Woodmere Academy,* 52 N.Y.2d 200; *Matter of Summit School v. Neugent,* 82 A.D.2d 463). Moreover, educational and religious institutions are generally entitled to locate on their property facilities for such social, recreational, athletic and other accessory uses as are reasonably associated with their educational or religious purposes (see e.g., *Matter of Brown v. Board of Trustees,* 303 N.Y. 484, 489; see also, *Matter of Community Synagogue v. Bates,* 1 N.Y.2d 445; *Shaffer v. Temple Beth Emeth,* 198 App. Div. 607; *Matter of Summit School v. Neugent,* supra). And while such institutions are not exempt from compliance with a zoning ordinance, neither are they required to affirmatively demonstrate a special "need" for any expansion (*Cornell Univ. v. Bagnardi,* 68 N.Y.2d 583, at 596–597). Greater flexibility than would attach to applications for variances made by commercial institutions is required and the "controlling consideration . . . must always be the over-all impact on the public's welfare" (*Cornell Univ. v. Bagnardi,* at 595).

We conclude that the appellants' determination that the petitioner is operating or intends to operate a "commercial camp" is totally without evidentiary basis (cf.,

Rorie v. Woodmere Academy, supra; *Matter of Summit School v. Neugent,* supra). Similarly without evidentiary basis is the determination that the swimming pools will adversely affect the surrounding community, particularly since the appellants concede that an increase in enrollment, regardless of whether or not the pools are installed, cannot be prohibited. It is also evident that the appellants used impermissible criteria in determining whether the application should be granted (see, *Cornell Univ. v. Bagnardi,* supra) and from the appellants' failure at the outset to pay heed to the requirements of ECL article 8 and General Municipal Law § 239-m, we can infer only that outright denial of the application was virtually a foregone conclusion and was thus arbitrary and capricious.

Since no persuasive expert or other evidence was offered to demonstrate that the addition of two pools would have a significant adverse impact on, among other things, traffic patterns, property values, or municipal services (see, *Cornell Univ. v. Bagnardi,* 68 N.Y.2d 583, 595, supra; see also, *Matter of North Syracuse First Baptist Church v. Village of N. Syracuse,* 136 A.D.2d 942), and since it would appear that reasonable conditions could both alleviate community hostility and address bona fide public welfare considerations, it would appear that the Supreme Court was otherwise correct in granting the petition and remitting the matter for consideration of appropriate conditions. Since this case involves the expansion of a prior nonconforming use to allow the construction of swimming pools, the authorization to do so must emanate from the appellants in the form of a variance with conditions, rather than in the form of a special permit which could be issued by the Board of Trustees. In any event, however, we also note that review of the petitioner's environmental assessment statements which should have been undertaken as early in the process as was possible and referral to the Nassau County Planning Commission which must precede any final action (see, *Matter of Old Dock Assocs. v. Sullivan,* 150 A.D.2d 695; see also, *General Municipal Law* § 239-m) have not been effectuated and we therefore remit the matter to the appellants for completion of the necessary procedures and a new determination in accordance herewith.

We direct that the appellants complete the necessary procedures with all deliberate speed and we thus discern no basis for disturbing the timetable fixed by the Supreme Court. We have also considered the appellants' remaining contentions and find them to be without merit.

Jo Ann Campbell v. City of Champaign, 940 F.2d 1111, U.S.
Court of Appeals, Seventh Circuit, 1991

Opinion by Posner.
The plaintiff was hired by the City of Champaign to be the City's Records

Manager (equivalent to City Clerk), pursuant to an ordinance which provides that the Records Manager "shall serve at the pleasure of the City Manager." She was fired—for rudeness to fellow employees—and brought this suit under 42 U.S.C. § 1983, claiming that she had a Fourteenth Amendment property interest in her job and therefore could not be fired unless accorded due process of law, which she claims she was not. The district judge granted summary judgment for the City and the other defendants.

How could the plaintiff have a property interest in her job when she served "at the pleasure of the City Manager"? That is the language of at-will employment, and how could an at-will employee be thought to have the sort of secure and dependable interest fairly describable as an entitlement and therefore as "property"? *Reed v. Village of Shorewood*, 704 F.2d 943, 948 (7th Cir. 1983). Well, he (or she) cannot, of course. *Simpkins v. Sandwich Community Hospital*, 854 F.2d 215, 218 (7th Cir. 1988); see also *Corcoran v. Chicago Park District*, 875 F.2d 609, 612 (7th Cir. 1989); *Lee v. County of Cook*, 862 F.2d 139 (7th Cir. 1988). But upon the commencement of her employment the plaintiff was handed a booklet entitled "Personnel Policies—Non-Bargaining Unit Employees," and she claims that this employment handbook made her an employee terminable only for cause and thereby conferred on her a property right in her continued employment so long as she did not give cause for being terminated.

This is not the first attempt to tack *Duldulao v. St. Mary of Nazareth Hospital Center,* 115 Ill. 2d 482, 505 N.E.2d 314, 106 Ill. Dec. 8 (1987), which holds that under the common law of Illinois an employee handbook can create an employment contract, to *Board of Regents v. Roth,* 408 U.S. 564 (1972), which holds that a tenure employment contract creates property within the meaning of the due process clause of the Fourteenth Amendment. The attempt fails here, as it did in *Simpkins, Corcoran,* and *Lee,* and does so for two reasons. This particular employee handbook does not create a contract; and not every employment contract creates a property right.

1. The idea behind *Duldulao* is that if an employee handbook contains a promise on which a reasonable employee would rely, the employee's action in taking up or continuing the employment after receiving the handbook is the acceptance of a unilateral offer and makes a legally enforceable contract. There is a lot that is questionable in this reasoning, *Enis v. Continental Illinois Nat'l Bank & Trust Co.,* 795 F.2d 39, 41–42 (7th Cir. 1986), but that is not our business now that the Supreme Court of Illinois has spoken; for it is a question of Illinois law. The question for us is whether the employee manual of the City of Champaign could fairly be interpreted as promising the plaintiff that her job was secure as long as she didn't misbehave. It could not. The ordinance under which she was hired made clear that she served at the

pleasure of the City Manager—that is, that she had no tenure, no job security. A reasonable person in the plaintiff's position would not have assumed that the ordinance could be overridden by a mimeographed handout addressed to all nonunion employees of the City. Moreover, the handbook contains no promissory language. This is not to make a fetish of particular words, but to remark the absence of any words even remotely indicative of an intention to confer legally enforceable rights.

The plaintiff asks us to infer such an intention from the fact that the handbook lists various grounds for dismissal or discharge and contains no catch-all that would make clear that she could also be terminated for no ground at all. This misunderstands the purpose of the handbook. It is not to confer rights but to warn employees about conduct or circumstances that will result in termination or other adverse personnel action. The handbook distinguishes between two types of termination—"dismissal" and "discharge," the former being nondisciplinary, the latter disciplinary. The former includes for example the elimination of the employee's position. With respect to disciplinary terminations the handbook states that "the City agrees with the concept of progressive disciplinary action"—that is, with the principle that you don't discharge an employee until lesser sanctions ranging from an oral reprimand to demotion have failed to rectify his misbehavior—but makes clear that the City can jump the queue as it were and discharge an employee without previous discipline if the infraction is particularly serious or has been committed repeatedly.

The City's commitment to "progressive disciplinary action" is too loose and vague to confer a legally enforceable right to such progressivity. Nor is that the focus of the plaintiff's argument, which is rather that since the handbook contains a finite list of grounds for termination (either by way of dismissal or by way of discharge), it contractually entitles her to continued employment provided none of those grounds is established. But if the handbook had meant to do this it would not we think have left the matter to be inferred from silence.

In essence the plaintiff is claiming that if a handbook doesn't expressly disclaim contractual obligation it creates such an obligation, so that if the City of Champaign wanted to reserve the right to fire employees on grounds not stated in the handbook—or on no grounds—it had to say so, had to add a provision stating in substance that, "by the way, don't think that if we fire you on a ground not stated in the handbook you have a right to sue us." Such a disclaimer might be prudent but it is not a sine qua non for avoiding liability.

2. Even if the plaintiff had a good claim for breach of contract against the City, it would not follow that she had a constitutional claim for a deprivation of property. Not every contract right is property. *Lim v. Central DuPage Hospital*, 871 F.2d 644, 648 (7th Cir. 1989); *Fontano v. City of Chicago*, 820

F.2d 213 (7th Cir. 1987) (per curiam); *Brown v. Brienen,* 722 F.2d 360, 363–65 (7th Cir. 1983). Prisoner-rights cases such as *Olim v. Wakinekona,* 461 U.S. 238 (1983), show that a contract which merely creates a right to specified procedures does not create an entitlement upon which a claim of deprivation of property without due process of law can be founded. See also *Archie v. City of Racine,* 847 F.2d 1211, 1217 (7th Cir. 1988) (en banc); *Doe v. Milwaukee County,* 903 F.2d 499, 503 (7th Cir. 1990). To bring the case within the orbit of the property concept there must be a substantive entitlement. When the claimed deprivation of property is the loss of a job, the entitlement must be to a job, rather than just to a set of disciplinary procedures. "[A] contract that creates merely a right to procedure does not create a property right within the meaning of the due process clause." *Lim v. Central DuPage Hospital,* supra, 871 F.2d at 648. So even if the contract in this case be construed as *entitling* the plaintiff to progressive discipline, the breach would not be a deprivation of *property.* We have already explained why we do not construe the contract to have entitled the plaintiff to keep her job unless specified grounds for dismissal or discharge were established.

The judgment for the defendants is Affirmed.

Discussion Questions

1. Discuss how the bundle of sticks metaphor and partial ownership affect government regulation of property.
2. Discuss public policy reasons to allow or limit deed restrictions.
3. What types of ordinances does your community have relating to owning pets or parking cars on the street? Consider whether these provide for the public health, safety, or welfare of the community.
4. Discuss whether zoning enforcement by responding to complaints, such as home businesses or yard signs, is an efficient, effective, and fair approach.
5. Compare government regulation affecting property uses to private nuisance actions. Which one is preferable?
6. Discuss the community interests versus individual property rights balance in eminent domain considerations. For example, consider what happens, who benefits and who is burdened when a state university seeks to expand its campus and uses eminent domain to achieve this plan.
7. Discuss how government as a property owner is different from individual ownership. Consider how this affects the responsibilities and tasks of public administrators.

8. Consider the social, political, administrative, and legal concerns related to the smelly pig-farm community situation. Discuss whether the three points in the editorial are accurate and fair.

9. Trace the steps and governmental reviews that the school followed to build a swimming pool in the *Lawrence School* case. Consider whether the approaches the Village took were evenhanded. Would you recommend any different procedures or ordinances in this type of situation?

10. Not all contracts are property, and not all situations where due process type hearings are based on constitutional provisions. Discuss how the *Campbell v. Champaign* case defines whether there is a property interest in government employment. What are the factors to determine if an employee manual provides a protected property right in a contract?

7
Contracts and Contracting

Individuals and businesses enter into agreements all the time. Consider this situation: You walk into a fast food place and you order a burger, no pickles, fries, and a cola, no ice. To go. You pay the tab. The server brings you a bag of food and a drink. When you sip the drink and open the bag, you discover you did not get what you paid for. You got a cheeseburger with everything on it, a diet soda with lots of ice, and no french fries. What do you do? Normally, you take the food to the counter and ask them to fix your order. If the server says something like "you got what you ordered or we didn't make a mistake," what do you do then? You may leave and decide to never return. You may ask to talk to the manager and request that your order be fixed. Normally, servers and managers correct the order; businesses do not want unhappy customers.

Is buying a meal or a buying a T-shirt a contract? This is an ordinary sales transaction. These exchanges rarely are in writing; they are normal business. Yet, the law of contracts applies to these situations. Most people would not bring a legal claim because they got the wrong food order. We normally expect that businesses will correct mistakes. When the exchange of goods for money does not go as intended—the wrong burger and soda and no fries in this scenario—then this can be considered a breach of contract. And as is typical, often the dispute is resolved by discussion and a request for correction. Of course, many situations that involve contracts are much more complex.

The existence and stability of contracts is seen as an essential element reflecting the rule of law. Contracts are legally binding agreements that are essential for commerce in a global economy. Contracts are used in government, and contracting is seen as both a management tool and skill. This chapter provides an overview of contract law and contracting practice as it applies to public managers.

Contract Law

Many different types of situations involve aspects of contract law. A simple purchase of a hamburger and soda is governed by the law of contracts. The purchases of a coat, a car, or a bushel of corn are also contracts. An insurance policy or a car loan involve contracts. The ongoing employment of an administrative assistant or accountant involves contracts. The ongoing purchase of services by an agency or city is also governed by contract law.

A contract may be written or oral. A contract may be explicit between the parties or recognized by law. Contracts can be based on a handshake, an oral agreement, or a signed written agreement. The law of contracts is based primarily on common law doctrine. There are some provisions that are included in statutes. For instance, commercial law regarding shipping, bills of lading, and writing checks may be covered under statutes that adopt portions of the Uniform Commercial Code.[1]

Although contracts and contracting are normal practices for individuals, businesses, and governments, the substantive law of contracts is very complex. Contract law developed through a long history of English and American common law. Contract law is still dominated by the common law, and it differs in specifics and details from state to state. Although the term contract is used in popular language as a promise, such as the "Contract with America,"[2] in law, a promise is not the same as a contract. In law, a contract consists of both the agreement made by the parties, and the legal rights, duties, and consequences that flow from the agreement. Understanding a general overview of contract law is important to many aspects of public management because governments enter into contracts in many forms. What is presented below is a brief overview.

Elements of a Contract

Law students may look to resources such as *Contracts in a Nutshell* for a basic overview of contract law; or they may look to a legal encyclopedia or treatise for a more thorough treatment or for citations to leading cases.[3] But the general overview or the black letter law on contracts requires seven elements to be present for a valid, legally enforceable contract. These are:

1. offer,
2. acceptance,
3. mutuality of agreement,
4. mutuality of obligations,
5. consideration,
6. competent parties, and
7. lawful subject matter.[4]

Each of these elements has particular meaning briefly discussed below.

Offer and Acceptance

An offer is a definite proposal to enter into a contract. It involves a promise by one party in exchange for a promise, act, or forbearance given by another party. Contracts involve agreements and exchanges, and so a promise or a gift by one party to another is not a contract. A party accepts when the party assents to the terms of the offer. Although there is not one way of acceptance, an acceptance must agree exactly to the terms of the offer in a way that can be clearly understood as an acceptance. A reply that changes the terms of the offer is considered a counter offer. Law has an extremely technical set of rules in determining offer and acceptance.

Mutuality of Agreement

Both sides must agree to the contract. If there is mutual mistake of fact then courts may find a contract did not exist, but a mistake of law or a mistake by one party does not invalidate a contract.

Mutuality of Obligations

Both parties must be obligated to do something under the contract or the courts may find no mutuality of obligation.

Consideration

Most people would say that to have a contract it must involve money, goods, or services, but this is not the definition in law. In contract law, each side must provide consideration. Consideration may be cash or its equivalent; it can also be an exchange of goods or services, and it can be an action or forbearance to act.

Competent Parties

Only competent parties can enter into binding contracts. A competent party can be an individual or an entity. Adults can enter into contracts, and the law presumes that parties willingly enter into contracts if they have negotiated the terms and considered possible outcomes. Courts presume individuals read, understand, and agree to the terms of written contracts, such as insurance contracts. Minors and legally incompetent adults cannot be held to the agreements they entered into; that means that a minor can cancel a contract when he reaches the age of majority.

But the definition of competent parties is different for governments and entities. A government official cannot enter into a contract without express authority to act; the same is true for other corporate entities, including non-profits. Officials are authorized to enter into contracts through statutes or by written orders issued by superiors who may delegate specific authority.

Legal Subject Matter

A contract must have lawful subject matter; the courts will not enforce contracts that violate the law, such as contracts to engage in criminal activity.

Stages and Enforcement of a Contract

A typical way to analyze and discuss contracts is through process or stages. Four stages are considered. The first is formation, which includes both pre-contract negotiation and making the agreement. In government contracts, this can include placing a contract up for bid and then drafting and completing a contract that may be hundreds of pages long. The second stage is performance where the contract terms are completed by both parties. Performance may be a one-time exchange; performance may be providing goods or services over a period of years.

The third stage, which all parties to a contract hope never occurs, is breach of contract or simply, breach, the legal phrase for a break in the terms and consequent contract failure. A breach happens when one or more parties fails to perform as agreed; the aggrieved party can begin by conversing with the other party about the disparity in performance and work out a resolution; the aggrieved party can ignore the inadequate performance of the breach; and finally the offended party can declare a breach and assert that the contract is no longer in force. The last conceptual stage is remedy; if there is a breach, the parties may be able to negotiate a resolution to the breach. A remedy may begin when one party demands that the other party cure the breach; if the parties cannot resolve the differences, the aggrieved party may proceed to lawsuit and judicial decree.

Court cases arising in contract occur when there is a breach or a violation of the contract. The preference of the courts is to encourage parties that enter into agreements to enforce what the parties agreed to. Sometimes the dispute centers on whether there was a contract in the first place, and this type of dispute focuses on the stage of formation. At other times these disputes address the terms of the contract, meaning what parties agreed to do. And occasionally, there are legal justifications why nonperformance is excused. Once a contract is established, then the question before the court is who caused the breach and the amount and type of damages that have occurred because of the breach.

The law of contract requires the person either to accept performance or to bring a suit to declare a breach and termination of the contract. The aggrieved party has a duty to mitigate or seek ways to reduce damages. In determining damages in contract cases, the law looks to provide what was agreed to in the contract and nothing more. The law calls this "making the parties whole." And here, the preference by the courts is to consider monetary damages. Finally, provisions in the contract to punish a party for nonperformance are rarely enforced by the courts; instead, the courts award only the actual damages suffered.

Statutes and Common Law

Almost all contract law is governed by state law, whether in statutes or common law. There is no federal common law of contracts, but there may be federal statutes that affect contracts. Although contract law has its origin in common law, there are aspects of contract law that are now governed by statute. Some contracts are required by statute to be in writing; for example, this is true regarding contracts to purchase property. Some aspects of employment law may be found in statutes; this is true of merit provisions for many governments. Federal law regulates many aspects of agreements in the field of banking and securities. States establish standards for certain types of contracts, such as insurance policies, or they provide consumer rights such as a time frame when certain sales contracts can be rescinded. Because contracts are essential elements of effective commerce and because many commercial transactions have common factors, the American Law Institute developed the Uniform Commercial Code as a model law. Many states have adopted some, but not necessarily all, of the provisions of this code.

Contracts are part of customary practices. The contract itself reflects the shared agreement of the parties, or the parties establish a legal relationships when entering into a contract, but their focus is accomplishing an exchange of goods or services. The parties typically determine what the contract means and expect to complete the contract without need for litigation. Although there are some aspects of contract law that are found in statutes and others that are developed by common law, it is the customs and relationships between the parties that reflect contract law in action.

Management Approach of Contracting

Contracts and contracting-out have been advanced as management improvement and cost-savings techniques for government. Unfortunately, the complexity of contracts and the difficulty of legal enforcement are often ignored or underplayed in these works. When parties enter into a contract, they are only obligated to follow the terms of the contract—not what was intended or discussed, only the written language of the contract. When a contract is questioned, then enforcing the terms of the contract by any dispute-resolution technique, be it litigation or alternative process, is costly in essential resources of time and money. Any dispute is a distraction from achieving the purpose or objective of an agency. Management by contract requires different and complex skills for public administrators that are not fully recognized in many of the new public management texts. Contracting-out is not so easy a technique as proponents may suggest.

Contracting is perceived as a transactional relationship, as in the burger purchase example. Contracting-out is presented as a management technique as a way to reduce costs and improve services that governments provide. Contracting-out describes a web of relationships between government and the private sector, nonprofit, and/or for-profit businesses to purchase goods or services. For instance, long-term service provider relationships have been contracted out for government services including trash hauling, probation review, counseling, and child-welfare screening.[5] This management approach has been advocated to be cheaper and more effective than government workers providing the service, but it has not been proven to be either. Critics of contracting-out have noted that it reflects a hollowing out of government, and they have questioned whether public-sector values are considered in the service delivery.[6]

Essential Considerations for Contracting-Out

As the respected public administration scholar Philip J. Cooper has detailed in his book, *Governing by Contract*, contract administration is essential to government operations and contract administration skills are a needed competency for public managers. Governing by contract involves skills and experience. In evaluating the success of contracting out, the six important considerations are:

1. Successful contracting operations require consistency with public values.
2. Contracts are an important part of the public law structures and do not exist outside of public law.
3. The common negative assumptions about contracts as opportunities for corruption do not accurately reflect practices.
4. Public contracts are used to achieve social goals through alliances between government and the contract providers.
5. When a government contracts, public policy is achieved through hybrid institutions that require careful attention from contract managers.
6. Elected officials need to be involved in and aware of the aspects of contract management.[7]

Contract Administration and Operation

Individuals enter into agreements all the time. Businesses buy and sell based on written or oral agreements. The ability to enter into contracts and agreements is an essential part of commerce. Contracts and agreements are also very important for government operations and are a needed competency for public managers. Whether considering old public administration, discussions of the hollow state, or the new public management, many scholars indicate that contracting for goods and services is an essential part of established government practices.

Government-by-contracting includes purchasing, construction, and services. Contracting is about capacity and capability. Contracts may be a one-shot exchange or purchase. Other contracts may be for providing public services in an ongoing relationships; Cooper calls them "contract alliances" and emphasizes how there is an alliance or partnership in providing government services in the public interest.[8] The legal term for these ongoing contracts is executory contracts, which recognize the ongoing execution of the contract provisions.

For government contracts, the making of the contract includes putting the specifications out to bid and providing opportunity for many businesses to do business with government. Usually, the requirement is that the "lowest and best" bid be accepted, but the concerns of effectiveness of achieving the goals should have as much, if not more, salience as the concern of the economy or the lowest cost contract.

The decision to contract and forming the contract involves political and management decisions as well as legal advice in drafting the contractual language. The desired outcome, output, and costs must be specified both in the requests for bids and in the provisions of the contract itself. It is no small wonder that many contracts have very detailed provisions and can go hundreds of pages.

Not all government contracts are between government and businesses. Often a government may contract with other governments. A town may contract with the county sheriff for police protection. Local governments may enter into mutual aid agreements for police or firefighting services. Such an agreement between governments is called a "Memorandum of Understanding" (MOU) or a "Memorandum of Agreement" (MOA).

Public attorneys and public managers have different priorities for contracts. In legal study and practice, it is the formation of contract and the breach of contract that receives most attention; these are disputes that lawyers address and that are present in the case law. Attorneys use the common law as guidance in drafting effective contracts to help managers achieve the desired agreement. Managers want good agreements and performance; managers care most about performance and operations of contracts to achieve program and policy objectives. For public managers contract administration includes monitoring, supervising, and achieving the contract's objectives. This operation and management of contract objectives is less often discussed and recognized in the public management literature, but it is an essential aspect of public management.

The operational aspects of contracts, or the contract administration, involve important management skills. It is a common problem that a contract may not be executed as intended or agreed upon. Often contract managers must monitor and work out these situations. Ways to address underperformance, delay, or adjustments—whatever might cause them—are often included in written provisions in the contract. An important consideration in executory contracts is the flow of information between the contracting agency and service provider; access by both parties to operational and management information may be required to ensure compliance of service delivery or timing of compensation.

There may be minor problems of interpretation and implementation, such as problems with supplies or timing, or the problem may go to the essential aspects of the contract. Within the legal approach to contract failure or breach, there are two options when the contract is not being carried out as intended by the parties: Either continue with the contract, or sue for breach of contract and terminate the agreements. These two options make it difficult for administering long-term service-related contracts.[9] These options also emphasize that the damages or award for the breach of contract must make the parties whole by fair compensation related to the agreement; damages in contracts are not intended to punish the wrongdoer or to enrich the aggrieved party. In fact, as mentioned above, when a contract is declared in breach, the aggrieved party must mitigate damages, meaning it must make efforts to find substitutes for performance, and make other efforts to keep the damages low.

In many public-service provision contracts, such as trash hauling, if a city were to declare breach for late or shoddy performance this immediately raises logistical problems of who will provide the service before the next contractor is engaged. Furthermore, the process of putting public contracts out to bid is long and difficult. Recognition and anticipation of possible difficulties in executory contracts is needed during the negotiation and contract-formation stages. Contracts need to address the potential situations where services are not being performed as required and establish protocols for the two sides to work out accommodations to address the conflicts.

One such approach is to include contract-resolution procedures within the contract itself. Often contracts involving ongoing delivery of services or ongoing relationships may include within the contracts ways to consider disputes without resort to a court cases. These contracts often include Alternative Dispute Resolution (ADR) techniques of arbitration or mediation. As a result, if small or larger disputes cannot be worked out between the parties and they want the contract relationship to continue, then by the terms of the contract the concern may be referred to mediation or arbitration rather than terminating the entire contract. One difficulty in using ADR is that to consider weak performance, the administrator needs information; it may be that the government entity purchasing the services does not have the records or information needed to effectively pursue its claim. Thus, providing management access to information on a regular basis needs to be included in the terms of the contract when the contract is made.

Contract modification is another way to address problems or gaps in performance during contract administration. If the difficulties in contract performance reflect differing views of the parties as to what was intended, or, if there are gaps in performance because of change in circumstances, then a contract can be amended. Contracts are legally binding agreements, but they certainly can be changed through agreement of the parties and these typically are amendments to the contract. Thus, part of contract administration may include coordinating contract adjustments or amendments to achieve the purpose of the contract.

In the contracts for ongoing services, it should never be forgotten that the ultimate responsibility for the service remains with the city or government agency that awarded the contract. Managing contractual relationships requires special attention be given to audit (keeping full and accurate records of costs), quality control (enforcement of contract terms), monitoring (interacting with service providers), prompt attention to complaints (from citizens, clients, or subcontractors). Managers need good interpersonal relations and supervisory skills in managing contracts. When citizens or clients who are receiving services complain about the contract providers, such as when a trash pickup is skipped or debris is spread along the street, administrators need to investigate and respond. The government that contracted for the service continues to be responsible that the services are delivered in a safe and effective manner.

Contracts are not indefinite. An important part of contract administration is the ending or renewal of the service contract. An ongoing contract alliance is typically made for a period of time to provide a particular service, but at some point the contract can be subject to renewal or it may end by its own terms. Often, ongoing service provisions may be subject to a new bidding procedure and the experience from current and prior contracts should be included in evaluating what is desired in a new contract. The best case for the end of the contract is that it is part of the natural progression of the contract;

the worst case is one where the contract is subject to dispute because of a claim of breach of contract.

Finally, not all relations between governments and an entity providing a service are based on contracts. Governments provide grants to individuals and businesses, but a grant is not a contract. In a grant issued by a government, the terms and requirements are found in statutory provisions authorizing the public policy and administration of this policy. Often, the notification of a grant and request for submissions provides detailed expectations for the grant applicants. An award letter from the granting agency or foundation then specifies what needs to be done for the distribution of funds to the recipients to carry out research or service activity. In some aspects, grants are more like gifts than contract agreements. Although the grantees are expected to perform in response to the receipt of funds, key bilateral agreement aspects of contracts do not exist in grants. Grants differ enough that traditional contract law does not apply to the relationship that arises out of a grant relationships.[10]

Special Considerations for Government

When agencies or governments decide to contract for services, there is the need for authority to enter into a contract or it is ultra vires. The phrase "ultra vires" means outside authority, and for a government to enter into a contract, the agent or the public administrator must have authority to act. For legal compliance, for public accountability, and for transparency, this means that contracts with government must be in writing and they must be preapproved or ratified by the legislature.

Authority for an administrator to act may be found in budget-spending authority, the enabling legislation for the policy, or the job description. Management considerations and democratic values both encourage clear expressions of the public administrator's authority to enter into an agreement. There have been instances where a public official enters into a contract without clear authority and the court found that the government was not liable to pay, but instead it was an individual obligation of that officer to pay or fulfill the contract terms. In other situations where a valid contract did not exist and where government benefited from the services provided, courts have found that there was an implied contract under the equity doctrine of quasi contract and required government to pay a fair amount for the services provided.

Some governments have specific criteria about when administrators may purchase goods or to enter into other contracts. For instance, detailed federal training is required in contracts before employees are authorized for purchasing or procurement. Requiring written authority to purchase is an important budgetary and management control. Within OMB, there is an Office of Federal Procurement Policy, which was established by law in 1974. Federal employees must be trained and certified to purchase goods as a measure for accountability. In addition, there are federal policies about what can and cannot be contracted-out and inherently government functions cannot be contracted-out.[11]

One common recommendation about contracting is that it be carefully evaluated as part of the policy-decision process, applying criteria regarding the appropriate uses of contracting. Contracting should be evaluated in context of other options for obtaining goods or services. Contracting should be chosen if four elements exist: It is the best choice; it will provide better services; it will lower costs; and it will provide greater flexibility.[12] Contracting is often used when the services are specialized, occasional, or experimental. Contracting is appropriate for one-time events or where government does not have the capacity or expertise. In short, contracting should be an efficient, economical, effective, and carefully reasoned policy choice. Managers need to be vigilant when contracting to avoid fraud, waste, and political favoritism both in awarding and executing the contract. Finally, in the decision to contract-out services, administrators must include the time and effort needed for effective governmental contract oversight.[13] The need for management capacity to oversee government contracts should not be underestimated.

Conclusion

Contracts are frequent and essential in business and government. Ordinary people regularly enter into situations governed by contract law and these sales, exchanges, or relationships are part of normal experiences. However, in government and business there are many situations that require detailed and thorough planning to address complex and ongoing relationships. Contract law may be complex, but contracting is now an important part of public management skills and practices.

Cases

There are two examples of government contract situations presented in the following cases. The *Space Master v. City of Worcester*[14] case considers problems with the construction of temporary school buildings, and the contract was not executed as expected. This case discusses bids being used in a government construction contract. The case illustrates that advance planning for contingencies may not alleviate problems. It also illustrates that contract management includes careful documentation of the costs incurred when the performance of services is late. The second case, *City of Miami v. Kory*[15] illustrates how employment relations involve contracts of different sorts. This case considers at-will employment, delegated authority of managers to act, and duress. Note that the contract in question on appeal is the employee's resignation letter, the offer, and the acceptance by her supervisor. Both of these cases demonstrate management practices and considerations that resulted in contract litigation.

Space Master International, Inc, v. City of Worcester, 940 F.2d 16, U.S. Court of Appeals, First Circuit, 1991

Opinion by Bownes.

This is an appeal from a summary judgment in favor of plaintiff-appellee Space Master International, Inc. ("Space Master"). The City of Worcester, defendant-appellant, hired Space Master to construct modular classrooms to alleviate overcrowding in the City's public schools. Under the publicly-bid contract, the City agreed to pay Space Master $1,514,559 to install within 120 days twenty-three modular classroom buildings at nine school sites. If performance exceeded 120 days, the City reserved the right to assess Space Master liquidated damages of $250 per day plus $100 per day per site.

Space Master completed its work over 200 days late; the city retained $254,400 in liquidated damages. Space Master then sued the City in the United States District Court of Massachusetts, seeking the withheld funds on the grounds that the liquidated damages provision was unenforceable. It alleged that the liquidated damages clause was not reasonably related to any anticipated or actual loss and that the liquidated damages withheld by the City were disproportionate to the damages incurred. Space Master claimed in the alternative that even were the liquidated damages clause found to be enforceable, plaintiff should not be held liable for the entire amount of liquidated damages because the delay was caused by acts of the City, subcontractors and factors beyond Space Master's control.

The City moved for partial summary judgment on the enforceability of the liquidated damages provision. It conceded that "the matter of how much in liquidated damages should be assessed against Space Master should be reserved until after a trial on the reasons for the delay." Space Master filed a cross-motion for summary judgment on the enforceability of the liquidated damages clause. After a hearing, the court granted Space Master's motion and denied the City's. The City appeals this ruling.

Standard of Review

. . .

"Summary judgment will not lie if the dispute about a material fact is 'genuine,' that is, if the evidence is such that a reasonable jury could return a verdict for the nonmoving party." *Anderson v. Liberty Lobby, Inc.,* 477 U.S. 242, 248, (1986). Massachusetts contract law "will identify which facts are material." See id.

Our review is plenary, and we "view the record in the light most favorable to the party against whom a motion for summary judgment is directed, and give that party the benefit of all the reasonable inferences to be drawn therefrom." *J.I. Corp. v. Federal Ins. Co.,* 920 F.2d 118 (1st Cir. 1990). We apply this standard as well where summary judgment motions were made by opposing parties. *Continental Casualty Co. v. Canadian Universal Ins. Co.,* 924 F.2d 370, 373 (1st Cir. 1991). "The [trial] court must evaluate each motion separately, being careful to draw inferences against each movant in turn." *Griggs-Ryan v. Smith,* 904 F.2d 112, 115 (1st Cir. 1990).

Liquidated Damages

Under the *Restatement of Contracts*: "Damages for breach by either party may be liquidated in the agreement but only at an amount that is reasonable in the light of the anticipated or actual loss caused by the breach and the difficulties of proof of loss. A term fixing unreasonably large liquidated damages is unenforceable on grounds of public policy." *Restatement (Second) of Contracts* § 356 (1) (1979). Two factors combine to determine whether an amount fixed as liquidated damages is not so unreasonably large as to be unenforceable. First, to be reasonable the amount must approximate actual loss or loss anticipated at the time the contract was executed. *Colonial at Lynnfield, Inc. v. Sloan,* 870 F.2d 761, 764 (1st Cir. 1989) . . . second, "the greater the difficulty either of proving that loss has occurred or of establishing its amount with the requisite certainty . . . the easier it is to show that the amount fixed is reasonable." *Restatement (Second) of Contracts* § 356 comment b.

Considerable deference is given to the parties' reasonable agreement as to the amount of liquidated damages where losses are difficult to quantify. *Lynch v. Andrew,* 481 N.E.2d at 1386; *Kroeger v. Stop & Shop Cos.,* 13 Mass. App. Ct. 310, 432 N.E.2d 566, 573 (1982). That deference, however, is not unlimited. In *Colonial at Lynnfield, Inc. v. Sloan,* we found that the liquidated damages provision at issue was a reasonable estimate of difficult to ascertain damages. We nonetheless found that the liquidated damages provision was an unenforceable penalty because no loss had been sustained as a result of the breach. 870 F.2d at 765. Liquidated damages must compensate for loss rather than punish for breach: "An exaction of punishment for a breach which could produce no possible damage has long been deemed oppressive and unjust." *Priebe & Sons, Inc. v. United States,* 332 U.S. 407, 413 (1947). See also *Dubinsky v. Wells Bros. Co.,* 218 Mass. 232, 105 N.E. 1004 (1914) (liquidated damages clause was unenforceable penalty because it was intended to secure performance; no substantial loss was sustained).

There can be no question that the injury sustained by the City is difficult to quantify in monetary terms. Because Space Master breached its promise to provide classrooms for the City within 120 days, children had to attend classes in hallways, gymnasiums, auditoriums, and libraries; educational programs were compromised; and morale among teachers, students and administrators suffered. These conditions continued for over 200 days past the contract deadline.

We have found no Massachusetts case directly on point; that is, where the injury involved harm to the public and was difficult to assess in monetary terms. Cases in other jurisdictions do allow such. See *Jennie-O-Foods, Inc. v. United States,* 217 Ct. Cl. 314, 580 F.2d 400, 413 (1978) (upholding liquidated damages for "costs to the public convenience and the temporary thwarting of the public goals that the particular contract served"); *United States v. Bills,* 639 F. Supp. 825, 831 (D.N.J. 1986) (liquidated damages upheld for loss of doctor's services in medically underserved area); *United States v. Swanson,* 618 F. Supp. 1231, 1243–44 (E.D. Mich. 1985) (same); *Abel Constr. Co. v. School Dist.,* 188 Neb. 166, 195 N.W.2d 744, 746–48 (1972) (upholding liquidated damages of $4,650.00 where late completion of athletic track resulted in expenses of $1,137.16, school was unable to use athletic facilities, and school and public suffered inconvenience to which no monetary value could be fixed). Cf. *In re D. Federico Co.,* 25 Bankr. 822, 833 (Bankr. D. Mass. 1982) (liquidated damages for delay in performance of public contract upheld without articulating type of damages caused by delay). As the Court said in *Priebe & Sons, Inc. v. United States,* "When they are fair and reasonable attempts to fix just compensation for anticipated loss caused by breach of contract, [liquidated damages provisions] are enforced. They serve a particularly useful function when damages are uncertain in nature or amount *or are unmeasurable,* as is the case in many government contracts." 332 U.S. at 411 (citations omitted, emphasis added).

Rulings on liquidated damages provisions in construction contracts are particularly deferential to the parties' agreement. Delay in performance prevents the possibility of use, "and it can seldom be shown that no use would in fact have been made, had completion been on time, or that no profit would have been made from such use." 5 Corbin, Corbin on Contracts § 1072 (1964). In *Norcross Bros. Co. v. Vose,* 199 Mass. 81, 85 N.E. 468 (1908), the court enforced liquidated damages for delay in construction without questioning the reasonableness of the amount. It is worthy of note that most construction contracts are the product of arms-length bargaining. In the present case, the contract was put out for bid.

Massachusetts applies general principles of contract law to public contracts. See *R. Zoppo Co. v. Commonwealth,* 353 Mass. 401, 232 N.E.2d 346, 349 (1967). We think it would apply the rule set forth in *Lynch v. Andrew,* 481 N.E.2d at 1386, and *Kroeger v. Stop & Shop Cos.,* 432 N.E.2d at 573, to the case at hand: Where losses are difficult to ascertain, considerable deference is due the parties' "reasonable" agreement as to liquidated damages. The basic question is whether the City intended the liquidated damages provision in the contract to compensate it for a loss difficult to quantify in monetary terms or intended it as a penalty to spur timely performance. We turn, therefore, to the evidence before the district court. Dr. John E. Durkin, Superintendent of the Worcester Public Schools, stated in an affidavit:

> When the contract was executed, it was difficult to ascertain the value of actual damages that would result from a delay in the contract's completion. The City could have incurred costs for the completion of the classroom delivery and installation by another contractor. The City might have decided to lease additional classroom space from a private party. The City could have paid to refurbish other public properties to be used as classroom space. The City could have incurred damages in the form of interest payments due on the borrowing that was done to pay for the contract at issue. The City could have incurred costs to pay for its own personnel for additional time that was required because of the need to supervise and monitor the completion of the necessary work to alleviate the overcrowding. The City could have been damaged by the continuing overcrowding problems and the impact such problems had on the quality of education that could be offered by the City.

This statement suggests that the liquidated damages clause was meant to compensate for loss that might be incurred rather than to penalize.

Other testimony by Durkin indicated that the liquidated damages clause was intended to penalize for late performance rather than to compensate the City for injury it would incur as a result of late performance. The deposition of Durkin reads in pertinent part:

> Q: Well, did you give them any instructions to insure that those provisions would be included in the contract?
> A: I didn't originate those figures, other than the fact that I knew that there were penalty clauses in the contract. The specifics came from—
> Q: And by penalty what do you mean, doctor, basically what is here?
> A: That's my interpretation of penalty, that if the modular classrooms

were not in place on time and accepted by the city, that there would be these assessments made against the provider.

Q: To penalize the contractor for his late performance?

A: I think more to encourage the contractor to deliver the modulars on time and to meet the provisions of the contract.

Q: So to provide a financial incentive to the contractor to finish the units on time?

A: I believe was the motivating factor, yes.

Q: That was the reason that those were put in as far as you know?

A: I think it was to motivate them and let them know if they were not, we would impose a penalty.

When asked in his deposition about the purposes of the liquidated damages provision, John C. Orrell, purchasing agent for the City, replied:

A: At the initiation of the preparation of the bid documents, we, of course, discussed the very crucial elements of the bid documents. Contained within those elements were the provisions for the liquidated damages.

Because of the severe overcrowding in the Worcester Public Schools, it was concluded that it would be imperative that we have some sort of liquidated damages provision in the contract to be certain that the project was completed on time.

Orrell did not recall how the amount of liquidated damages had been determined, but he remembered that a main function of the provision was to serve as an incentive for Space Master to finish its work on time.

In light of the contradictory and ambiguous statements, there was a genuine issue of material fact as to whether the City intended the liquidated damages provision to provide reasonable compensation or impose a penalty in the event of Space Master's breach. The grant of Space Master's motion for summary judgment was error.

For the reasons already stated, we affirm the district court's denial of defendant's motion for partial summary judgment on the liquidated damages clause.

Reversed in part, Affirmed in part. Remanded for trial.

Costs on appeal to the City.

City of Miami, Florida, et al. v. Delores Kory, 394 So.2d 494,
Court of Appeal of Florida, Third District, 1981

Opinion by Schwartz.

This is an appeal by the City of Miami from a declaratory judgment, rendered after a non-jury trial, which determined that Delores Kory's resignation as a probationary city employee was void because it was executed under duress. We reverse.

The facts are almost entirely undisputed. Under the civil service rules, an employee may be discharged without cause or explanation at any time during the first six months of employment, after which he attains permanent civil service status. On October 1, 1978, the appellee began work for the city in the Department of Management and Budget. At 1:00 p.m. on March 30, 1979, the last working day of Ms. Kory's probation, her supervisor, Manohar S. Surana, the Assistant Director of the Department, handed her a memorandum, signed by him, which stated that she would be terminated "effective 2:00 p.m. today, Friday, March 30, 1979." After reading the memo, and without prompting from Surana, Ms. Kory told him that she was seeking another position with the city. She asked if, in order to avoid being fired, which would have precluded her securing another city job, it would be possible for her to resign instead. Surana replied that he had no objection to a resignation but that the decision was entirely up to her. After going out to lunch to "give this some thought," Ms. Kory returned at 1:50 p.m. with a handwritten resignation, which bore the time "1:55 p.m.," intended specifically to become effective prior to her discharge. The note stated: "As I can no longer comply with the requirements of the position I occupy, I am tendering my resignation, effective immediately." Surana accepted the resignation.

During April Ms. Kory made several attempts to obtain other employment from the city and to extend her probationary status with the Department of Management and Budget. After all such efforts proved unsuccessful, she sought the advice of counsel on April 26, 1979. It was then that she first learned the fact which the trial court found to be decisive in granting her relief; although, he testified at the trial, he (like Ms. Kory) did not know it at the time, Surana, as the assistant director of his department, did not have the authority to discharge a probationer. Under the city code, only the director of a department, with the approval of the City Manager, possesses the power to do so.* Thus, if Surana's letter had been the cause of Ms. Kory's termination, it would have been ineffective as contrary to the requirements of the city's own regulations. *City of Hialeah v. Stola,* 330 So.2d 825 (Fla. 3d Dist. Court App. 1976).

---

*Section 6(d) of the *City of Miami Civil Service Rules and Regulations* provides: Said probationary employee may be returned to his former classification or, in the event he holds no permanent status in any class, may be discharged or reduced in rank at any time prior to the expiration of the probationary period upon receipt by said probationary employee of a written notice of discharge or reduction in rank from the Director of the Department, approved by the City Manager.

This was the basis of Ms. Kory's action below, which was to set aside the instrument which did end her employment with the city, her own resignation of March 30. She contended essentially that the resignation was the product of duress created by the invalid notice of dismissal. The trial judge agreed, set aside the resignation, and ordered the plaintiff restored to the position she would have occupied had it not been tendered that is, as a non-probationary civil service employee with full back pay and emoluments. We are unable to approve this conclusion.

An early, and often-cited definition of duress is contained in *Herald v. Hardin,* 95 Fla. 889, 116 So. 863, 864 (1928): "Duress is a condition of mind produced by an improper external pressure or influence that practically destroys the free agency of a party and causes him to do an act or make a contract not of his own volition." Accord, e.g., *Cooper v. Cooper,* 69 So.2d 881 (Fla. 1954); *Corporacion Peruana de Aeropuertos Aviacion Comercial v. Boy,* 180 So.2d 503 (Fla. 2d DCA 1965). As this formulation of the rule and all the equivalent ones indicate, there are in essence two factors which must coexist in order to establish duress, one which deals with the party allegedly under duress; the other, with the party allegedly imposing it. It must be shown (a) that the act sought to be set aside was effected involuntarily and thus not as an exercise of free choice or will and (b) that this condition of mind was caused by some improper and coercive conduct of the opposite side. "Underlying all definitions of "duress' is the dual concept of external pressure and internal surrender or loss of volition in response to outside compulsion." 17 *C.J.S. Contracts,* § 168 at 943 (1963). Although both elements of this duality are indispensable to a finding of duress, we think that neither existed in the present circumstances.

Resignation Voluntary Act of Plaintiff

As was said in *Azalea Drive-In Theatre, Inc. v. Sargoy,* 394 F. Supp. 568, 574 (E.D.Va. 1975), rev'd on other grounds, 540 F.2d 713 (4th Cir. 1976): "The authorities are in agreement that the ultimate fact to be determined whenever the question of duress is raised is whether the purported victim's will was so overcome as to deprive him of free choice."

On the facts of this case it is clear that Ms. Kory's resignation was to the contrary of this requirement, entirely the product of her own choice. The idea of her resigning was initiated entirely by her, and was not suggested, much less forced upon her by Surana. The case is thus completely different from those cited by the appellee, in which the resignation was affirmatively requested, indeed required by the employer as the only alternative to a similarly unlawful discharge. See, e.g., *Paroczay v. Hodges,* 219 F. Supp. 89 (D.D.C. 1963); *Motto v. General Services Administration of U.S.,* 335 F. Supp. 694 (E.D. La. 1971), aff'd without opinion, 502 F.2d 1165 (5th Cir. 1974), cert. denied, 420 U.S. 927 (1975). In a word, Surana did not tell Ms. Kory to "quit or be fired"; he said, "you're going to be fired," and Ms. Kory asked, "may I quit first?" Furthermore, after she herself raised the possibility of resignation, the plaintiff made a conscious decision to take that course for reasons which seemed to render it in her own best interests to do so. When, as here, a particular course of action is raised on one's own volition, see, *Taylor v. United States,* 219 Ct. Cl. 86, 591 F.2d 688 (Ct. Cl. 1979); *Joseph F. Egan, Inc. v. City of New York,* 18 A.D.2d 357, 239 N.Y.S.2d 420, 423 (App. Div. 1963), rev'd on other grounds 17 N.Y.2d 90, 268 N.Y.S.2d 301, 215 N.E.2d 490 (1966), and is finally decided upon in a deliberate and considered choice between alternatives, see, *Coffman v. Bolger,* 590 F.2d 1366 (5th Cir. 1979); *Johnson, Drake & Piper, Inc. v. United States,* 209 Ct.Cl. 313, 531 F.2d 1037 (1976); *McGucken v. United States,* 187 Ct. Cl. 284, 407 F.2d 1349 (Ct. Cl. 1969), cert. denied, 396 U.S. 894 (1969); *Autera v. United States,* 182 Ct.Cl. 495, 389 F.2d 815 (1968), no finding of involuntariness, and thus no conclusion of duress may be sustained.

Resignation not Product of Improper Conduct of City

Turning to the other side of the coin, the conduct of the city, we find the plaintiff's case equally inadequate. As has been demonstrated, the act supposedly coerced must be caused by some improper or illegal conduct of the defendant. See also, *Fuller v. Roberts,* 35 Fla. 110, 17 So. 359 (1895). In this regard, it is not improper and therefore not duress to threaten what one has a legal right to do. *Spillers v. Five Points Guaranty Bank,* 335 So.2d 851 (Fla. 1st DCA 1976), and cases and authorities cited; *Scutti v. State Road Department,* 220 So.2d 628, 630 (Fla. 4th DCA 1969). To the extent that any action of the city brought about Ms. Kory's resignation, it was obviously and only her proposed discharge. But it is undisputed that the city had the perfect right to do just that, fire Ms. Kory as a then-probationer without cause. See, *City of Miami v. Fraternal Order of Police,* 378 So.2d 20 (Fla. 3d DCA 1979), cert. denied, 388 So.2d 1113 (Fla. 1980). The only aspect of that anticipated action which was arguably improper was the means by which it was about to be effected, that is, by Mr. Surana, rather than the head of the department. It was demonstrated, however, that this irregularity had absolutely nothing to do with Ms. Kory's decision to resign. To carry the burden of establishing the required causal connection between the unlawful conduct of the defendant and a resulting coerced action of the plaintiff, Ms. Kory would have had to show that she would not have resigned if the memo had been executed by the proper official, and thus that she was forced into resigning by the fact that it was signed by the wrong one. The record shows the exact opposite. Ms. Kory was not aware of the procedural deficiency and her actions were completely unrelated to its existence. A voluntary action cannot be deemed the result of duress because the surrounding transaction involves a technical impropriety which is discovered long afterwards and which has no influence on the result. See, *Mills v. Forest Preserve Dist. of Cook County,* 345 Ill. 503, 178 N.E. 126 (1931).

Even if, as it did not, the "improper" feature of the discharge had something to do with the resignation, the actions of Surana could not be deemed coercive. As the trial judge found, he was totally unaware of the contrary rule, and believed in good faith that he had the authority himself to fire the plaintiff. Thus, the principle stated as follows in 13 *Williston on Contracts* § 1606, at 672–73 (3d ed. Jaeger rev. 1970) is directly applicable: "[A] threat to bring a civil action or to resort to remedies available under a contract is not such duress as will justify rescission of a transaction induced thereby. This is true even though it is subsequently determined that there is no legal right to enforce the claim, provided the threat is made in good faith, i.e., in the reasonable belief that a possible cause of action exists." Accord, e.g., *Weiner v. Minor,* 124 Conn. 92, 197 A. 691 (1938); *Morrill v. Amoskeag Savings Bank,* 90 N.H. 358, 9 A.2d 519, 524 (1939). In submitting a memo he sincerely believed was effective to terminate her, Surana simply did nothing wrongful toward the plaintiff, which could vitiate her subsequent decision to resign.

Approaching the issue from a somewhat different point of view, the plaintiff's position is really that the anticipated discharge was in breach of the civil service rules. If that were so, she had a perfectly satisfactory remedy for reinstatement in the courts, just as did the plaintiff in the case upon which she so heavily relies, *City of Hialeah v. Stola,* supra. The rule is, however, that threatened action cannot constitute duress, when there are adequate legal remedies available with which to challenge it. E.g., *Hartsville Oil Mill v. United States,* 271 U.S. 43 (1926); *Vines v. General Outdoor Advertising Co.,* 171 F.2d 487 (2d Cir. 1948) (per L. Hand, J.); *Tri-State Roofing Co. of Uniontown v. Simon,* 187 Pa.Super. 17, 142 A.2d 333 (1958). This principle is particularly applicable to employment situations such as this "because a suit will effectively supply damages or other reparation." 13 *Williston,* supra, § 1621, and cases collected at 764, n. 4. Had the plaintiff desired to challenge the discharge, she should and could have done so; her choice not to take that course cannot be deemed the result of duress. See, *Christie v. United States,* 207 Ct.Cl. 333, 518 F.2d

584, 587 (1975) ("Plaintiff chose to resign and accept discontinued service retirement rather than challenge the validity of her proposed discharge for cause. The fact remains, plaintiff had a choice. She could stand pat and fight. She chose not to.") [e. o.]; *C. & J. Michel Brewing Co. v. State,* 19 S.D. 302, 103 N.W. 40 (1905) (tax payments made, without filing protective suit, pursuant to non-coercive request of state officials, held voluntary and not product of duress even though statutory authorization for taxes subsequently ruled unconstitutional).

In the last analysis, what Ms. Kory did was take a voluntary action which seemed like a good idea at the time. In hindsight, it turned out to have been a mistake; what she should have done was let herself be improperly fired and then inevitably win the subsequent lawsuit. But "it cannot therefore be held that she acted under duress, for, if so, every settlement of a disputed matter made under a mistake of law could be overturned." *Mills v. Forest Preserve Dist. of Cook County,* supra, 345 Ill. 503, 178 N.E. at 131.

For the reasons stated, the judgment below is reversed and the cause remanded with directions to dismiss the complaint.

Reversed and remanded.

Discussion Questions

1. Discuss how the legal elements of contracts serve democratic public purposes such as transparency and accountability.
2. How do managers make sure that agreements are clear, consistent, and understood by all?
3. Discus the strengths and weaknesses of contracting-out from the viewpoint of economy, efficiency, equity, and political responsiveness.
4. Discuss reasons to have special training for contract managers. What are some of the skills contract managers need to have to succeed?
5. Can you identify examples of contracting-out government services in your community?
6. In the *Space Master* case, the date of the completion of construction was important to the city. Why was "time of the essence" for the city? What would happen if the city spent money for alternate classrooms—do you think they would be reimbursed?
7. Note the court stated that penalties were against public policy in the *Space Master* case. What are some policy reasons to prohibit penalties (hint, consider how much Space Master would receive from the contract and how much the liquidated damages would reduce this amount).

8. What are other ways managers can achieve timely delivery of goods or completion of projects, taking into account that the courts prohibit penalties?

9. In the *Miami v. Kory* case, the court was deciding the validity of what contract?

10. The courts did not find a problem with the lack of authority for Surana to talk to Kory about her release from employment. Is this a good decision from a legal viewpoint? Should courts consider general public impressions when deciding duress?

8

Tort Actions and Government Considerations

Laws reflect the standards society expects individuals, businesses, and governments to meet. This is the purpose for the statutes, regulations, and procedures that governments enforce. These laws and policies are developed in response to social needs and social norms. In the common law, torts is the substantive area that deals with how society expects individuals and entities to behave toward one another. Thus, when a property owner knows that the wooden front steps to his business are not stable, he is expected to repair them before someone is injured. When a person is driving down the street, we expect her to follow the traffic signs and lights, and if she runs a red light and her car hits another, we expect that she will pay to repair the car she hit. These scenarios all relate to ideals of duty and responsibility to others, and they fall under the substantive law of negligent torts.

Substantive tort law changes quite frequently, and the expenses involved in tort judgments have been a source for policy discussions to reform tort law. Torts involve wrongdoing; they are civil wrongs where the offender must pay damages or compensation. The law of torts is based on substantive state law, not federal law. Torts are not criminal nor regulatory actions, but all three areas of law relate to ideas of wrongdoing and fault. In criminal and regulatory actions, the government is seeking to gain compliance with authoritative societal standards and enacted laws, by either by punishing criminal actions or seeking compliance with regulatory standards.

Tort actions often involve one individual suing another. In recent decades, individuals have sued government more and more often to seek compensation or to change policies. It is common to discuss individuals suing government. Some class actions involve individuals suing to change government actions, practices, and/or policies. Other suits may be individual actions where one person is seeking compensation for harm they allege is caused by government negligence. Governments also use tort suits to address public interest or community harms, as is discussed later.

Traditionally, in common law, individuals could not sue the government. This doctrine of sovereign immunity was adopted by American courts and it serves as a defense to litigation. In this chapter, these general principles of tort law will be presented first and concerns of immunity and limits of government liability will be addressed in a later section. The final section provides an introduction to constitutional torts.

Tort Law Principles

A fundamental principle in tort law is that the burden or costs of injuries should be paid by the wrongdoer. The ideas of compensation, cost, and risk allocation are important in tort actions. There is a social aspect of tort theory as well, and that is that a person will try to avoid causing harm to another and will behave as a reasonable person if they know they will be liable for the harm they cause. In contract law, the law presumes that people knowingly and after deliberation enter into agreements. In tort law, the relationship between the parties is involuntary, and the duties are community standards imposed through the common law.

Torts are civil actions where one party seeks damages for the harm intentionally or negligently caused by another. When the aggressor deliberately harms another, this act is called an "intentional tort." This chapter will address "negligent torts." The four elements of actionable negligence are:

1. a duty to exercise reasonable care,
2. a breach of that duty,
3. legal or proximate cause, and
4. actual harm.[1]

The substantive area of negligent torts keeps expanding. Claims of negligence are based on a foreseeable injury, proximately caused by another (the tort-feasor) because that person failed a duty to use reasonable care. The duty of care can be based on a social expectation, a law or rule, or even a standard for an industry or practice. A duty of care can be established through case decisions or through the development of standard business practices, and entities are expected to keep up with common standards of practice. For example, many individuals get infections while receiving inpatient treatments at hospitals and there is federal guidance for hand hygiene in hospital settings; but whether this guidance is an industry standard for duty of care would be a question of fact in a tort action. Thus determining what the duty is and whether it is violated are questions of fact. The question is often phrased as: "What would a reasonable prudent person do in that situation?" This involves a subjective evaluation. The question of whether an injury is foreseeable is another area that involves evaluation of the facts based on whether the risks or consequences of an action are what an ordinary prudent person might expect to occur.[2]

In ordinary discourse, "cause" is not a constant or agreed-upon term. In law, the question of tort causation, or proximate causation, is difficult as well. *Barron's Law Dictionary* defines proximate cause as "that which in natural and continuous sequence unbroken by any new independent cause produces an event, and without which the injury would not have occurred."[3] Proximate cause is legal causation and relates to an act that sets in motion a chain of events leading to an injury. Often in cases, the courts use a "but for" test that is presented in the form of: "But for the defendant's action, the harm would not have occurred." Proximate cause may be found from an act or an omission. If causation involves a failure to act, then there must have been a duty to act.

In addition, there are duties of care for everyone to act reasonably. Both parties may be partially at fault in a situation. The law at one point was harsh when the law of contributory negligence said that if some plaintiff was partially at fault, he could not recover any damages from the other person involved. Now it is far more common to use a comparative negligence standard that if both parties are at fault, then the damages are reduced by the percentage the plaintiff was at fault. Sometimes possible harm is well-known and recognized, and in this case there may be questions of assumption of the risk. That means a person knew an activity had risks, participated, and got injured, and in these situations courts may find an assumption of the risk.

As an element of tort suits, harm to the plaintiff must be shown. The harm can include personal injury or death, emotional suffering, property injury, and economic injury such as lost earnings or damage to a person's reputation. When there is a finding of liability in torts, the defendant must pay the actual damages to the injured party based on the harm caused. The damages can include payment to repair or replace property, medical expenses, lost wages, and pain and suffering. In rare instances when the defendant's conduct is shown to be so outrageous, so willful, or wonton that it shocks the conscious, then courts may allow the plaintiff to seek an award of punitive damages. As the word "punitive" indicates, punitive damages are used to punish and make an example of the wrongdoer. Often states limit punitive damages (such as no more than three times the actual damages award).

Finally, there are some activities that are seen as so dangerous or ultra-hazardous there may be strict liability, where there needs to be no showing of fault. Situations where courts have applied strict liability include extremely dangerous activities such as maintaining electrical power lines, keeping wild animals like lions, or for some defects not easily discernible in manufactured products. Thus strict liability means the manufacturer must include the costs for potential liability within the charges for the good or service, and this means the loss is often spread around to those who use a product that is subject to strict liability.

In torts, what constitutes the duty of care—whether the duty was breached, whether a reasonable person would foresee the harm, and what is the amount of damages—are all questions that rely on the factual situation. The amount of damages or monetary injury also can be open to factual interpretation. In addition, new arguments are often proposed of new or expanding duties of care. Thus the law of torts is not as predictable, or it changes more rapidly than contracts or property. Often torts are managed by insuring for risks and seeking negotiated settlements. Torts, more that other areas of common law, involve moral questions of fault, duties, and responsibility.

Government Bringing Tort Actions

It is far more common to have government defending tort suits than for governments to be bringing tort suits. This is because there are many areas the government regulates pursuant to statutes and promulgated regulations. Government brings action under this express rule of law power rather than common law theories. It is far more common for government enforcement to be done under rule-based authority and regulatory standards; however, there are occasions where government has pursued litigation based on tort claims.

For instance, respected scholar Martha Derthick's book, *Up in Smoke,* details the multistate tobacco litigation. In this litigation, many states joined together to seek compensation for medical expenses the states incurred to pay for illness caused by tobacco smoking.[4] The legal theory was that the cigarette manufacturers engaged in fraud and received unjust enrichment. States claimed individuals' injuries were caused by tobacco, and these companies should compensate the expenses states incurred to treat the injured. The states' attorneys general pursued these suits by hiring private firms to pursue the cases, and they paid the private attorneys a percentage of the award. The legislatures did not authorize these suits. After protracted litigation of four years, a settlement was reached where tobacco companies would pay forty-six states an estimated $246 billion between 2000 and 2025. In addition, the companies would fund public- service announcements about the hazards of tobacco use.

Cities and states have not fared as well in bringing other public interest tort actions. For instance, in 2000 New York City sued gun manufacturers under a theory of nuisance, but in 2008 a U.S. Court of Appeals dismissed the suit because the Protection of Lawful Commerce in Arms Act banned suits unless the plaintiff proved the gunmakers violated state or federal statutes in sales and marketing practices.[5] In July, 2008 the Rhode Island Supreme Court overturned a $2.4 billion verdict the state obtained by alleging the inclusion of lead in paint was a public nuisance. The paint manufacturers convinced the Supreme Court that public nuisance law did not remedy this type of harm.

Illinois, Missouri, and New Jersey appellate courts have also rejected similar state suits against paint manufacturers based on nuisance theories.[6]

Nuisance, under tort, argues that a person or company uses its property or causes a condition that interferes with another's enjoyment of their property. Examples of activities found to be nuisances include loud noises, noxious odors, air pollution, or keeping pets and livestock without cleaning up after them. Through zoning and code provisions, local governments often make certain types of nuisance subject to misdemeanor or municipal offenses. However, enforcement by citation does not necessarily remove offending practices. Instead, there may be a need to seek injunctions to obtain a cease-and-desist order to stop the offending action, either during certain times or even permanently. Individuals can seek injunctions, but if the nuisance is causing problems for an entire neighborhood then it seems appropriate and efficient for government to take action. In addition, in situations that extend beyond one community or where there is no existing statute or ordinance on the books, it is possible for government attorneys to bring a tort action.

One objection to this approach of government regulation through tort lawsuits is based on rule-of-law considerations. That is, there is no written statutory notice of inappropriate or illegal conduct. Another objection to this approach challenges whether the government attorney bringing tort actions is subject to sufficient legislative oversight or executive control. The third objection asserts that government attorneys bringing tort suits is an approach that is subject to an abuse of discretion.

Sovereign Immunity

Sovereign immunity began as political doctrine that served as an absolute defense to government liability. If a government was sued, it claimed sovereign immunity and the case was dismissed. When parties are sued, they can raise defenses. First, they may raise technical defenses such as lack of jurisdiction, no cause of action, statutes of limitations have passed, and so forth.

Historically, the sovereign was immune from being sued in courts of law. Individuals who believed they were harmed by the sovereign could petition and ask for redress, but when the sovereign was a king, the courts, being subject to the king, were not allowed to find that the king acted improperly or did wrong. The principle of sovereign immunity has long existed in history, and it was adopted early in American history by the courts as well. Sovereign immunity is a court-made doctrine and courts interpreted it to mean that to sue the government, there must be specific authority to sue the government; this authority could exist either by statute, by written approval, or by waiving this defense in a suit. The strict interpretation of sovereign immunity meant that in the nineteenth century, individuals with contracts with the government could not sue for breach of contract. Instead, individuals had to petition the legislature for redress. In the late 1800s federal legislation allowed suits in the Court of Claims, but the government still retained sovereign immunity from tort actions and liability.

Federal Immunity and Tort Claims Act

There were inroads into sovereign immunity. In the United States, there is no federal constitutional source of sovereign immunity and so sovereign immunity developed under the common law, where courts generally held government could not be sued without its consent. The justification for common law sovereign immunity had to do with the treasury and operations of government. The arguments for this type of sovereign immunity had a number of points:

1. claims, if paid, would be a strain on the public treasury;
2. defending the claims would cause interference with duties and administrative expenses;
3. the government provided the same sort of care for all, and so the tort justification of encouraging due care and reasonable conduct did not justify lawsuits against government.

Individuals had to petition members of Congress to introduce private bills to be compensated for torts or harm caused by the government before 1946 when Congress passed the Tort Claims Act.[7] This law allowed individuals to sue the federal government for some torts, such as ordinary situations where others could be sued as in the example of car accidents. Congress also left some government immunity in this act. There also are other statutory provisions that may limit a party from suing government or another party, which will be discussed below.

The federal government also retained sovereign immunity for certain actions through legislation. For instance in 1928, when Congress enacted the Flood Control Act, it retained immunity for actions relating to flood control, and this included actions even if the government was negligent.[8] In addition, under the Stafford Act, the federal government retains immunity for tort claims in emergency responses and only allows claims to be made through a more limited claim type of process.[9] Many states have retained sovereign immunity for emergency responders during declared disasters; other states may also have limits on the provision that allows individuals to sue government. Aspects of state sovereign immunity are discussed below.

Most people would think that if the government waives sovereign immunity under a tort claims law, then the government policy is to allow parties to prove that government employees were negligent in carrying out their jobs. The law only allows people to sue government for tort that an ordinary person would be liable for. This means in effect that some governmental activities are not subject to findings of liability, but often a case proceeds through discovery and motion practice before the court dismisses based on an immunity defense. The statutory provisions and court interpretations of the law limit the types of claims that can be brought.

Claims are excluded under four important and broad exceptions:

1. When a government employee acts with due care executing a statute or regulation;
2. when a government employee's act or omission occurs when the employee is carrying out a discretionary function or making a policy decision;
3. when a government contractor's work, including actions or omissions, would be exempt if performed by a government employee; and
4. when a public employee commits an intentional tort, because the Tort Claims Act only addresses negligent torts.

There are differing views about the appropriateness of allowing individuals to sue government. For instance, public managers argue that the very nature of defending litigation is distracting from achieving the job that involves large expenses in both time and money. Others argue that tort suits are an incentive for proper conduct in society, and this proper conduct incentive should include the government. The assertion is that whether an action is done by government or an individual, the same tort rationales apply. For example, under theories such as respondeat superior, an employer and manager pay closer attention to the actions of employees when they can be held liable for the negligent tort of an employee during the course of their job. Others argue that the ability of government or large businesses to pay damage is a way to redistribute costs or allow society to pay for harms. Some call this a "deep-pocket view." The argument of ability to pay requires the government or business to include litigation as part of its ongoing expenditures and then to spread those costs to its customers or constituents.

State and Local Immunity

There are different types of immunity that governments have and that governments have granted based on public policy reasons. Some states have waived sovereign immunity for torts but limited the amount of damages plaintiffs can receive. The extent of state and local government sovereign immunity and tort liability depends on each state's laws. The immunity for state employees also is a question of state law, but states and their employees can be sued under federal law, 42 U.S.C.§1983, for violating someone's constitutional rights; these are called "constitutional torts" or "1983 actions." Local government sovereign immunity and tort liability also depend on state laws.

There is one aspect of state tort laws that is worth examining: the limits on damages amounts even if liability is shown. Some states have statutes that place caps on the amount of damages the state may be responsible for because of an event. This applies to catastrophes and mass casualties. Here is a situation from Colorado to consider. Colorado had liability limits that caused public outcry after a disaster. Colorado capped the liability of the state at $100,000 per individual and $400,000 per event. On August 10, 1987, when a state road worker operating a frontloader pushed on a seven-ton boulder near Berthoud Pass, it rolled down the mountain, landed on a tour bus, and killed nine people and seriously injured nineteen others. Although Governor Roy Romer promised to pay for the medical expenses of the injured, the state legislature refused to authorize additional expenses beyond the liability cap. A case reached the Colorado Supreme Court that upheld the statute that capped damages. As an alternative, the attorneys representing the injured passengers proceeded under federal constitutional rights theories. Finally in 1993, the state agreed to compensate the injured for a total of 2.5 million dollars.[10]

When a mass disaster or a catastrophe occurs, limits on damages such as Colorado's law means that many who are injured may not be compensated for their medical expenses. In addition, the ability to persuade the legislature to act to provide compensation may be difficult, even when they have a compassionate executive. In the Colorado bus crash, in one interview a municipal league representative agreed that the decision was a tradeoff.[11] This means that the Colorado limitations on governmental liability were a policy choice where there was a tradeoff in either imposing costs on the taxpayers or making the victims bear the brunt of the financial burden from the accident.

Limits and Alternatives to Tort Lawsuits

Legislatures determine the public policy reasons to enact legislation that allows parties to sue government or limits the ability of parties to sue government. The public policy exception to the tort claims acts is justified as providing for administrative discretion in carrying out legislative policy. This places a limit on judicial involvement, or some would call it "judicial interference," with policy decisions. For example, courts do not want to monitor the choice a manager makes between setting a speed limit at 20 mph or 25 mph. Applying the public policy doctrine shifts the issue of harm caused by government;

it moves it from court review to the political arena. There are five general categories of limitations or alternatives to tort litigation.

First are laws that limit liability. Two examples of this type of policy include Good Samaritan laws and child abuse reporting exemptions. Good Samaritan laws are statutory provisions that serve the public purpose of encouraging individuals to help one another if there is an accident. Under common law, there is no obligation to stop and help another person. Under Good Samaritan laws, the injured person cannot sue someone who stops to help. This is seen as especially useful to encourage those with medical training to aid in emergencies. Many states limit the ability to sue someone that in good faith reports child abuse. Again, there is a public policy here that it is more important for individuals to report child abuse and to protect the child than to allow lawsuits for damage to a person's reputation.

Second are tort reform laws. Businesses and professions, particularly doctors, have argued that defending lawsuits increases insurance costs even before a judgment is entered, and that these costs impose excessive burdens on business. They have argued that the tort system is out of control and needs to be adjusted to aid the economy. Many of the tort reform laws that have been proposed and enacted place limits on who sues, how much they may seek in damages, limit punitive damages, or otherwise make it more difficult for plaintiffs to bring actions against others. In response, individuals argue that if businesses are exempt from potential liability, then the incentive to act in a reasonable manner and to avoid harm to others will be missing.

The third category of laws limiting public, and private, liability are victims' compensation funds. There are compensation funds that are established as alternatives to litigation. Sometimes government has stepped in to limit liability for some activities or to provide risk pools for other activities. The reason for these liability limits is that the activity involved serves the public interest.[12] For example, individuals injured after an immunization cannot sue and instead must present their claims to the federal program.

An example is workers compensation programs that many states enacted to provide for set amounts for injuries on the job without resort to litigation. Workers compensation is distributed through an administrative system, where the amount of the award is established by schedule and the facts of the situation are often determined in an administrative setting. Employers must contribute to the funds based on number of employees and claims made by their employees. In some ways, workers compensation is like insurance. One of the purposes for workers compensation is to reduce the adversarial nature of claims between a worker and an employer. The workers compensation system simplified the claims process, but many observers have noted that the amounts awarded for injuries have not been adjusted for inflation and are inadequate.

The fourth type is the use of disability insurance programs that provide some resources for those unable to work and that serve as a social safety net. The development of the federal Social Security disability payments as a social welfare program has provided minimal payments to those who are unable to work. Disability claims do not require finding fault or responsibility when someone is unable to work. Instead, if the person meets the minimum requirements for eligibility and made payments into the Social Security disability insurance fund, they may be eligible. This system is criticized for the low amounts that are paid to individuals and the difficulty in demonstrating during hearings the petitioner's inability to work.

Finally, there are unusual circumstances where government may provide humanitarian payments through legislative largesse. After the attacks of September 11, 2001, a highly unusual government program provided for compensation for those who were injured or died because of the terrorist attacks. There were a number of rationales for the Victims' Compensation Fund. First, the airline industry argued that it would not be able to continue in business if the possibility of litigation remained. Although they believed that they could ultimately win such litigation, the distraction and expense of defending the litigation and the public relations concern of passenger trust in the airlines made their industry particularly vulnerable. In effect, this argument was that there was an economic necessity to rescue an industry. Second, there were arguments regarding patriotism and sympathy for those that were injured. The view was that the entire country was under attack and that it was only right and appropriate for government to compensate them.[13]

While it seemed that Congress wanted to do something and acted quickly after 9/11 to provide for victims of this massive catastrophe, this approach seems to be a rare occurrence. No humanitarian or nationalism arguments were successful to provide compensation for victims of a mass natural catastrophe of the hurricanes Katrina and Rita. Over 300,000 cases have been filed in the U.S. District Court in New Orleans against the U.S. government for negligence in the construction and maintenance of levees and canals, and some cases claimed the government failed to warn the public about the limits on protection from severe storms.[14] What is normally provided to the victims of hurricanes and other mass disasters is a small one-time assistance grant provided by the Federal Emergency Management Agency (FEMA).

Constitutional Torts

Most tort claims against governments and their employees arise under the authority of state tort laws. There is one exception where tort claims can be brought under federal constitutional authority. These are called constitutional torts. Simply stated, administrators can be found personally liable for damages if they violate an individual's constitutional rights. For example, a violation of an individual's due process rights or an illegal search can be the basis of a suit alleging a public administrator's personal liability. The term constitutional torts is another way to discuss claims brought under the Civil Rights Act (42 U.S.C. § 1983) and so these claims are often called "1983 actions."

This statute was passed in 1871 as part of the enforcement mechanisms of the Fourteenth Amendment. Although it can be seen as part of the Civil War reconstruction laws, it only became more widely used after the Civil Rights movement of the 1960s. In practice, Section 1983 provides jurisdiction and a right of action in federal courts. It is not limited to constitutional violations of racial discrimination and it has been broadly applied. This statute, which authorizes redress for violations of constitutional and statutory rights is not itself a source of substantive rights, but rather a method for vindicating federal rights elsewhere conferred by those parts of the United States Constitution and federal statutes that it describes.

This law gives a right of action against a person who acts under color of state law, and so this subjects state and local governments, and their employees, to federal jurisdiction. Public administrators have been found personally liable under this law. This law imposes constitutional competence on governments and their public administrators. This law has several purposes: It overrides certain kinds of state laws; it provides remedy where state law is inadequate; and it provides federal remedy where state remedy, though adequate in theory, is not available in practice. Because state and local officials and their governmental employers can be sued for constitutional torts, every public manager needs to know how the constitution applies to them. This why public managers need constitutional competence.[15] The text of this statute is provided below.

Civil Action for Deprivation of Rights 42 U.S.C. § 1983

> Every person who, under color of any statute, ordinance, regulation, custom, or usage, of any State or Territory or the District of Columbia, subjects, or causes to be subjected, any citizen of the United States or other person within the jurisdiction thereof to the deprivation of any rights, privileges, or immunities secured by the Constitution and laws, shall be liable to the party injured in an action at law, suit in equity, or other proper proceeding for redress, except that in any action brought against a judicial officer for an act or omission taken in such officer's judicial capacity, injunctive relief shall not be granted unless a declaratory decree was violated or declaratory relief was unavailable. For the purposes of this section, any Act of Congress applicable exclusively to the District of Columbia shall be considered to be a statute of the District of Columbia.

Conclusion

Lawsuits alleging negligence have to show that there was a duty of care owed to that particular plaintiff and that a breach of duty caused harm. The tort system is seen as a way to encourage individuals, businesses, and government to act in a reasonable manner to avoid harming others. A regulatory system is one alternative to unequal power relationships or an alternative to individuals seeking to change business practices that may cause harm to the community.

The ability of individuals to sue government or public officials provides managers feedback on operations. Governments can act to minimize harm as part of normal operation, and tort liability is an incentive to affirmatively minimize harm. Individual public administrators also have an incentive to know what constitutional rights are when they, as state actors, can also be sued for denying a person their constitutional rights. Tort litigation can also be seen as part of the democratic values of allowing individuals to seek redress for government actions. But balancing government concerns for effectiveness and tax burdens against individual responsibility and injury is an important but complex aspect of governance.

Cases

The following cases demonstrate some of the negligence tort law aspects of duty, foreseeability, and fault. Both of these cases involved public administrators making decisions that affect the health, safety, and welfare of the general public and specific individuals. Note the discussion of responsibility and risk in the first case, *Schiffman v. Spring and Bright*. The coaches in this case are public administrators because they work for a state university. The second case is more complex as it considers three types of immunity under Texas law that were raised as defenses by an administrator in the *Gonzales v. Avalos* case.[16] Note what the court says is required for immunity regarding discretionary or mandatory administrative decisions, and also note what the administrator was accused of misusing. Consider as you read the cases what managers in similar situations could do to reduce the likelihood, extent, or frequency of injuries.

Michele Schiffman v. John Spring and Fred Bright, 609 N.Y.S.2d 482, Supreme Court of New York, Appellate Division, 1994

Opinion.
Order unanimously reversed on the law without costs, motion granted and complaint dismissed. Memorandum: Supreme Court [the trial court] should have granted the motion of defendants, John Spring and Fred Bright, for summary judgment dismissing the complaint.

Plaintiff, a member of the women's varsity soccer team at the State University of New York at Brockport, was injured on September 22, 1987, when her foot became stuck in mud on the playing field while she was participating in a soccer game held at the State University of New York at Geneseo (Geneseo). Plaintiff alleged that Spring and Bright, the athletic director at Geneseo and the coach of the Geneseo women's varsity soccer team, respectively, were negligent in electing to hold the soccer game on a field that was wet, slippery and muddy. Plaintiff testified at an examination before trial that, before play commenced, she was aware of the condition of the surface of the playing field. Additionally, plaintiff testified that she and other members of the team discussed that condition and complained about it to their coach. Nonetheless, plaintiff voluntarily elected to participate in the game and played the first half without incident. She voluntarily returned to the field to play the second half. Plaintiff sustained her injury shortly after the second half commenced.

"As a general rule, participants properly may be held to have consented, by their participation, to those injury-causing events which are known, apparent or reasonably foreseeable consequences of the participation" (*Turcotte v. Fell,* 68 N.Y.2d 432, 439; see, *Maddox v. City of New York,* 66 N.Y.2d 270, 277–278; *Lamey v. Foley,* 188 A.D.2d 157, 163). On the other hand, a defendant generally has a duty to exercise reasonable care to protect such participants from "unassumed, concealed or unreasonably increased risks" (*Benitez v. New York City Bd. of Educ.,* 73 N.Y.2d 650, 658). "To establish plaintiff's assumption of risk, a defendant must show that plaintiff was aware of the defective or dangerous condition and the resultant risk, although it is not necessary to demonstrate that plaintiff foresaw the exact manner in which his injury occurred" (*Lamey v. Foley,* supra, at 164, citing *Maddox v. City of New York,* supra, at 278). Whether that conclusion can be made depends on "the openness and obviousness of the risk, plaintiff's background, skill, and experience, plaintiff's own conduct under the circumstances, and the nature of defendant's conduct" (*Lamey v. Foley,* supra, at 164; see, *Benitez v. New York City Bd. of Educ.,* supra, at 657–658; *Turcotte v. Fell,* supra, at 440, 442). "Perhaps the most important factor, however, is whether the risk is inherent in the activity" (*Lamey v. Foley,* supra, at 164).

Defendants sustained their initial burden on their motion for summary judgment. They submitted evidentiary proof in admissible form to establish that plaintiff voluntarily participated in the soccer game, fully aware of the condition of the playing field and of the risk of injury. Defendants' proof established that plaintiff's injury "was not the consequence of a failed duty of care on the part of the defendants" but was "a luckless accident arising from the vigorous voluntary participation in competitive interscholastic athletics" (*Benitez v. New York City Bd. of Educ.,* supra, at 658–59). In opposition to the motion, plaintiff failed to raise a triable issue of fact whether defendants breached their duty to exercise reasonable care to protect plaintiff from "unassumed, concealed or unreasonably increased risks" (*Benitez v. New York City Bd. of Educ.*, supra at 658). Plaintiff failed to dispute defendants' proof that she voluntarily participated in the soccer game with knowledge and appreciation of the risks inherent in playing on a field that was wet, slippery and muddy.

Order unanimously reversed on the law without costs, motion granted and complaint dismissed.

Ernesto Gonzalez, Appellant v. Jesus R. Avalos, Sr., father of deceased, Appellee, 866 S.W.2d 346, Court of Appeals of Texas, El Paso, 1993

Opinion by Koehler.

This is a case involving defenses of official and governmental immunity. In this interlocutory appeal from a denial of summary judgment, an employee of the Department of Human Services contends that because he is immune from liability in a suit brought against him for the wrongful death of a child, the court erred in denying his motion for summary judgment. We affirm.

Relevant Facts

Jesus Avalos, Appellee (Avalos), was the father of two children: Andres, age two, and Ricardo, age five. The children were in the custody of his former wife, Linda Avalos. On November 23, 1988, Avalos entered the El Paso office of Child Protective Services Division (CPS) of the Texas Department of Human Services (DHS) to report his concerns that his children were being abused by their mother's live-in boyfriend, Jesus Alvarez. His report was taken down by Elvia Caldera, a DHS social worker. The allegations made by Avalos to Ms. Caldera were that Ricardo was being physically abused, that he had three or four scratches or bruises on his neck, that he would not talk about the abuse for fear of retaliation, and that he had lost weight during the two month period Alvarez had been living with his mother. Caldera's report was forwarded to her supervisor, Ernesto Gonzalez (Gonzalez), the Appellant, the same day. On November 28,1988, Gonzalez closed the Avalos case without assigning it for investigation.

On December 14, 1988, Andres was admitted to Vista Hills Hospital for treatment of severe injuries, injuries from which he subsequently died. Avalos, acting as surviving father and administrator of Andres' estate, sued DHS and Gonzalez for the wrongful death, alleging negligence and negligence per se. Gonzalez, who was sued in both his individual capacity and as a DHS employee, sought a summary judgment on several theories of immunity.

Gonzalez has brought this interlocutory appeal from the order denying his motion for summary judgment.

Standard of Review

When reviewing a summary judgment appeal, we must determine whether the movant in the trial court carried his burden of showing that there is no genuine issue of a material fact and that he is entitled to judgment as a matter of law. *Nixon v. Mr. Property Management Co., Inc.,* 690 S.W.2d 546, 548 (Tex. 1985). In deciding whether or not there is a disputed fact issue precluding summary judgment, evidence favorable to the nonmovant is to be taken as true, and in that connection, every reasonable inference must be indulged in favor of the nonmovant and any doubts resolved in his favor. *Nixon,* 690 S.W.2d at 548–49. Where the defendant is the movant, in order to prevail, he must by appropriate summary judgment evidence either (1) disprove at least one element of each of the plaintiff's theories of recovery or (2) plead and prove conclusively each essential element of an affirmative defense. *Bradley v. Quality Service Tank Lines,* 659 S.W.2d 33, 34 (Tex. 1983); *Zep Mfg. Co. v. Harthcock,* 824 S.W.2d 654, 657 (Tex.App.–Dallas 1992, no writ); *Rayos v. Chrysler Credit Corporation,* 683 S.W.2d 546, 547 (Tex.App.–El Paso 1985, no writ). The basic issue presented to us then is, did Gonzalez establish as a matter of law his nonliability for his alleged negligence by reason of some form of immunity.

Liability and Immunity of State Employees

A state employee may be sued in either of two capacities: in his individual capacity, in which event he is personally liable for any judgment rendered against him; or in his official capacity, in which event any adverse judgment is paid by the state. An employee sued in his official capacity may raise any defense available to the state, including sovereign immunity. *Bagg v. University of Texas Medical Branch at Galveston,* 726 S.W.2d 582, 586 Tex. App.–Houston [14th Dist.] 1987), writ ref'd n.r.e.); *Russell v. Edgewood Independent School Dist.,* 406 S.W.2d 249, 252 (Tex.Civ.App.–San Antonio 1966, writ ref'd n.r.e.). When sued in his individual capacity, the employee is entitled to raise the defense of official immunity, rather than sovereign immunity. *Baker v. Story,* 621 S.W.2d 639, 643 (Tex.App.–San Antonio 1981, writ ref'd n.r.e.). Avalos sued Gonzalez in both his official and his individual capacity. Gonzalez argues that he was entitled to summary judgment because he is protected from liability by official immunity, by the statutory immunity created by Family Code, Section 34.03, and by sovereign immunity.

Official Immunity

In his first point of error, Gonzalez contends that as a state officer, he is immune from both criminal and civil liability. Public officials and employees whose jobs are classified as "quasi-judicial" are shielded from liability when they act in good faith within the scope of their employment. *Eakle v. Texas Dep't of Human Services,* 815 S.W.2d 869, 875 (Tex.App.–Austin 1991, writ denied); *Russell v. Texas Dep't of Human Resources,* 746 S.W.2d 510, 513 (Tex.App.–Texarkana 1988, writ denied); *Austin v. Hale,* 711 S.W.2d 64, 66 (Tex.App. 1986). To prevail on this theory, Gonzalez needed to prove: (1) that he held a quasi-judicial position as director of CPS; (2) that he acted within the scope of his authority as a quasi-judicial employee; and (3) that he acted in good faith. *Eakle,* 815 S.W.2d at 875; *Austin,* 711 S.W.2d at 66.

A quasi-judicial position is one that involves the exercise of discretionary, rather than ministerial, acts. *Eakle,* 815 S.W.2d at 875.Though the distinction is not always easy to draw, discretionary actions require personal deliberation, decision, and judgment, while ministerial actions require obedience to orders or the performance of a mandated duty. *Travis v. City of Mesquite,* 830 S.W.2d 94, 102 (Tex. 1992). *Austin,* 711 S.W.2d at 67. Quasi-judicial actions include discretionary acts such as gathering information in connection with an investigation and making decisions based upon that information. The fact that an employee of the state has partly or primarily quasi-judicial duties does not eliminate the possibility that he may have some ministerial duties as well.

Gonzalez, as a supervisor of CPS, was required to make decisions and exercise discretion as to the extent of investigations and the priorities to be given reported abuse cases. His position with DHS was therefore quasi-judicial. See *Austin,* 711 S.W.2d at 67–68 (DHS employees who investigated a child abuse case held quasi-judicial positions).

Avalos contends, however, that Gonzalez did not act within the scope of his discretionary authority because he had no discretion under the Texas Family Code Section 34.05(a) to decide whether or not to investigate Avalos' allegations of abuse. We agree. Section 34.05(a) provides that "the Texas Department of Human Services . . . *shall make a thorough investigation* promptly after receiving either the oral or written report of child abuse or neglect by a person responsible for a child's care, custody, or welfare. . . . The department *may assign priorities to investigations* based on the severity and immediacy of the alleged harm to the child. . . ." [emphasis added]. Tex. Fam. Code Ann.§ 34.05(a) (Vernon Supp. 1993). Under Subsection (c), certain requirements for the investigation are specified: "The investigation *shall* include a visit to the child's home, unless the alleged abuse or neglect can be confirmed or clearly ruled out without a home visit, and an interview with and examination of the subject child. . . ." [emphasis added]. Tex. Fam. Code Ann. § 34.05(c) (Vernon Supp. 1993). Other provisions in the section state what "the investigation *may* include" and where it "*may* be conducted." It is obvious from a reading of the statute that the legislature chose the uses of the mandatory "shall" and the discretionary "may" very carefully. We hold that those provisions that use "shall" in relation to investigations and by their wording leave the employee no choice are mandatory. The provision requiring DHS to make a thorough investigation leaves no room for an employee to decide that no investigation is necessary when child abuse has been reported. Thus, Gonzalez' decision not to investigate was not within the scope of his authority and discretion. On the other hand, those provisions of Section 34.05 that use "may" or clearly give the employee some choice in how much investigation is necessary and what action is to be taken after completion of the investigation are discretionary. Thus in Austin, the Court held that the two DHS employees had official immunity from liability for alleged negligence in conducting the investigation and in failing to remove the child from the dangerous environment. *Austin*, 711 S.W.2d at 67–68.

Gonzalez argues that under the system of investigative priorities established by DHS pursuant to the provisions of Section 34.05(a) (quoted above), he was entitled to give Avalos' report of abuse a Priority III classification, which he claims required no investigation. The DHS administrative rules in effect at the relevant time set forth three priorities for intake and investigation. 40 Tex. Admin. Code §§ 49.501 et seq. (West 1989). Section 49.502 provided for the assignment of priorities to reports based upon the employee's evaluation of the harm or threatened harm to the child, the legal base for the services, and DHS and community resources for providing the services. Section 49.503 established Priority I for children who were alleged or found to be abused or neglected and were in immediate danger of death or serious physical harm. Priority II, under Section 49.504, was to be assigned to other children who were alleged or found to be abused or neglected (and who were presumably not in immediate danger of death or serious harm). Priority III, as set forth in Section 49.505 was "for children who are not alleged or found to be abuse or neglected . . ." It is obvious that under all three priorities, a child could not be found to be abused and neglected without CPS having made at least the minimal investigation required by Family Code Section 34.05. Because Avalos had made allegations of abuse, Gonzalez had no discretion to give the report a Priority III classification but was required to give the case either a Priority I or II assignment and to initiate an investigation within the appropriate period specified by the rules. His action in assigning the report Priority III being outside the scope of his discretionary authority, Gonzalez had no official immunity. Point of Error No. One is overruled.

Statutory Immunity

Gonzalez asserts in his second point that the trial court erred in denying him a summary judgment because he has an absolute immunity from liability by virtue of the statutory immunity granted by Section 34.03 of the Family Code (1993). That section provides:

> § 34.03. Immunities
>   (a) Except as provided by Subsection (b) of this section, a person reporting or assisting in the investigation of a report pursuant to this chapter is immune from liability, civil or criminal, that might otherwise be incurred or imposed. Immunity extends to participation in any judicial proceeding resulting from the report.
>   (b) Persons who report their own conduct or who otherwise report in bad faith or malice, or assist in the investigation of a report in bad faith or malice, are not protected by this section.

Gonzalez claims that as a person who investigates and determines the validity of child abuse allegations generally, he is absolutely immune. Of course, the language of the statute grants immunity to a person who assists in the investigation, not in investigations generally. Gonzalez by deciding to close the Avalos case without investigation was not "a person . . . assisting in the investigation of a report." Because of that fact, we conclude that Gonzalez cannot claim immunity under Section 34.03. Point of Error No. Two is overruled.

Sovereign Immunity

In his third point of error, Gonzalez asserts that he was entitled to a summary judgment because having been sued in his official capacity, he is protected from liability by the same sovereign or governmental immunity defense available to the state. *Bagg*, 726 S.W.2d at 586.

Generally, the state as sovereign is immune from suit unless it has expressly given its consent to be sued. Moreover, even where it has given consent to be sued, the state is immune from liability. *Missouri Pacific R.R. Co. v. Brownsville Navigation Dist.*, 453 S.W.2d 812, 813 (Tex. 1970); *Dillard v. Austin Indep. Sch. Dist.*, 806 S.W.2d 589, 592 (Tex.App.–Austin 1991, writ denied). One exception to this rule is provided by the Texas Tort Claims Act (TTCA), which waives the state's immunity from suit and from liability in certain cases. Tex. Civ. Prac. and Rem. Code Ann. §§ 101.001 et seq. (Vernon 1986 and Supp. 1993). This waiver of immunity, however, is limited to the express provisions of the TTCA. *Wenzel v. City of New Braunfels,* 852 S.W.2d 97, 99 (Tex.App–Austin 1993, no writ); see *McKinney v. City of Gainesville,* 814 S.W.2d 862, 865 (Tex.App.–Fort Worth 1991, no writ).

Despite the state's waiver of its immunity under TTCA, Gonzalez urges that Section 101.026 of TTCA preserves his immunity from being sued in his official capacity. That section reads:

§ 101.026. Individual's Immunity Preserved

To the extent an employee has individual immunity from a tort claim for damages, it is not affected by this chapter.

Gonzalez interprets this provision to mean that the sovereign immunity of a state employee sued in his official capacity is retained even though the state has waived its immunity from suit and liability under the TTCA. This interpretation, however, ignores the word "individual" preceding "immunity" in the statute. Section 101.026 does not preserve sovereign immunity for a state employee sued in his official capacity; it preserves the official immunity of an employee sued in his individual capacity. See *Salcedo v. Diaz,* 647 S.W.2d 51, 53 (Tex.App.–El Paso, writ ref'd n.r.e.) (as to relevant party), 650 S.W.2d 67 (Tex.), rev'd on other grounds, 659 S.W.2d 30 (Tex. 1983) (applying Section 101.026's predecessor statute to official immunity of defendant sued in individual capacity). The reason for the rule is that a suit against a state employee in his official capacity is, in substance, a suit against the state. *Eakle,* 815 S.W.2d at 871, citing *Lowe v. Texas Tech,* 540 S.W.2d 297, 298 (Tex. 1976) (suit against a state agency is a suit against the state); see also *Edelman v. Jordan,* 415 U.S. 651, 663 (1974). As a result, the employee enjoys immunity only to the same extent that the state itself does. *Bagg,* 726 S.W.2d at 584); *Russell v. Edgewood Independent School Dist.,* 406 S.W.2d 249, 252 (Tex.Civ.App.–San Antonio 1966, writ ref'd n.r.e.). Gonzalez' interpretation of Section 101.026 would provide an employee of the state with sovereign immunity greater than the state's, even though the suit against the employee in his official capacity is considered substantially a suit against the state. No such rule exists by virtue of Section 101.026 or otherwise. An employee's immunity is equivalent to the state's, except when an employee is immune for another reason, such as official immunity. As held above, Gonzalez has no official immunity which would be preserved by Section 101.026.

Avalos pled that the TTCA waives the state's immunity from his suit, on the ground that the suit arises from Gonzalez' misuse of tangible property, i.e., the CPS intake report. Gonzalez has not argued otherwise on this appeal. . . . Because Avalos alleged that his son's death resulted from "the use, misuse, or failure to use" tangible personal property (the CPS intake report belonging to DHS), the state's immunity from the suit has been waived by the TTCA and Gonzalez is not entitled to a summary judgment based on the sovereign immunity doctrine. Point of Error No. Three is overruled.

We affirm the trial court's denial of Gonzalez' motion for summary judgment.

Concurring Opinion by Larsen

I concur with the majority opinion in this case, but write to address an impossible assignment given the appellate courts by our legislature: interlocutory review of issues involving subjective good faith.

. . .

The legislature passed this statute allowing interlocutory appeal of immunity issues to echo that available for officials sued under federal civil rights laws such as 42 U.S.C. § 1983. What the legislature has ignored, however, is that qualified immunity in federal cases (also called "good faith" immunity) is judged by an objective standard, amenable to summary disposition, while Texas law employs a subjective standard in defining official immunity. An examination of the law granting official immunity in state and federal jurisprudence makes the problem clear.

The Federal Standard

Before 1982, federal civil rights law recognized that officials could avoid liability for violating citizens' civil rights by meeting a two-pronged test, containing both subjective and objective elements, that: (1) the official held a subjective good faith belief that the challenged actions were lawful; and (2) this belief was objectively reasonable in light of the existing law. *Procunier v. Navarette,* 434 U.S. 555 (1978); *Butz v. Economou,* 438 U.S. 478 (1978); *Wood v. Strickland,* 420 U.S. 308 (1975). This test changed dramatically with the U.S. Supreme Court's decision in *Harlow v. Fitzgerald,* 457 U.S. 800 (1982). There, the Court announced a new standard which abandoned the subjective element of good faith, substituting the following:

> Government officials performing discretionary functions generally are shielded from liability for civil damages insofar as their conduct does not violate clearly established statutory or constitutional rights of which a reasonable person would have known. On summary judgment, the judge appropriately may determine, not only the currently applicable law, but whether that law was clearly established at the time an action occurred.

If the law at that time was not clearly established, an official could not reasonably be expected to anticipate subsequent legal developments, nor could he fairly be said to "know" that the law forbade conduct not previously identified as unlawful. *Until this threshold immunity question is resolved, discovery should not be allowed.* [emphasis added.] *Harlow v. Fitzgerald,* 457 U.S. at 818, 102 S. Ct. at 2738.

In 1987, the Supreme Court further refined this standard in *Anderson v. Creighton,* 483 U.S. 635 (1987), holding that even where conduct appears to have violated a clearly established constitutional principle, good faith immunity will attach where a well-trained officer would not have known that the challenged conduct violated plaintiff's rights. This refinement retained the federal court's objective focus. Thus, under federal law, the internal thought-processes and motivations of an individual defendant are not dispositive or even relevant; rather, good faith immunity is defeated upon summary judgment only where well-established law is violated, and a reasonable officer in defendant's place would have known that the actions were illegal. *Harlow,* 102 S. Ct. at 2736; *Anderson,* 483 U.S. at 647.

. . .

The legislature, in passing Tex. Civ. Prac. & Rem. Code Ann. § 51.014(5) adopted federal procedure without this accompanying federal substance.

The State Standard

Texas state law (in a doctrine analogous to federal good faith immunity) recognizes official immunity for a state employee whose status or actions may be classified as quasi-judicial, no matter how erroneous or negligent those actions may be, so long as the official acts in good faith and within the scope of authority. *Russell v. Texas Department of Human Resources,* 746 S.W.2d 510, 513 (Tex.App. 1988); *Austin v. Hale,* 711 S.W.2d 64, 66 (Tex.App.1986). It is the good faith element of this immunity which I find problematic. In contrast to the federal *Harlow* standard, Texas case law contemplates a subjective good faith standard, and characterizes unprotected conduct as that done "willfully and maliciously." *Campbell v. Jones,* 153 Tex. 101, 264 S.W.2d 425, 427 (Tex. 1954); *Russell,* 746 S.W.2d at 514; *Baker v. Story,* 621 S.W.2d 639, 644 (Tex. App.–San Antonio 1981, writ ref'd n.r.e.).

In *Travis v. City of Mesquite,* 830 S.W.2d 94, 103–04 (Tex. 1992) (Cornyn, J. concurring), Justice Cornyn noted some of the difficulties in reviewing good faith immunity under the present law. He suggested adopting the old federal standard, containing both subjective and objective elements. In formulating a good faith standard under the specific facts of Travis (which involved a high-speed car chase by off-duty police officers with a resulting collision and damages to a bystander), Justice Cornyn wrote that he would find a defendant failed to establish good faith if:

(1) the officer knows that a clear risk of harm to the public in continuing the pursuit substantially outweighs the need to immediately apprehend the suspect (the subjective element); or

(2) a reasonably prudent police officer, under the same or similar circumstances, would know that the clear risk of harm to the public in continuing the pursuit substantially outweighs the need to immediately apprehend the suspect (the objective element). *Travis*, 830 S.W.2d at 104.

Those courts which have wrestled with determining subjective good faith on interlocutory appeal of a summary judgment have, understandably, glossed over the issue: indeed, these cases commonly, and erroneously, shift the well-established burden of proof on summary judgment. Frequently they require plaintiffs to produce evidence of bad faith, rather than requiring defendants to conclusively establish their good faith motivations. *Travis*, 830 S.W.2d at 103; see *Eakle v. Texas Department of Human Services,* 815 S.W.2d 869, 876 (Tex.App.–Austin 1991, writ denied) ("The record contains no showing of bad faith on behalf of the commissioners. . . ."); *Austin v. Hale,* 711 S.W.2d 64, 68 (Tex.App.–Waco 1986, no writ) ("The record did not contain any evidence that [defendants] had acted in bad faith when they conducted the investigation."). This awkward solution, in my opinion, has the undesirable effect of simply eliminating the good faith element of official immunity. Neither trial courts nor courts of appeals can, nor should we be asked to, perform the task set for us here: to determine a defendant's state of mind, whether good or bad, on summary judgment or on interlocutory appeal from its denial.

Procedure Is Incompatible with Standard

The legislature has grafted federal procedure for reviewing official immunity onto an incongruous body of substantive law. Internal motivation and state of mind, upon which subjective good faith determinations turn, are peculiarly fact-dependent. More than other findings, they depend upon assessment of credibility, surrounding circumstances and demeanor, all things which summary judgment and interlocutory appeal cannot measure. Although we did not reach the good faith element of defendant's official immunity claim here, I write to point out the antagonistic relationship between procedure and substance here.

Conclusion

Appellate courts cannot ascertain an official's subjective good faith on interlocutory appeal from summary judgment. Federal courts have never been required to do so: they adopted simultaneously an objective standard and a procedure for early, summary review of immunity questions. I believe our adoption of federal procedure, without altering the substance of official immunity, effectively eliminates an essential element of that defense. I cannot think this is an outcome either the Texas Legislature or the Texas courts contemplated. I urge both to examine it.

Discussion Questions

1. Discuss how tort actions compare to government enforcement of statutes and regulations.
2. Discuss how tort law includes consideration of duty, fault, and other moral concepts. Are these appropriate concepts for substantive law?
3. Discuss the situation where government attorneys use tort actions to enforce standards. What are some of the public policy concerns that occur when government attorneys use common law as compared to statutory authority for enforcement actions?
4. What were the historic reasons for sovereign immunity? What are current policy considerations for providing immunity to government or to limit the liability of government for torts?
5. What are the five alternatives to tort? Discuss the strengths and weaknesses of these alternatives to tort liability.
6. If a judgment is entered against an administrator for a constitutional tort, that administrator can be personally liable, meaning that they must pay the damage awards from their own assets. How does this responsibility affect how administrators carry out their jobs?
7. State entities such as hospitals and universities are government actors for tort purposes. In the *Schiffman* case, how do normal practices of competitive soccer or NCAA standards affect what a coach or athletic director decides regarding calling off a game because of bad field conditions? Does the doctrine of assumption of risk affect individual or government responsibilities in other situations?
8. There are statutory duties and statutory grounds for immunity that exist. What are the key considerations regarding mandatory or discretionary duties that are discussed in the *Gonzales* case?
9. What is the difference between official and individual capacity? Of the three types of immunity that are considered in the *Gonzales* case, which are appropriate to apply to public administrators?

9

Dynamic Public
Administration and Law

This book has shown that public managers must understand the constitutional framework and doctrines as they implement legislative policy and respect judicial decisions. Administration and governance involves good decision-making built on both delegated and discretionary authority. It involves providing fair and accountable public services. Earlier chapters provided a general overview of the following areas of substantive law: constitutional law, administrative law, property law, contract law, and tort law. However, many aspects of legal interpretation and application depend upon the type of agency, the government activity, or the particular situation.

Although law is often associated with adversarial practice and court review, this is not the only way law affects administrators. Public managers must act within the bounds of legality and respect the constitutional rights of individuals. Legality is defined as "a process that encompasses the diffusion of legalistic reasoning, procedures, and structures."[1] Litigation and conflict are often the most visible involvement of law in public administration, and conflicts are often emphasized over routine practices. Even if many aspects of administration will never be challenged in a court case or become the subject of public discussion, administrators should apply public law in these situations. That is, public law values and practices should be incorporated and institutionalized as normal governance.

There are a number concerns about public management and law that remain to be addressed in this chapter. The following sections consider society's governing mechanism, obtaining specific legal knowledge, common criticisms of law and government, and seeking changes through democratic processes. The final section concludes by linking dynamic administration to governance and law.

Governing Mechanisms

This book emphasizes how law is an important and indispensable part of public management and governance. But law is a *part* of administration. Laws are not the only consideration, and they may not be the first consideration for administrators in making decisions or carrying out their governmental responsibilities. Government would not exist without law and law is important in society, but law is one of a number of social-control mechanisms.

Societies have a number of governing mechanisms that are used to encourage preferred organizational goals, community practices, or individual behaviors. The legal scholar and theorist Peter Schuck considered three major social-control mechanisms: social norms, competitive markets, and law.[2] All these mechanisms affect public management.

Schuck begins by considering the broad category of social norms. "*Social norms*—the shared beliefs, common practices, and mutual expectations among members of a group—are modes of social ordering, in all collectivities, including states, families, and friendships."[3] These social norms shape individual behavior and their strength often depends on factors such as status, reputation, shame, or approval. The government's ability to change social norms through laws or mandates, such as prohibiting segregation or prohibiting employment discrimination based on gender, is difficult to achieve and perhaps impossible. Shuck also notes that social norms develop slowly, that different groups may have different norms, and that some norms may be very slow to change. Finally, Schuck notes that social norms may have little effect on some individuals or businesses

Public administration studies of organization theory and ethics discuss the importance of norms and relationships. There are many examples of studies of public and private organizations and norms. Here are three examples of well-respected scholarship. How group membership affects an individual factory worker's effort was demonstrated in the Hawthorne Studies, beginning in the mid 1920s, that were published in 1941.[4] In the public sector, Herbert Kaufman's research on administrative behavior in the Forest Service was published in 1960,[5] and Rosemary O'Leary recently, in 2002, analyzed environmental agencies and dissent.[6] Other studies also consider how the norms of an agency or community affect accomplishing organizational goals. In the study of public-sector ethics, the debate between institutional rules and professional norms as sources of responsibility and accountability began with the seminal 1940s debate between administrative scholars Carl Friedrich and Herman Finer.[7] Many current theorists also discuss constitutional values, statutory mandates, and delegations as part of public-sector ethics.[8]

Schuck's second category is market influences. "*Markets* are systems of voluntary exchanges through which people buy and sell goods (broadly defined) that they value."[9] Markets may be formal or informal exchanges; markets are considered in the context of economic theory that incorporates the purpose of trade and exchange to make the individuals involved better off.

Markets emphasize consensual, competitive, and informed exchanges. Market controls are most closely associated with business practices. Businesses have developed patterns of interaction and trade that are based on relationships or common practices. Businesses have integrated common law rules, particularly contracting, into market practices. But Schuck notes that market mechanisms are known for favoring the larger and powerful entities over the infrequent or individual participant.[10]

Despite that fact, the market is often considered an ideal situation of free exchange between individuals with equal bargaining power. Although it is common to equate business and government, often the desire is for government to run like a reasonable, efficient, and responsible business.[11] There are many differences between businesses and government; the most important is the Constitution.[12] Businesses are allowed to take risks in order to make money. Businesses and the market do not have to consider the effect of their actions on the general public or future generations, but public servants must.

Schuck presents *law* as the third type of social control, and he says law competes with social norms and market controls.[13] In his discussion of law, including both public and private law, Shuck explains how law is a dominant factor in American society for establishing rights between private parties, for regulating behaviors, and for defining priorities and interests. Schuck notes that law affects relationships between individuals and that private enforcement using law is part of this area of social control. Schuck notes that the three forms of social control reinforce each other and are intermingled in action. Finally, Schuck notes that the threat of government enforcement, punishment, or criminal charges, like the other types of social controls, has its strengths and weaknesses.

Some implications from Schuck's comments are that even though laws are not just imposed or used by government, they affect social norms and business exchanges. In addition, in considering these social controls, it is worth emphasizing that public law in the form of statutes, regulations, benefits, or taxes encompasses a wide array of techniques to affect the community, but American law depends first on voluntary compliance by the population and then on legal enforcement through individual or governmental action. Finally, public managers use a number of techniques and tools in administering policies and programs. Established administrative practices vary and may look like norms or market devices such as providing incentives, information, education, contracts, or grants, more than they look like regulations, enforcement, or litigation. Often commentators, theorists, and politicians provide suggestions for change, innovation, and reforms to achieve public objectives.[14] Administrative practices involve many types of established mechanisms, as well as seeking and developing improved tools and practices.

Gaining Specific Legal Knowledge

In addition to understanding the overview of public law that affects them, administrators may need more specific legal knowledge. The legal information that is generalized in law often emphasizes constitutional and judicial process; these are important fundamentals that administrators need to know. Earlier chapters addressed different management techniques, approaches, and controls that generally apply to public administrators. However, the particulars of an administrator's duties within a particular agency are much more focused and specific. Lawyers call the specialized law that affects one area "substantive law." Consider how different child dependency and neglect practices are from environmental law, or how the practices of a state health inspector of restaurants, differs from those of federal securities regulators. There is specialized substantive law in each of these areas. Administrators must learn and apply the substantive law for their specialization.

In many agencies, substantive law components are thoroughly integrated and infused into the standard routines. In the example of emergency management, state and local emergency-management agencies develop response plans as encouraged by federal law through guidance documents and as required to be eligible for federal grants.[15] These plans are followed, and they are beginning points for the operational elements to manage responses to different types of emergencies. For other agencies, there may be specific manuals issued that provide up-to-date guidance on legal authority in statutes, regulations, and court decrees that affect administrative actions. Administrators learn the particular substantive legal requirements on the job through new-employee orientation, regular training, and continuing education. Developing and maintaining legal knowledge is essential to administrative competence.

Administrators are not expected to be legal experts, but they are expected to know the law that applies to them and to do this they often need to work with their legal advisors. Managers receive advice from their attorneys. This may be part of a regular practice or a response to a problem. Changes in law or requirements should generate legal advice from the lawyer to the agency. In addition, agencies and officers often request opinions from their council, and sometimes these opinions are collected and available for evaluation. This is true when the Attorney Generals Offices' for states and the United States answer legal questions and issue opinions. These Attorney General opinions are collected and published, and now they are often available online. In addition to managers discussing with legal counsel problems or potential lawsuits, managers and their legal counsel may offer day-to-day considerations or recommend the agency seek legal opinions.

As Doyle Buckwalter and Ivan Legler explain, the way a lawyer or public administrator may consider a problem differs.[16] There are different professional norms and emphases. Public lawyers have subject matter expertise and professional training in law. Legal counsel provides legal research and advice on specific situations; litigators represent government agencies in court, and they often want to win their case. Managers are more focused on accomplishing goals and improving everyday operations.

Buckwalter and Legler emphasize that, despite distinct professional specialization and emphasis, public administrators and legal counsel must work together. They point out that administrators need to understand that legal advice takes time to produce because it involves research and analysis of relevant legal authority that relates to a particular problem. In other words, legal advice is specific to facts and circumstances of a situation. Often lawyers provide narrow opinions based on legal interpretations, rather than give managers general advice about governing. Buckwalter and Legler recommend that administrators should ask lawyers to consider the *what* and *how* of the tasks that administrators seek to accomplish, rather than asking if something is legal. In response, legal counsel needs to provide opinions on how the agency may reach their goals without incurring legal problems.[17]

Other resources exist for administrators who wish to keep up-to-date on law. Professional associations, such as a state municipal league, may provide synopses or updates on important legislation or court decisions. However, managers need to realize that what may affect them about a new law or a recent appellate decision may be different than what an association may summarize.

Public Perceptions and Administrative Practices

It is easy to gripe about laws and government. People's perceptions about administrative practice, legislative actions, and court decrees may be presented as comments or criticisms; some of these are resentments, discontent, or complaints. Because it is common to criticize public administrators and what they do, this is called "bureaucrat bashing." However, the ability to discuss and complain about laws, governing, and administration is part of the democratic fabric. This section considers some common public complaints and discusses how these relate to administrative practice.

First, a common assertion of critics conflates law with bureaucracy, and concludes that law is static, inflexible, and mechanistic. Law is not static or inflexible, although it may be presented this way as a starting point for critique. "Sometimes there is a tendency for those outside the legal system to view the law in mechanistic terms, as consisting of rigid and self-evident rules, which leave little room for interpretation or for blending with the very factual circumstances that arise. The legal realist [scholars], however, have demonstrated that legal rules are not so inflexible, but there is discretion in the formulation and application, that [decisionmakers] can take account of human features of a dispute."[18] As this book has shown, public law is not automatic or inflexible. In their work, public managers have to be sophisticated in their interpretation and application of law. They have to take into account both existing laws and rules and the human features of public services.

Second, sometimes a law is presented as weird or strange in news stories. This was the case in 1983, when water in the Great Salt Lake reached historic high levels and was flooding over parks, wildlife refuges, farmland, and roads. The water threatened businesses and major highways. In fact, this flooding was due to natural causes because a large winter snowfall had made a large snow pack in the mountains and as that melted in early summer there was also greater than normal rainfall. The lake was at a historic high, with the "largest seasonal rise since the nineteenth century."[19] The Great Salt Lake does not have any streams or outlets where water flows out; evaporation is the normal way that the lake levels recede. Although the Utah Department of Natural Resources and Energy was monitoring the rising waters and it was developing engineering plans to divert the water, public administrators projected that they could not act in time to prevent damage to the businesses and highways. This was a crisis. The legislature responded by passing a law setting the lawful height of the lake, and within days the lake became "the biggest lawbreaker" as the water exceeded the established height.[20] This law was presented in the news as weird, nonsense, or merely symbolic.[21]

Symbolic laws are laws that do not contain enforcement provisions, and they are often called "toothless." Toothless laws have no real power and effect, like an old toothless guard dog. The idea of a symbolic law also means that the legislature needs to do something to demonstrate the seriousness of the situation. Even if this lake-height law was merely symbolic, there was a public problem that the legislature, governor, and public managers were working on to protect the public. That is, although this law was not enforceable in court, it still was important to Utah citizens and public managers as a statement of policy.

Third, administrators may have more knowledge or information than newspaper reporters or the general public. The information presented in a news story may not tell the whole story. There may be alternate explanations and valid reasons for legislation and government actions that are not readily apparent. It is possible there were other reasons for Utah to pass legislation about the height of the lake and to retain that law until this day. One plausible but not verified reason for a law establishing the height of a lake is that for citizens, businesses, or governments to be eligible for federal flood or disaster relief, the lake must be at flood stage—above the normal limits. Whether there were any other reasons for the lake water-level statute was not included in the press reports. The context and details of how laws are applied in normal governing operations are part of the specialized expertise and experiences of administrators. Administrators may need to share this information with affected individuals.

Fourth, public administration and law may not be clear to the public. Sometimes the lack of clarity is because of the technical or specialized language. Although there have been repeated pleas to write laws in plain English, legislation, regulation, and court cases all involve technical jargon that administrators learn but may not be easily comprehended by the public. In addition, as explained in the previous paragraph, administrators involved in the situation may have a better understanding of the reasons why a particular process or rule is adopted. Public administrators often must explain to the affected individuals the meaning of laws, rules, and practices.

Fifth, a very common theme in commentators' discussions about law and administration is that laws interfere, laws stifle, or laws constrain. There is a good law-bad law aspect to these discussions. "Bad laws" interfere with what an individual wants to do. This type of opinion may be included in the media or in day-to-day conversations. There may be a general resentment for laws and administrative procedure that affect individuals. For instance, people dislike filing taxes or standing in line to renew driver's licenses. People complain about the paperwork and the steps to determine eligibility for government benefits. "Red tape" is the common term used for the public law, rules, regulations, and procedures that government applies. Red tape is often shorthand for government interference or bureaucracy; it is normally a negative phrase. However, as Herbert Kaufman said: "One person's red tape may be another's treasured safeguard."[22] People may want to be "liberated" from legal requirements or consequences, but some procedures are required by constitutional law decisions or by statutes. Administrators can evaluate whether the laws are still appropriate and if the procedures used are necessary. Then, administrators can take action and seek changes to reduce red tape.

Sixth, administrators are criticized when they enforce the laws or do their jobs properly. For instance, a newspaper reported how a fourteen-year-old boy was fired by a minor league team because the U.S. Department of Labor told the team that the batboy's employment violated child labor laws. The child labor laws stated that "14- and 15-year olds must not work past 7 on school nights or 9 during the summer."[23] The article accused an "insensitive bureaucrat" of limiting the kid's work options. Public administrators in the department of labor were criticized by the Labor Secretary who issued a statement that "termed the application of labor-laws to batboys 'silly.'" [24]

The public attention and outcry lead to internal governmental criticism of how these administrators did their job and this led to an agency review of the labor laws it was tasked to enforce. The article did not consider the history of exploitation of child labor. Also absent from the news was the analysis the agency conducted to reach a decision. The agency considered the child's age, the number of hours worked in week, the hours worked in a day, and how late the child worked in the night game. For administrators, being criticized for doing a job as required and with competence can be demoralizing, but this is part of democracy in action.

It is unusual for commentators or news reports to focus on administrators doing their jobs well. Public attention is typically pointed toward allegations of improper or excessive government action. In short, common assertions are that there are government problems. However, these assertions can lead to reviews of processes, rules, and laws. Public attention to perceived problems is feedback, and this public feedback is an important part of democratic government. It often generates review of governmental policies, and sometimes it generates revision of public policy.

Finally, many of the complaints about law or government have merit. Some of the complaints are thoughtful and detailed based on evidence and analysis. Some complaints reflect frustration or misunderstanding about administrative practices. Other comments or complaints may reflect political or ideological positions and debates. Unfortunately, some of the citizen complaints are posited as conclusions or common knowledge. That is, rather than the complaint being a starting point for a discussion or debate, the complaints are taken as givens and as immutable; the statement may be overinclusive, underinclusive, or just false. But administrators need to listen to the stories, problems, and complaints of citizens and see if the agency can address the individuals' concerns. Public administrators and elected officials must consider actions to address serious disparities and systematic unfairness. As part of normal operations, administrators and agencies must consider the substance of complaints.

Seek Change Through Democratic Process

Sometimes public managers may find the laws they work with and that affect them to be obsolete, undesirable, or outmoded. The agencies may find public complaints about their government to be valid and in need of attention. At other times, statutes, regulations, and court decrees that affect administrative practices and procedures may be contradictory or limit the agency's effectiveness. There are also situations where administrators lack clear authority or where there are contradictory mandates. The question becomes: What can public administrators do to address problems with laws that are obsolete, incomplete, undesirable, or unclear?

Agencies and administrators interpret laws, but there are many occasions where the law is either unsettled, unclear, or subject to alternative interpretations. In these situations, agencies should advance a reasonable interpretation. At other times, a shift in policy interpretation follows elections or a shift in political preferences. That is, reforms are proposed and developed outside the agency or the reforms are new policy interpretations of existing authority. During elections, bureaucrats are often criticized as inefficient or self-interested, and often systematic reforms are recommended to fix the government. Some systematic reforms are related to political goals, such as proposing a smaller government or more executive power.

Agencies and administrators can take action when law or procedures are undesirable, contradictory, unjust, or outdated. Agencies and administrators should work within the democratic processes to seek change. There are four valid approaches administrators can take if current practices and legal authority are in conflict.

First, administrators can comply with the express language and common understanding of the statutes. Following the express language is called "following the letter of the law," and following the intent or purpose of the law is "following the spirit of the law."

The second approach applies when there is room for interpretation—for example, when the law is unsettled or unclear—then agencies can develop and apply new interpretations that are within the bounds of delegated administrative powers.

The third approach is to use the adversarial and appellate process to challenge existing precedent or to advocate for new interpretations; that is, administrative agencies use the court process to develop legal doctrine.

The fourth approach is to seek legislative action to change the statutory language. Legislative approval can be obtained to permit innovation, to allow creative administrative practices, or to develop pilot projects. Seeking authoritative court decisions or seeking legislative actions can take considerable time and persuasive powers. But both are part of the established democratic and participatory practices to change governmental authority. In short, the time and effort to work within the system to change the laws demonstrates democratic values in action.

Administrators can act within democratic processes to interpret and change their responsibilities and authority. An example of how this may include different or combined approaches occurred in the *Federated Distributors v. Johnson* case that is included in Chapter 3. In this case the Department of Revenue had to choose between two tax classifications for the "new product," a juice-based drink that had alcohol in it. The agency chose the more literal definition, based on the specific type of spirits included in the drink, but they also considered using the definition based on how the "new product" compared to wine coolers. That is, the agency used its discretion to evaluate and assess the tax.

The *Federated Distributors* case, like most presented in this text, originated when an affected party, business, or individual challenged government action through the courts. When Federated sued and then appealed the court's ruling, the agency presented its arguments. However, when the agency's interpretation was rejected by the Illinois Court of Appeals, the agency then pursued an appeal to the Illinois Supreme Court. These were steps within the democratic process of litigation to challenge or defend agency interpretations. The agency did not entirely prevail because the Supreme Court reversed in part and affirmed in part. The Court affirmed that the legislative classifications violated the state Constitution, but it also found that wine and wine coolers should not be taxed at the same rate.

Legislative action was also an option in *Federated Distributors v. Johnson*. Although the published cases do not address this point, it is likely that public administrators in this case or in a similar situation to the one in *Federated Distributors v. Johnson* would seek legislative action to clarify the gap in tax categories for juice-alcohol mixed drinks. There are a number of possible points where the difficulties in the statutory scheme might be conveyed to the legislative committee responsible for taxes. These include when Federated submitted new products for tax classification, when Federated sued, or when the Illinois Appellate or Supreme Courts issued their decisions. Finally, the Supreme Court also noted that determination of tax levels, consistent with state constitutional limits, was the legislature's responsibility. Here the court indicated what branch has the ability to correct ambiguities or constitutional flaws in statutes.

Finally, there are some things administrators should not do when they face statutes and court cases that prohibit a manager from acting as they would prefer. Administrators should not ignore or circumvent the law. Some commentators suggest that public managers should merely ignore "bad laws," or ignore laws that are hassles. Some "entrepreneurial government" advocates suggest that public managers should focus on their goals even if this meant "circumventing or subverting political and institutional obstacles."[25] These two suggestions are wrong; they violate the public administrator's duty to act in accordance to the law; they show disrespect for the democratic process; and they undermine the legitimacy of all government actions.

Acting in disregard for the clear language and intent of a law also subjects the individual administrator and government to lawsuits and liability for improper actions. Ignoring laws and breaking laws has led to corruption charges, scandals, and criminal convictions. As the Supreme Court said, "No man in this country is so high that he is above the law. No officer of the law may [defy the law] with impunity. All the officers of government, from the highest to the lowest, are creatures of the law, and are bound to obey it."[26]

Dynamic Public Administration

Public administration is dynamic. It is active. It is powerful. It requires continuous productive activity. Public administration involves not just rules or goals but the government activities needed to achieve them. It is dynamic because policies, priorities, and practices change. As the public administration scholar Marshall Dimock has argued, public administration is much more dynamic than law.[27] Governance, the exercise of public authority, requires managers and the public to be involved in public affairs. Administrative involvement in governance is active and it is infused with public law.

What this book has demonstrated is that public law requires public administrators to make good decisions. Public law imposes rational deliberation and due process in administrative decision-making. Decision-making in dynamic public administration involves principled pragmatism.[28] The idea of pragmatic decision-making, based on evaluating the standards, the evidence, and the situation while considering the community interest, was an attribute of democratic statesmanship that Philip Selznick discussed. Selznick is a well-respected scholar and theorist of democratic administration. He said, "In the philosophy of pragmatism all policy-making, indeed all of life, should reflect informed awareness of what is worth having, doing and being. Pragmatism is not a flight from principle. It is an argument for discovering principles and making them relevant to everyday life."[29]

Administrative decisions involve a principled pragmatism that incorporates constitutional structure and values with statutory authority and policy goals. An important part of administrative discretion is at the point when agencies select what actions to emphasize and enforce. Discretionary decisions must include consideration of what is worth doing and why it is relevant to the public welfare.

Principled pragmatism also exists in the administrative-decision process, which emphasizes reasoned consideration based on laws, rules, and evidence. Administrative decision-making now incorporates due process values that require public managers to enunciate the problem, and evaluate the relevant laws and evidence, and to be able to articulate reasons for their actions. These steps may take time and effort, but they provide transparency and accountability. Good administrative decision-making accomplishes constitutional values.

Balancing the dynamics of administration with public law is part of the administrator's craft. There are numerous points where administrative discretion and interpretation are exercised. When public managers evaluate a particular problem, they must understand that problem and how it fits within the agency's mission, political preferences, executive goals, and public interest, and, public managers must recognize and respect the limits of their legal authority as an integral part of this evaluation. Dynamic administration must also consider the present and future as agencies seek to accomplish public goals.

Public administration, governance, and public law exist to serve the citizens. In this endeavor, public managers have to consider constitutional and democratic values as they seek to accomplish the public policies and responsibilities entrusted to them.

Case

Government responsibility and legal liability can be two different concepts. For federal civil rights liability under 42 U.S. C. § 1983, there must be state action and whether there is state action is the first question in the final case, *Jones v. City of Carlisle.*[30] In this case, the court must consider issues about individual versus government responsibilities and questions about the government's duties to protect the public. This case also raises some interesting considerations about what happens when administrators make seemingly benign discretionary decisions to not enforce the law. Finally, when the government is not found liable for damages in a court case, it does not always address whether the government took the appropriate action. This case raises the problem of the appropriate venue to remedy management problems.

James Ricky Jones and Vera Jones, et al. v. City of Carlisle, et al.,
3 F.3d 945, U.S. Court of Appeals for the Sixth Circuit, 1993

Opinion by Dowd.

I.

The appellants, James Ricky Jones (hereafter "Mr. Jones") and his wife Vera Jones (hereafter collectively "the Joneses") challenge the district court's dismissal of their action brought against the City of Carlisle, Kentucky (hereafter "the City") under 42 U.S.C. § 1983. The Joneses also challenge the district court's remand to state court of their claim against defendant Preferred Risk Mutual Insurance Company (hereafter "Preferred Risk") for declaratory relief.

The Joneses claim that the appellee City of Carlisle is liable pursuant to

§ 1983 for money damages for the physical injuries Mr. Jones suffered in the November 13, 1990 automobile accident cause by Mark Byrd (hereafter "Byrd"), a private citizen of Kentucky. The Joneses also seek a declaration from the court that they are entitled to $100,000 on Mr. Jones' underinsured motorist policy.

The Joneses allege that the City incurred § 1983 liability for Mr. Jones' injuries when it allowed Byrd, a known epileptic prone to uncontrollable seizures, to maintain a driver's license. The Joneses also challenge Preferred Risk's position that under the terms of the underinsured motorist policy, it does not incur liability until after the policy holder obtains a judgment against the tort-feasor and the tort-feasor's insurance is insufficient to cover the insured's judgment.

The district court dismissed the § 1983 claim against the City for failure to state a cause of action under Fed. R. Civ. P. 12(b)(6). The district court found that Byrd was not acting as the agent of the City at the time of the accident, and that Mr. Jones, as distinguished from the public at large, was not placed in special danger as the result of the City's inaction and Byrd's continued activity. Further, the district court found that no special relationship existed between the City and Mr. Jones nor between Byrd and Mr. Jones which would impose upon the City a duty of care owed to Mr. Jones. The district court remanded the Joneses' declaratory judgment claim against Preferred Risk to Nicholas County, Kentucky.

II.

. . .

The complaint alleges that Mark Byrd is an epileptic who has suffered from an uncontrolled seizure disorder since birth. In 1983, Kentucky issued Byrd a driver's license. Between 1983 and 1987, Byrd was involved in at least seven automobile accidents in the City of Carlisle. Each accident was allegedly caused by Byrd experiencing a seizure while driving, and each accident resulted in either property damage, personal injury, or both. The City police investigated each accident; however, no accident report was ever filed. No citation was ever issued and no law enforcement action was ever taken against Byrd.

In the accident involving Mr. Jones, Byrd, as in his other accidents, was operating a motor vehicle when he experienced an epileptic seizure. He lost control of his vehicle, crossed over the center line into the oncoming lane of traffic, and struck head-on the motor vehicle operated by Mr. Jones, who was severely and permanently injured. Byrd was never cited and no law enforcement action was taken against him as a result of this accident.

A. Section 1983 Analysis

The Joneses bring the present lawsuit claiming that the City was aware that Byrd presented a danger to motorists but took no action to revoke his driver's license. Under Kentucky statutes, law enforcement officials are required to file with the Department of State Police a written report of any motor vehicle accident resulting in personal injury or property damage. Ky. Rev. Stat. § 189.635(3). This report must also be submitted to the Kentucky State Police. Ky. Rev. Stat. § 189.635. Further, Kentucky will suspend the license of a driver upon notice from law enforcement officials that the driver is subject to epileptic seizures. 601 Ky. Admin. Regs. 13:010.

The Joneses advance three claims under 42 U.S.C. § 1983 against the City. First, they claim that it was the policy of the City both to fail to report accidents involving individuals suffering from epileptic seizures and to allow Byrd, a known epileptic prone to seizures, to maintain a driver's license and operate a motor vehicle. Second, the Joneses claim that the City's failure to train and supervise its police has caused the City Police to be inadequate to the tasks performed by them, especially as concerns the duty of the police officer as regards unfit and unsafe operators of motor vehicles. This failure to train, the Joneses allege, also results in § 1983 liability attaching to the City. Third, the Joneses claim that Mr. Jones, as a citizen of the United States and of Kentucky, is entitled to the protection of the laws of both, and that the City's actions, policies, or customs deprived Mr. Jones of this entitlement. The Joneses argue that, absent these policies, individual officers would have reported the prior accidents as required under state law, Byrd's license would have been revoked, and the accident involving Mr. Jones would never have occurred.

The Due Process Clause of the Fourteenth Amendment provides that "no State shall deprive any person of life, liberty, or property, without due process of law." However, the Due Process Clause does not "protect the life, liberty, and property of its citizens against invasion by private actors. The Clause is phrased as a limitation on the State's power to act, not as a guarantee of certain minimal levels of safety and security." *DeShaney v. Winnebago County Soc. Serv. Dept.*, 489 U.S. 189, 195 (1988).

In *DeShaney*, a mother and her son brought suit against a county agency claiming that it was responsible for the brutal beating the son received at the hands of his father. After a divorce, the court had awarded custody of the boy to his father. On numerous occasions, the boy was brought to the emergency room with injuries that suggested child abuse. Further, the defendant agency was made aware of these suspicious injuries. Nonetheless, the agency took no steps to protect the boy from his abusive father. The child was eventually beaten so severely by his father that he suffered permanent brain damage.

The Court held that the defendant agency did not violate the son's due process rights because the boy's injuries were caused by a private actor, and that the agency had no control over the father. The Court noted that the agency did not cause the injuries and there was no special relationship between the boy and the agency or between the father and the agency which would trigger an obligation to take affirmative action to prevent future abuse. According to the DeShaney Court, the fact that the defendant agency was aware of the potential danger was not sufficient to impose a duty to act.

In the earlier case of *Martinez v. California*, 444 U.S. 277 (1980), the Court held that the state officials were not liable when a parolee murdered a fifteen year old girl. The Court found that the officials did not cause the crime, that the parolee was not acting as an agent of the state, and that the victim did not face any special danger apart from the rest of society.

The Sixth Circuit has also applied the analysis employed in *DeShaney*. In *Janan v. Trammell*, 785 F.2d 557 (6th Cir. 1986), a case filed two years prior to *DeShaney*, a boy was murdered by a parolee. The boy's family brought suit against the Parole Board claiming that it was aware of the parolee's dangerous propensities and had a duty to protect society from him. The court held for the Parole Board, finding no duty to protect the victim from the parolee. The court first noted that the parolee was not a state officer acting under color of state law. The court then announced the rule to be applied in the Sixth Circuit regarding injuries suffered and damages incurred at the hands of private actors: "The proper analysis is whether a special relationship exists between the criminal and the victim or between the victim and the state or whether there is some showing that the victim, as distinguished from the public at large, faces a special danger by the parolee's release. In so holding, we follow other circuits that have held that absent a special relationship between the criminal and the victim or the victim and the state, no due process violation can occur." Id. at 560 (citations omitted). See also *Cornelius v. Town of Highland Lake, ALA,* 880 F.2d 348 (11th Cir. 1989).

A due process violation was found in *Nishiyama v. Dickson County, Tenn.,* 814 F.2d 277 (6th Cir. 1987), where a county prisoner was entrusted with a patrol car for his private use, absent any supervision. While driving the police car, the prisoner used the flashing blue light to pull over the decedent's car and then beat her to death. At trial, it was determined that it was the policy of the Sheriff's Department to allow the prisoner to drive the car unsupervised. It was also determined that the Sheriff was aware that the prisoner had been using the patrol car to pull motorists off the road for several hours before the victim was killed but did nothing to stop this conduct.

The court found a special relationship between the defendant Sheriff's Department and the prisoner, as the prisoner was being held in custody, albeit with substantial privileges. Further, the court noted that, unlike *Martinez* and *Janan*, the defendants put into motion the actions which eventually caused the victim's death. The court observed that "the officers gave [the prisoner] the car *and* the freedom to commit the crime." Id. at 281 (emphasis in original).

Unlike the defendant in *Nishiyama*, the City of Carlisle did not cause plaintiff's injuries; the injuries were caused by Byrd, a private individual. Byrd was not acting as the agent of the City, nor was there a special relationship between the City and Byrd or between the City and Mr. Jones. Further, while Byrd was a definite danger behind the wheel of a motor vehicle, he was no more a danger to Mr. Jones than to any other citizen on the City streets. Finding that the Joneses have failed to establish a special relationship required to invoke the due process protection of the Fourteenth Amendment, the district court was correct in granting the City's motion to dismiss the Joneses' § 1983 claim based on an alleged policy of not submitting accident reports in cases involving epileptic seizures.

In support of their claim of failure to train, the Joneses cite *Canton v. Harris,* 489 U.S. 378 (1989). In *Harris*, police officers failed to provide the plaintiff with medical attention once she was taken into custody. The Court found a due process violation because of the special relationship that the plaintiff and the city had based upon the custody of the plaintiff. However, the Court noted that "a municipality can be liable under § 1983 [for a failure to train] only where its policies are the 'moving force [behind] the constitutional violation.'" Id. at 389 (citation omitted).

As the district court held, the Joneses' reliance on *Harris* is misplaced. It is true that the Supreme Court in *Harris* held that a municipality may be liable under § 1983 for failure to train or supervise law enforcement officials where such failure constitutes "deliberate indifference" to the rights of an individual. However, the analysis of a § 1983 failure to train claim does not stop there. As the *Harris* Court noted, to prevail, a § 1983 plaintiff must demonstrate that the policy "actually caused injury." Id. at 390. In *Harris*, the plaintiff suffered injury at the hands of a state actor. In contrast, Mr. Jones' injuries were caused by a private actor. While the City did nothing to prevent Byrd from driving, this inaction was not the "moving force" behind Mr. Jones' injuries. His injuries were directly caused by the epileptic seizure Byrd experienced while he was operating his vehicle. As a result, the Joneses' § 1983 claim of failure to train or supervise was appropriately dismissed by the district court.

The district court also appropriately dismissed the Joneses' "entitlement" claim against the City. This claim that Mr. Jones was entitled to the protection of the laws of the United States and Kentucky represents nothing more than a "failure to protect" claim under the Fourteenth Amendment. As previously noted, the *DeShaney* Court definitively held that while the Due Process Clause of the Fourteenth Amendment prevents a State from depriving individuals of life, liberty, or property without due process of law, it does not impose upon the State an affirmative obligation to protect private individuals from the conduct of other private citizens. *DeShaney*, supra at 195.

As the *DeShaney* Court observed, this type of § 1983 analysis often renders harsh results, especially when innocent individuals suffer injuries while local governments stand idly by. *DeShaney*, supra at 203. However, this Court, like the *DeShaney* Court, is unable to extend the reach of the Due Process Clause of the Fourteenth Amendment to cover common law tort actions between private citizens.

B. Declaratory Judgment Analysis

. . .

The declaratory judgment action against Preferred Risk was originally filed in district court. It was consequently improper for the district court to remand it to a state court. Therefore, the Joneses' declaratory judgment action is remanded to the district court for entry of an order of dismissal without prejudice.

III. Conclusion

For the reasons stated above, the judgment of the district court is Affirmed in Part and Remanded in Part for entry of an order consistent with this opinion

Discussion Questions

1. How do the social-control attributes of social norms and market exchange affect public administration?
2. Discuss how public managers can respond to public criticisms about silly laws or unclear processes.
3. What are the four ways public managers can seek changes to laws, rules, and court decisions?
4. What is dynamic public administration, and how is it related to good administrative decision-making?
5. In *Jones v. Carlisle,* the court considered whether a pattern of police behavior was a city policy. Discuss the strengths and weaknesses of considering a pattern of behavior an agency policy. Although the City may not have been held legally liable, consider what other processes exist to hold the city accountable for its failure to enforce the law.

Notes

Notes to Chapter 1

1. Janet V. Denhardt and Robert B. Denhardt, *The New Public Service: Serving, Not Steering,* expanded ed. (Armonk, NY: M.E. Sharpe, 2007), 86.

2. Julia Beckett, "Five Great Issues in Public Law and Public Administration." In *Handbook of Public Administration,* 3rd ed., ed. Jack Rabin, W. Bartley Hildreth, and Gerald J. Miller (New York: Taylor and Francis, 2006), 697–719.

3. David H. Rosenbloom and Rosemary O'Leary, *Public Administration and Law,* 2nd ed. (New York: Marcel Dekker, 1997); Ronald C. Moe and Robert S. Gilmour, "Rediscovering Principles of Public Administration: The Neglected Foundations of Public Law," *Public Administration Review* 55 (1995): 135–146.

4. John A. Rohr, *To Run a Constitution: The Legitimacy of the Administrative State* (Lawrence: University of Kansas Press, 1986); Gary L. Wamsley, Robert N. Backer, Charles T. Goodsell, Philip S. Kronenberg, John A. Rohr, Camilla M. Stivers, Orion F. White, and James F. Wolf, *Refounding Public Administration* (Newbury Park, CA: Sage, 1990); Gary L. Wamsley and James F. Wolf, *Refounding Democratic Public Administration: Modern Paradoxes, Postmodern Challenges* (Thousand Oaks, CA: Sage, 1996).

5. Phillip J. Cooper and Chester A. Newland, eds., *Handbook of Public Law and Administration* (San Francisco: Jossey-Bass, 1997); Charles Wise and Rosemary O'Leary, "Is Federalism Dead or Alive in the Supreme Court? Implications for Public Administrators," *Public Administration Review* 52 (1992): 559–572.

6. Alexander Hamilton, James Madison, and John Jay, *The Federalist* (New York: Barnes & Noble Books, 2006); Many of the phrases that we associate with constitutional authority such as separation of powers, checks and balances, freedom of speech, and so forth are not included within the Constitutions or Amendments. These phrases, found in commentaries and court decisions, help shape our understanding of government and law.

7. David H. Rosenbloom, *Building a Legislative-Centered Public Administration: Congress and the Administrative State, 1946–1999* (Tuscaloosa: University of Alabama Press, 2000).

8. Michael W. Spicer and Larry D. Terry, "Legitimacy, History and Logic: Public Administration and the Constitution," *Public Administration Review* 53 (1993): 239–245.

9. John A. Rohr, "Public Administration, Executive Power, and Constitutional Confusion," *Public Administration Review* 49 (1989): 108–114.

10. Frederick C. Mosher, *Democracy and the Public Service,* 2nd ed. (New York: Oxford University Press, 1982).

11. H. George Frederickson, "Public Administration and Social Equity," *Public Administration Review* 50 (1990): 228–237.

12. John Adams is frequently cited, but this phrase is also in the Massachusetts Constitution.

13. The Constitutional Convention approved the Constitution on September 7, 1787. Nine states ratified it by June 21, 1788, and all states ratified by May 29, 1790.

14. Andrew Altman, *Arguing About Law: An Introduction to Legal Philosophy*, 2nd ed. (Belmont, CA: Wadsworth, 2001), 1–8.

15. Donald F. Kettl and James W. Fesler, *The Politics of the Administrative Process*, 3rd ed. (Washington, DC: CQ Press, 2005), 10.

16. Woodrow Wilson, "The Study of Administration." In *Classics of Public Administration*, 2nd ed., ed. Jay M. Shafritz, Albert C. Hyde, and Sandra J. Parkes (Chicago, IL: Dorsey Press, 1978), 22–34. Originally published in *Political Science Quarterly* 2 (June 1887).

17. Rohr, *To Run a Constitution*.

18. Terry L. Cooper, *The Responsible Administrator: An Approach to Ethics for the Administrative Role*, 4th ed. (San Francisco: Jossey-Bass, 1998); Montgomery Van Wart, *Changing Public Sector Values* (New York: Garland Publishing, 1998).

19. Michael W. Spicer and Larry D. Terry, "Legitimacy, History and Logic: Public Administration and the Constitution," *Public Administration Review* 53 (1993): 239–245.

20. Leonard D. White, *Introduction to the Study of Public Administration* (New York: Macmillan, 1926).

21. Moe and Gilmour, "Rediscovering Principles."

22. Ibid. pp. 138–139.

23. Laurence E. Lynn, Jr., "Restoring the Rule of Law to Public Administration: What Frank Goodnow Got Right and What Leonard White Didn't," *Public Administration Review* 69 (2009): 803–812; Rosemary O'Leary, "Response to John Rohr," *Public Administration Review* 49 (1989): 115.

24. *Harlow v. Fitzgerald*, 457 U.S. 800, 819 (1982).

25. Luther H. Gulick, "Notes on the Theory of Organization." In *Papers on the Science of Administration*, ed. Luther H. Gulick and Lyndall F. Urwick (New York: Institute of Public Administration, 1937), 3–13.

Notes to Chapter 2

1. *Brown v. Board of Education of Topeka*, 347 U.S. 483 (1954).

2. *Miranda v. Arizona*, 384 U.S. 436 (1966).

3. *Mathews v. Eldridge*, 424 U.S. 319 (1976).

4. *Harlow v. Fitzgerald*, 457 U.S. 800, 819 (1982).

5. David H. Rosenbloom, James D. Carroll, and Jonathan D. Carroll, *Constitutional Competence for Public Managers: Cases and Commentary* (Itasca, IL: Peacock, 1999).

6. Lee Epstein and Thomas G. Walker, *Constitutional Law for a Changing America*, 2nd ed. (Washington, DC: CQ Press, 2000).

7. Rosenbloom, Carroll, and Carroll, *Constitutional Competence*.

8. *Marbury v. Madison*, 5 U.S. (1 Cr.) 137 (1803); Epstein and Walker, *Constitutional Law*, 69.

9. *McCullough v. Maryland*, 17 U.S. (4 Wheat) 316 (1819).

10. Epstein and Walker, *Constitutional Law*, 110–115.

11. Ibid., 228–246.

12. Thomas C. Marks, Jr. and John F. Cooper, *State Constitutional Law in a Nutshell* (St. Paul, MN: Thomson West, 2003).

13. Ibid.

14. U.S. Constitution, Art. 1, § 8, cl 3.

15. U.S. Constitution, Art. 1, § 8, cl 1.

16. U.S. Constitution, Art. 1, § 7, cl 1.

17. Albert M. Sbagria, *Debt Wish: Entrepreneurial Cities, U.S. Federalism and Economic Development* (Pittsburgh: University of Pittsburgh Press, 1996); Irene Rubin, *The*

Politics of Public Budgeting: Getting and Spending, Borrowing and Balancing, 5th ed. (Washington, DC: CQ Press, 2006).

18. Donald F. Kettl and James W. Fesler, *The Politics of the Administrative Process,* 3rd ed. (Washington, DC: CQ Press, 2005), 85–86.

19. M. David Gelfand, Joel A. Mintz, and Peter W. Salsich, Jr., *State and Local Taxation and Finance in a Nutshell* (St. Paul, MN: Thomson West Group, 2007).

20. *Daimler Chrysler v. Cuno,* 547 U.S. 332 (2006).

21. *Raines v. Byrd,* 521 U.S. 811 (1997).

22. *Clinton v. City of New York,* 524 U.S. 417 (1998).

23. Ibid., 449.

24. Ibid., 496.

25. *New State Ice Co. v. Liebman,* 285 US 262, 311 (1932) (Concurring Op.).

26. Catherine Drinker Bowen, *Miracle at Philadelphia; The Story of the Constitutional Convention, May to September, 1787* (Boston: Little, Brown, 1966); Herbert J. Storing, *What the Anti-Federalists Were For* (Chicago: University of Chicago Press, 1981).

27. *Joint Anti-Fascist Refugee Committee v. McGrath,* 341 US 123, 163 (1951) (Concurring Op.).

28. *Griswold v. Connecticut,* 381 U.S. 479 (1965).

29. *Yick Wo v. Hopkins, Sheriff,* 118 U.S. 356 (1886).

30. *Plessy v. Ferguson,* 163 U.S. 537 (1896).

31. *Brown v. Board of Education of Topeka,* 347 U.S. 483 (1954).

32. *Regents of the University of California v. Bakke,* 438 U.S. 265 (1978).

33. *Parents Involved in Community Schools v. Seattle School District No. 1,* 551 U.S. 701 (2007).

34. *Ricci v. DeStefano,* 557 U.S. ____, 129 S. Ct. 2658, 174 L. Ed. 2d 490 (2009).

35. *Adarand Contractors v. Pena,* 512 U.S. 200, 214 (1995) internal quote and citation omitted.

36. *O'Connor v. Ortega,* 480 US 709, 721–22, 725 (1987).

37. *Garcetti v. Ceballos,* 547 U.S. 410 (2006); Robert Roberts, "Developments in the Law: *Garcetti v. Ceballos* and the Workplace Freedom of Speech Rights of Public Employees," *Public Administration Review* 67 (2007): 662–672.

38. "Byzantium." In *The Concise Oxford Companion to Classical Literature,* ed. M.C. Howatson and Ian Chilvers (Oxford: Oxford University Press, 1996), Oxford Reference Online, www.oxfordreference.com (Accessed September 20, 2009).

Notes to Chapter 3

1. Sally Engle Merry, "Everyday Understandings of Law in Working-Class America," *American Ethnologist* 13 (1986): 253–270.

2. Rosemary O'Leary, "Response to John Rohr," *Public Administration Review* 49 (1989): 115.

3. Charles Savage, "Bush Declares Exceptions to Sections of Two Bills He Signed Into Law," *New York Times,* October 15, 2008, A17.

4. Editorial, "On Signing Statements," *New York Times,* March 17, 2009, A26.

5. David H. Rosenbloom and Rosemary O'Leary, *Public Administration and Law,* 2nd ed. (New York: Marcel Dekker, 1997), 87–112.

6. Anne Schneider and Helen Ingraham, "Improving Implementation Through Framing Smarter Statutes," *Journal of Public Policy* 10 (1990): 67–88.

7. Theodore J. Lowi, *The End of Liberalism: Ideology, Policy, and the Crisis of Public Authority* (New York: Norton, 1969).

8. Jerry L. Mashaw, "Prodelegation: Why Administrators Should Make Political Decisions," *Journal of Law, Economics, and Organization* 1 (1985): 80–100, 81.

9. Schneider and Ingraham, "Improving Implementation."

10. R. Shep Melnick, "Administrative Law and Bureaucratic Reality," *Administrative Law Review* 44 (1992): 245–260.

11. Paul H. Appleby, *Policy and Administration* (Tuscaloosa: University of Alabama Press, 1949), 6–7.

12. *McBoyle v. U.S.,* 283 U.S. 25 (1931).

13. This case has been edited by removing some redundant citations.

14. *Federated Distributors Inc v. Thomas Johnson,* 125 Ill.2d 1 (1988).

15. Ibid., 21–22.

Notes to Chapter 4

1. Zhiyong Lan, "A Conflict Resolution Approach to Public Administration," *Public Administration Review* 57 (1997): 27–35.

2. Lester M. Salamon, ed., *The Tools of Government: A Guide to the New Governance* (New York: Oxford University Press, 2002).

3. *Marbury v. Madison,* 5 U.S. (1 Cr.) 137 (1803).

4. Lloyd Bonfield, *American Law and the American Legal System in a Nutshell* (St. Paul, MN: Thomson/West, 2006).

5. Lief H. Carter, *Reason in Law,* 4th ed. (New York: HarperCollins, 1994).

6. Julia Beckett and Heidi O. Koenig, eds., *Public Administration and Law* (Armonk, NY: M.E. Sharpe, 2005).

7. Nancy J. Manring, "ADR and Administrative Responsiveness: Challenges for Public Administrators," *Public Administration Review* 54 (1994): 197–203.

8. Phillip J. Cooper, *Public Law and Public Administration,* 3rd ed. (Itasca, IL: F.E. Peacock Publishers): 247–250.

9. Roger C. Cramton, "Judicial Law Making and Administration," *Public Administration Review* 36 (1976): 551–555.

10. Charles R. Wise and Rosemary O'Leary, "Breaking Up Is Hard to Do: The Dissolution of Judicial Supervision of Public Services," *Public Administration Review* 63 (2003): 177–191.

11. The footnote was omitted from this case.

12. The footnotes were omitted from this case.

Notes to Chapter 5

1. The Transportation Security Agency was formed as part of the Aviation and Transportation Security Act, Nov. 19, 2001, and was originally part of the Department of Transportation. It was transferred to the Department of Homeland Security in March 2003. The Department of Homeland Security was established by the Homeland Security Act of 2002, on November 25, 2002. http://www.tsa.gov/research/tribute/history.shtm and http://www.tsa.gov/research/laws/law_regulation_rule_0010.shtm (accessed July 30, 2009).

2. Security Regulations Overview [of TSA], http://www.tsa.gov/research/laws/regs/editorial_multi_image_with_table_0205.shtm (accessed July 30, 2009).

3. Christine B. Harrington and Leif H. Carter, *Administrative Law and Politics: Cases and Comments,* 4th ed. (Washington, DC: CQ Press, 2009); John M. Scheb and John M. Scheb II, *Law and the Administrative Process* (Belmont, CA: Thomson Wadsworth, 2005); and Ernest Gellhorn and Ronald M. Levin, *Administrative Law and Process in a Nutshell,* 5th ed. (St. Paul, MN: Thomson/West, 2006).

4. Donald F. Kettl and James W. Fesler, *The Politics of the Administrative Process*, 3rd ed. (Washington, DC: CQ Press, 2005), 32–45.

5. Upton Sinclair, *The Jungle* (New York: Modern Library, 2002; originally published in 1906).

6. Frank J. Goodnow, *Comparative Administrative Law: An Analysis of the Administrative Systems National and Local, of the United States, England, France and Germany* (New York: Putnam's Sons, 1893).

7. Henry M. Hart, Jr. and Albert M. Sacks, *The Legal Process: Basic Problems in the Making and Application of Law* (Westbury, NY: Foundation Press, 1994; originally prepared for publication in 1958).

8. Woodrow Wilson, "The Study of Administration." In *Classics of Public Administration*, 2nd ed., ed. Jay M. Shafritz, Abert C. Hyde, and Sandra J. Parkes (Chicago, IL: The Dorsey Press, 1978), 22–34. Originally published in *Political Science Quarterly* 2 (June 1887); Leonard D. White, *Introduction to the Study of Public Administration* (New York: MacMillan, 1926).

9. Lee Epstein and Thomas G. Walker, *Constitutional Law for a Changing America*, 2nd ed. (Washington, DC: CQ Press, 2000), 228–238.

10. *Panama Refining Co. v. Ryan*, 293 U.S. 388 (1935).

11. *Schechter Poultry Corp. v. U.S.*, 295 U.S. 495 (1935).

12. John A. Rohr, *To Run a Constitution: The Legitimacy of the Administrative State* (Lawrence: University of Kansas Press, 1986), 154. The full title of the report is "Report of the Committee on Administrative Procedure, Appointed by the Attorney General, at the Request of the President, to Investigate the Need for Improvements Therein." Many scholars call it "The Attorney General's Report on Administrative Procedure." For a discussion of the history of administrative law and process, see, Anthony M. Bertelli and Laurence E. Lynn, Jr. *Madison's Managers: Public Administration and the Constitution* (Baltimore: Johns Hopkins University Press, 2006), 72–102.

13. Ibid., 154–170.

14. James M. Landis, *The Administrative Process* (New Haven, CT: Yale University Press, 1938).

15. Administrative Procedure Act, 5 U.S.C. §551.

16. Richard T. Sylves, *Disaster Policy and Politics: Emergency Management and Homeland Security* (Washington, DC: CQ Press, 2008).

17. This flu is also called Swine Flu or the H1N1 Novel Flu. Pandemic flu information is posted on the Centers for Disease Control and Prevention (http://www.CDC.gov) and Flu.gov (http://www.pandemicflu.gov) Web sites.

18. "Agency Good Guidance Practices," 72 *Federal Register* 3432–3440 (January 25, 2007). This is part of "Regulatory Planning and Review," Executive Order 12866 of September 30, 1993, as amended by E.O. 13258 of February 26, 2002 and E.O. 13422 of January 18, 2002.

19. Cornelius M. Kerwin, *Rulemaking: How Government Agencies Write Law and Make Policy*, 3rd ed. (Washington, DC: CQ Press, 2003).

20. Kettl and Fesler, *The Politics*, 158–159.

21. Kerwin, *Rulemaking*, 73–85.

22. "Presidential Memorandum of January 30, 2009," *Federal Register* 5977–78 (February 3, 2009).

23. *Immigration and Naturalization Service v. Chada*, 462 U.S. 919 (1983).

24. Gellhorn and Levin, *Administrative Law*.

25. Lester M. Salamon, ed., *The Tools of Government: A Guide to the New Governance* (New York: Oxford University Press, 2002).

26. *Goldberg v. Kelly*, 397 U.S. 254 (1970).

27. Phillip J. Cooper, *Public Law and Public Administration*, 3rd ed. (Itasca, IL: F.E. Peacock), 250.

28. See also, David H. Rosenbloom, *Administrative Law for Public Managers* (Boulder, CO: Westview Press, 2003).

29. A place to start searching for federal and state statutes and regulations is the U.S. Government Official Web Portal (http:// www.usa.gov).

30. Lotte E. Feinberg, "Managing the Freedom of Information Act and Federal Policy," *Public Administration Review* 46 (1986): 615–621.

31. This case was edited and the court's footnotes are omitted here.

32. The U.S. Social Security Web site is http://www.socialsecurity.gov.

Notes to Chapter 6

1. U.S. Constitution Article I, Sect. 8. "To promote the Progress of Science and useful Arts, by securing for limited times to Authors and Inventors the exclusive Right to their respective Writings and Discoveries."

2. "The Code of Hammurabi." In *The Ancient Near East*, vol. 1, ed. James B. Pritchard (Princeton, NJ: Princeton University Press, 1958), 138–168.

3. Bruce E. Altschuler and Celia A. Sgroi, *Understanding Law in a Changing Society*, 2nd ed. (Upper Saddle River, NJ: Prentice Hall, 1996), 202.

4. Ibid., 202–204.

5. Ibid.

6. Patricia Salkin, "Land Use: Blending Smart Growth with Social Equity and Climate Change Mitigation." In *Agenda for a Sustainable America*, ed. John C. Dernbach (Washington, DC: ELI, 2009), 349–364.

7. Dennis R. Judd and Todd Swanstrom, *City Politics: The Political Economy of Urban America*, 5th ed. (New York: Pearson Longman, 2006), 276–293.

8. Ibid.

9. U.S. Constitution Article I, Sect. 8.

10. *District of Columbia v. Heller*, 554 U.S. ___, 128 S. Ct. 2783, 171 L.Ed.2d 637 (2008).

11. Judd and Swanstrom, *City Politics*, 285–293; Stewart Meck, Paul Wack, and Michelle J. Zimet, "Zoning and Subdivisoin Regulations." In *The Practice of Local Government Planning*, 3rd ed., ed. Charles J. Hoch, Linda S. Dalton, and Frank S. So (Washington, DC: ICMA, 2000), 343–374.

12. Jane Jacobs, *The Death and Life of Great American Cities* (New York: Random House, 1961).

13. *Yick Wo v. Hopkins, Sheriff*, 118 U.S. 356 (1886).

14. John M. Scheb and John M. Scheb II, *Law and the Administrative Process* (Belmont, CA: Thomson Wadsworth, 2005), 385–393.

15. Lee Epstein and Thomas G. Walker, *Constitutional Law for a Changing America*, 2nd ed. (Washington, DC: CQ Press, 2000), 330–345.

16. Ibid., 330.

17. Clayton P. Gillette, *Local Government Law: Cases and Materials* (Boston: Little Brown, 1994), 895.

18. *Loretto v. Teleprompter Manhattan CATV Corp.*, 458 U.S. 419, 426 (1982).

19. Ibid.

20. *Nollan v. California Coastal Commission*, 483 U.S. 825 (1987).

21. *Dolan v. City of Tigard*, 512 U.S. 374 (1994).

22. *Susette Kelo v. City of New London, Connecticut*, 545 U.S. 469 (2005).

23. *McCulloch v. Maryland*, 17 U.S. (4 Wheat.) 316 (1819).

24. *Citizens to Preserve Overton Park v. Volpe,* 401 U.S. 402 (1971).

25. Andrew I. Batavia, "Inclusion in Public Accommodations." In *Implementing the Americans with Disabilities Act,* ed. Jane West (Cambridge, MA: Blackwell, 1996), 263–298.

26. David H. Rosenbloom and Rosemary O'Leary, *Public Administration and Law,* 2nd ed. (New York: Marcel Dekker, 1997), 87–112.

27. Editorial, "Of Hogs and Houses," *St. Louis Post Dispatch,* June 3, 1995, 14B.

28. Ibid.

Notes to Chapter 7

1. American Law Institute, *Uniform Commercial Code: Official Text and Comments* (St. Paul, MN: Thomson West, 2005).

2. Ed Gillespie and Bob Schellhas, eds., *Contract With America: The Bold Plan by Rep. Newt Gingrich, Rep. Dick Armey and the House Republicans to Change the Nation* (New York: Times Books, 1994).

3. Claude D. Rohwer and Anthony M. Skrocki, *Contracts in a Nutshell* (St. Paul, MN: Thomson/West, 2006); an example of a treatise is Joseph M. Perillo, ed., *Calamari and Perillo on Contracts,* 5th ed. (St. Paul, MN: Thomson West, 2003).

4. Bruce E. Altschuler and Celia A. Sgroi, *Understanding Law in a Changing Society,* 2nd ed. (Upper Saddle River, NJ: Prentice Hall, 1996), 268–71.

5. Phillip J. Cooper, *Governing by Contract: Challenges and Opportunities for Public Managers* (Washington, DC: CQ Press, 2003).

6. Donald F. Kettl, *Government by Proxy* (Washington, DC: CQ Press, 1988); H. Brinton Milward and Keith G. Provan, *The Hollow State: Private Provision of Public Services* (Washington, DC: Brookings Institution Press, 1993).

7. Cooper, *Governing by Contract,* 160–164.

8. Ibid., 54–60.

9. Grant Gilmore, *The Death of Contract* (Columbus: Ohio State University Press, 1974).

10. Paul G. Dembling and Malcolm S. Mason, *Essentials of Grant Law Practice* (Philadelphia: American Law, 1991).

11. Office of Federal Procurement Policy, Policy Letter 72–1, September 23, 1992.

12. Cooper, *Governing by Contract,* 74–76.

13. Ibid.

14. This case has been edited and the court's footnotes have been omitted.

15. This case has been edited; the court's footnotes have been omitted, except for Footnote 2, which is now an asterisked footnote.

Notes to Chapter 8

1. Bruce E. Altschuler and Celia A. Sgroi, *Understanding Law in a Changing Society,* 2nd ed. (Upper Saddle River, NJ: Prentice Hall, 1996), 343–345.

2. Steven H. Gifis, *Barron's Law Dictionary* (Hauppauge, New York: Barrons, 1996), 206–7.

3. Ibid., 69.

4. Martha A. Derthick, *Up in Smoke: From Legislation to Litigation in Tobacco Politics,* 2nd ed. (Washington, DC: CQ Press, 2005).

5. Alan Feuer, "US Appeals Court Rejects City's Suit to Curb Guns," *New York Times,* May 1, 2008, B2.

6. Abha Bhattarai, "Rhode Island Court Throws Out Jury Finding in Lead Case," *New York Times,* July 2, 2008, C4.

7. Henry M. Hart, Jr. and Albert M. Sacks, *The Legal Process: Basic Problems in*

the Making and Application of Law (Westbury, NY: Foundation Press, 1994; originally prepared for publication in 1958.), 943–53.

8. Tort Claims Act, 1945 as amended. 28 U.S.C. § 1346 et seq.

9. The Stafford Act (also known as the Disaster Relief and Emergency Assistance Act), 42 U.S.C. § 5148. Daniel A. Farber and Jim Chen, eds., *Disasters and the Law: Katrina and Beyond* (New York: Aspen Publishers, 2006); Ernest B. Abbott and Otto J. Hetzel, eds., *A Legal Guide to Homeland Security and Emergency Management for State and Local Governments* (Chicago: ABA Publishing, 2005).

10. "Colorado law deprives accident victims of compensation" *Street Stories Show*, reported by Bob McKeown, June 25, 1992. CBS News Transcript, http://www.lexisnexis.com/us/lnacademic/search (accessed October 7, 2008); "A settlement of $2.5 million negotiated," *Business Wire*, March 18, 1993, http://www.lexisnexis.com/us/lnacademic/search/newssubmitForm.doc (accessed October 7, 2008).

11. "Colorado Law Deprives Accident Victims," 4.

12. This discussion of victims compensation funds, workers compensation, and disability insurance is based on Robert L. Rabin and Suzanne A. Bratis, "United States." In *Financial Compensation for Victims of Catastrophes: A Comparative Legal Approach*, ed. Michael Faure and Ton Hartlief (New York: Springer-Verlag/Wein, 2006), 303–359.

13. Kenneth R. Feinberg, *What Is Life Worth? The Unprecedented Effort to Compensate Victims for 9/11* (New York: Public Affairs, 2005).

14. Adam Nossiter, "In Court Ruling on Floods, More Pain for New Orleans," *New York Times*, February 1, 2008, A16. *In re Katrina Canal Breaches Consolidated Litigation*, 533 F.Supp. 615 (E.D. LA 2008).

15. David H. Rosenbloom, James D. Carroll, and Jonathan D. Carroll, *Constitutional Competence for Public Managers: Cases and Commentary* (Itasca, IL: Peacock, 1999).

16. The court's footnotes were omitted here.

Notes to Chapter 9

1. W. Richard Scott, "Law and Organizations." In *The Legalistic Organization*, ed. B. Sitkin and Robert J. Bies (Thousand Oaks, CA: Sage, 1994), 9.

2. Peter H. Shuck, *The Limits of Law: Essays on Democratic Governance* (Boulder, CO: Westview Press, 2000), 434.

3. Ibid.

4. Fritz J. Roethlisberger, "The Hawthorne Experiments." In *Classics of Organization Theory*, 6th ed., ed. Jay M. Shafritz, J. Steven Ott, and Yong Suk Jang (Belmont, CA: Thomson/Wadsworth, 2005), 158–166. (Originally published in *Management and Morale*, ed. F.J. Roethlisberger [Cambridge MA: Harvard University Press, 1941].)

5. Herbert Kaufman, *The Forest Ranger: A Study in Administrative Behavior* (Baltimore: Resources for the Future and Johns Hopkins University Press, 1967; copyright 1960).

6. Rosemary O'Leary, *The Ethics of Dissent: Managing Guerrilla Government* (Washington, DC: CQ Press, 2005).

7. Debra W. Stewart, "Professionalism vs. Democracy: Friedrich vs. Finer Revisited," *Public Administration Quarterly* 9 (1985): 13–25.

8. Terry L. Cooper, *The Responsible Administrator: An Approach to Ethics for the Administrative Role*, 4th ed. (San Francisco: Jossey-Bass, 1998); Montgomery Van Wart, *Changing Public Sector Values* (New York: Garland, 1998); and Janet V. Denhardt and Robert B. Denhardt, *The New Public Service: Serving, not Steering*, expanded ed. (Armonk, NY: M.E. Sharpe, 2007).

9. Schuck, *The Limits*, 434.

10. Ibid., 434–35.

11. Julia Beckett, "'The Government Should Run Like a Business' Mantra," *American Review of Public Administration* 30 (2000): 185–204.

12. Graham T. Allison, "Public and Private Management: Are They Fundamentally Alike in All Unimportant Respects?" In *Classics of Public Administration*, 5th ed., ed. Jay M. Shafritz, Albert C. Hyde, and Sandra J. Parkes (Belmont, CA: Wadsworth, 2004), 396–413. (Originally published in 1979.)

13. Schuck, *The Limits*, 435–36.

14. Examples include Albert Gore, Jr., *Creating a Government that Works Better and Costs Less: Report of the National Performance Review* (Washington, DC: Government Printing Office, 1993); Robert D. Behn, *Rethinking Democratic Accountability* (Washington, DC: Brookings Institution Press, 2001).

15. Richard T. Sylves, *Disaster Policy and Politics: Emergency Management and Homeland Security* (Washington, DC: CQ Press, 2008).

16. Doyle W. Buckwalter and J. Ivan Legler, "City Managers and City Attorneys: Associates or Adversaries?" *Public Administration Review* 47 (1987): 393–403.

17. Ibid.

18. Mark G. Yudof, "Preface." In *The Legalistic Organization*, ed. Sim B. Sitkin and Robert J. Bies (Thousand Oaks, CA: Sage, 1994) vii–x, ix.

19. Jay Matthews, "Great Salt Lake Runneth Over, Contrary to Lawmakers' Orders," *Washington Post*, April 3, 1983, p. A2.

20. Ibid.

21. Dan Harrie and Judy Fahys, "Weird Utah laws; Nonsense Clutters Code Book; Weird Laws Clutter the Utah Code," *Salt Lake Tribune*, January 18, 1998, p. A1.

22. Herbert Kaufman, *Red Tape: Its Origins, Uses, and Abuses* (Washington, DC: Brookings Institution Press, 1977), 7.

23. "Batboy is Called Out by Labor Officials, Who Vow a Review," *New York Times*, May 28, 1993, A10.

24. Ibid.

25. Martin A. Levin and Mary B. Sanger, *Making Government Work: How Entrepreneurial Executives Turn Bright Ideas into Real Results* (San Francisco: Jossey-Bass. 1994), 269.

26. *United States v. Lee*, 106 U.S. 196, 200 (1882).

27. Marshall E. Dimock, *Law and Dynamic Administration* (New York: Praeger, 1980).

28. Hugh Heclo, "The Statesman: Revisiting Leadership in America." In *Legality and Community: On the Intellectual Legacy of Philip Selznick*, ed. Robert A. Kagan, Martin Krygier, and Kenneth Winston (Lanham, MD: Rowman and Littlefield, 2002), 295–310, 307.

29. Philip Selznick, *Leadership in America: A Sociological Interpretation* (Berkeley: University of California Press, 1984), vii, as quoted by Heclo, "The Statesman," 307–8.

30. The footnotes have been omitted from this case.

Index

About the Author

Julia Beckett is an associate professor in the Department of Public Administration and Urban Studies at the University of Akron. She earned a Bachelor
of Arts degree in art and archaeology and a Juris Doctorate degree from
Washington University in St. Louis. She earned a Master of Public Administration and a Doctor of Philosophy degree from the Graduate School of
Public Affairs at the University of Colorado at Denver. She teaches courses in
public law, public organization theory, public budgeting, and urban policy in
the masters and doctoral programs in public administration and urban studies
at the University of Akron. Her research interests include public law, public
administration and budget history, and emergency management. She coedited
an American Society for Public Administration Classics volume on public law.
She has contributed chapters to scholarly books on public law, legal research,
budget theory, intergovernmental relations, and public bureaucracy. She has
published journal articles in *The American Review of Public Administration,
Journal of Public Policy and Analysis, Public Management and Social Policy,
Public Budgeting, Accounting and Financial Management,* and *Journal of
Public Administration Education.*